JEFF HORN

THE HORNET

WITH GRANTLEE KIEZA

ABC BOOKS

The ABC 'Wave' device is a trademark of the Australian Broadcasting Corporation and is used under licence by HarperCollins*Publishers* Australia.

First published in Australia in 2017
This edition published in 2019
by HarperCollins*Publishers* Australia Pty Limited
ABN 36 009 913 517
harpercollins.com.au

HarperCollins*Publishers*
Level 13, 201 Elizabeth Street, Sydney NSW 2000, Australia
Unit D1, 63 Apollo Drive, Rosedale, Auckland 0632, New Zealand
A 53, Sector 57, Noida, UP, India
1 London Bridge Street, London, SE1 9GF, United Kingdom
Bay Adelaide Centre, East Tower, 22 Adelaide Street West, 41st floor, Toronto, Ontario M5H 4E3, Canada
195 Broadway, New York NY 10007, USA

A catalogue record for this book is available from the National Library of Australia
ISBN: 978 0 7333 4043 7 (paperback)
ISBN: 978 1 4607 0994 8 (ebook)

Cover design by Luke Causby, Blue Cork
Cover image by Chris Hyde/Getty Images
Photographs are from the collection of Jeff Horn, except as noted.
Colour section picture credits: page 3 Jack Guez/AFP/Getty Images (top); page 4 Chris Hyde/Getty Images (top); page 6 Peter Wallis/Newspix (top), Bradley Kanaris/Getty Images (bottom); page 7 Peter Wallis/Newspix (top), Chris Hyde/Getty Images (middle), Annette Dew/Newspix (bottom); page 8 Steve Marcus/Getty Images (top), Annette Dew/Newspix (bottom).
Typeset in Sabon LT by Kirby Jones
Printed and bound in Australia by McPherson's Printing Group
The papers used by HarperCollins in the manufacture of this book are a natural, recyclable product made from wood grown in sustainable plantation forests. The fibre source and manufacturing processes meet recognised international environmental standards, and carry certification.

For my wife, Jo, and all my family and friends.
With love and thanks.

1

All it takes to reach the stars is a leap of faith.

– My trainer, Glenn Rushton, wrote this on a pair of boxing gloves that he gave me for my twenty-first birthday

HAVE YOU EVER HAD a dream to achieve something great? A goal that you hunger for and that keeps you awake at night; a goal that makes you work and work and work to reach it? Where do you want to go in life? What will you have to do to get there?

These are questions we all ask ourselves and ones that I pondered every day in the lead-up to the biggest boxing match ever staged in Australia. Here I was, the most unlikely boxer you could imagine, about to go toe to toe with one of the greatest fighters in history at Suncorp Stadium in Brisbane. The fight turned out to be one of the biggest international sporting events staged in Australia and, thanks to the incredible support from my country, it ended up generating a greater economic benefit for the state of Queensland than the G20 summit in Brisbane when political heavyweights Barack Obama and Vladimir Putin faced off in 2014.

It was a warm winter's afternoon on 2 July 2017. All around me, roaring with excitement, were more than 51,000 people, the largest crowd ever to attend a boxing match in Australia and the largest crowd anywhere in the world to see Manny Pacquiao fight.

People were there to witness the most audacious title attempt ever by an Australian fighter, as I took on boxing's Superman, a buzzing whirlwind who had been a world champion for almost twenty years and had earned more than A$660 million from the sport.

Reporters called my challenge for Pacquiao's title the most astonishing story in world sport – a rank outsider who somehow found himself facing one of the biggest names in boxing history and a high-ranking Filipino politician to boot.

What the hell was I even doing here in the first place?

In fact, when you looked at our careers logically, the fight seemed like a bizarre match-up. No wonder, going into it, I'd been ridiculed by know-alls around the world. The idea of me fighting for a world title – and especially against a living legend of sport – seemed like some ridiculous movie storyline, one of those science-fiction or fantasy flicks, in which an inoffensive kid is somehow transported to another world and given superpowers to face the ultimate challenge.

For one thing, I don't come from a boxing background. I didn't follow the sport when I was a kid and 'world boxing champion' was hardly on the top of preferred jobs suggested to me when I was a school nerd. The first fights I ever saw live were the Australian amateur titles in 2007.

Growing up, I had a pretty comfortable home life in the Brisbane suburbs. In contrast, Pacquiao had been born into abject poverty and grew up in a dirt-floor thatched hut in the jungle in a remote corner of the southern Philippines. Through his iron will and blazing hands he had battered his way through the top tiers of boxing and become a dominant force in the sport.

Pacquiao has a long inventory of palaces he calls home in the Philippines and the United States. I live in a modest house in a working-class suburb of Brisbane. He learned to fight by watching roosters peck and claw each other to death in cockfighting tournaments in the Philippines. I've got a docile Staffordshire terrier that never barks but comes running into my lounge room if she hears the codeword 'pizza', a word I don't say often. Pacquiao has held eleven world titles. I'm a schoolteacher and a qualified childcare worker.

Pacquiao had arrived in Brisbane a week before the fight on a specially chartered jetliner carrying his entourage of 160 family members, friends, trainers, managers and bodyguards. He booked out a huge section of the Sofitel hotel in Brisbane's CBD. While Pacquiao and his team rested up in one of Brisbane's flashest hotels, on the night before the fight, I was snoring loudly next to my pregnant wife, Jo, in our little house in the suburbs. Jo normally elbows me in the ribs to quieten me when I snore too loudly but she thought I might have a busy day ahead of me.

I used to joke that working with children had prepared me for any stressful situation in life. But it certainly hadn't prepared me for the Filipino volcano when, about a minute into the ninth round of my fight for his world welterweight title, he started erupting in centre ring. Pacquiao was doing his best to destroy me, to crush all my dreams and aspirations, with a burst of heavy punches like those he had used to annihilate some of the toughest men of all time. Who did I think I was to stand up to him?

Eleven years earlier I had been a geeky kid who didn't even know how to throw a punch properly. Even now I don't regard myself as a 'tough guy' and I try to avoid trouble at all costs. By nature I'm not a rough or confrontational person and I still suffer from the anxiety condition called claustrophobia. I was glad this fight was out in an open space rather than in a small dark room where I would have suffered a panic attack even before the first bell. I had made a good start in the fight, but now I was having a hard time holding everything together as Pacquiao tried to corner me and punch my lights out. I thought I'd been in front after eight rounds, but that meant nothing as Pacquiao saw a big bullseye on my chin. After missing the target so many times early in the fight, he had found his range and I was feeling his power.

Don't go down, I kept imploring myself. *Don't go down.*

Blood was dripping into my eye and my head was spinning. My eyesight was blurry and my legs felt like jelly. But my hearing was fine and the voice inside my head pleaded with me to stay strong.

The whole world is watching this, it said. *You've got millions of dollars riding on this fight – millions. You can set your family up for life if you win. You can make history or be a footnote. Think of what this means to your family and your friends.*

SMASH.

A huge Pacquiao left hand cannoned into my chin and my knees wobbled.

I tottered.

Don't go down. Don't go down, the voice roared at me once more.

I'd been hurt like this before and been dazed just as badly. Pacquiao is a tremendous puncher, but when I was thirteen a bully at my high school hit me with a coward-punch that was every bit as devastating as the world champion's left crosses. Just for a laugh, the bully had smashed a fist into the side of my head when I wasn't looking.

It wasn't the first time I'd been bullied at school. I'd been picked on a lot as a kid because I was shy and quiet. The bullying got so bad that I questioned whether there was any point to my life. At different stages of adolescence I had suicidal thoughts and very low self-esteem. I would cry in my mother's arms.

It was why I took up boxing when I was eighteen, something I don't regret. Boxing turned my life around, transforming me from a shy, frightened teenager into a world-class athlete. And now, here I was fighting one of the biggest names in sport before hundreds of millions of people on global television. Here, at Suncorp Stadium, my dream to set up my family for life and reward the faith of my friends and supporters with a world title was so close.

And yet Pacquiao was on the verge of snatching it back from me and leaving me humiliated.

CRASH.

He nailed me again.

Now I was fighting not just Pacquiao but gravity, as I tried to stay upright.

The eleven-time world champion opened up with a series of savage punches at my head. I could hear the groans as many of the crowd suspected that my dream was about to go belly-up and that I would leave that dream on the canvas. Even my most ardent fans must have feared that Pacquiao was about to vindicate the bookies who had made him a raging favourite. After all, Pacquiao is one of the greatest finishers in boxing. He had beaten-up great fighters inside the distance, including Oscar De La Hoya, Ricky Hatton and Miguel Cotto. Who did I think I was to be standing in his way?

The enormity of the task before me was all too real. Painfully real. I had pushed myself to the absolute limits of mental and physical exhaustion and now Pacquiao was pushing me over the edge as the bright Brisbane sun cast a long shadow over my future.

My right eyebrow was badly cut and blood was cascading down my face. I had lumps and bumps all over my scalp from where our heads were repeatedly cracking together as we traded punches in close. Pacquiao also had deep cuts on both sides of his scalp but the blood he could smell was all mine.

Before the fight, Pacquiao's American trainer Freddie Roach, one of the most successful boxing coaches of all time, had told a press conference that his fighter could knock me out any time he chose. Even though I had proved him wrong over the first half of the fight, it looked like the champ had decided to put me away now. As much as I tried to fend him off, Pacquiao was getting his own way.

All around me my family and friends were going through a tough time. In those few desperate minutes, they felt every hurtful energy-sapping, soul-destroying punch as the big heavy blows crashed into my head. My trainer,

Glenn Rushton – who had taught me how to throw my first real punch – my cut man Stephen Edwards, my brother, Ben, and my mate Adam Copland all twisted in their seats in my corner.

I had planned to announce to the world after the fight that Jo was expecting our first child and I wanted to make that announcement as a winner. Jo was sitting at ringside with my mum, Liza, and my grandparents, Marie and Jack Dykstra. Even though the crowd's roar was deafening, I could hear their voices almost as loudly as the one in my head telling me not to go down.

'Come on Jeffrey,' they yelled. 'You can do it. We believe in you.'

I was getting hammered by one of the great power-punchers of all time. My dad, Jeff Snr, seated near my corner, is acutely aware of boxing's risks and, as the round grew darker and darker and more dangerous for me, he thought about coming over and stopping the fight if the barrage continued in Round 10.

In the fifteen hours before the official weigh-in I had lost 4.6 kilograms and onlookers had commented on how gaunt and drawn I appeared.

Under Pacquiao's red-hot assault I could feel my energy evaporating as the champion tried to land the finishing punch. Teddy Atlas, an American boxing trainer with a mouth as big as the Grand Canyon, was one of the ringside commentators for the ESPN network. He was almost ecstatic that I was badly hurt. Before the fight he had told anyone who cared to listen that I had no chance, that I didn't deserve to be sharing the ring with Pacquiao and that the great champion would knock me out.

As Pacquiao came on strong, Atlas gleefully told viewers around the world that I was about to melt in the Australian sun and that soon I would be a puddle on the canvas.

With the roar of the crowd reaching a crescendo, Atlas's co-commentator, the former world champion Timothy Bradley, who felt it was a close fight and that I had proved myself on the world stage, said Pacquiao was now trying to step up the pace and was fighting with a sense of urgency.

The third ESPN commentator Joe Tessitore took over. 'Pacquiao surging, hunting, seeking to destroy with that left hand,' Tessitore said, breathlessly. 'Manny comes back ... You can barely hear yourself think ringside as blood is pouring from the right eye of Jeff Horn.'

Tessitore's voice rose as Pacquiao poured it on. 'And Pacquiao is on target. Punch after punch. Can Horn hold up now? He has given so much.'

I *had* given so much. But Pacquiao was swinging with everything he had and my face was ripped apart. My right cheekbone was purple and badly swollen and my face was bloodied. I looked like I'd been in a car accident and Pacquiao was trying to run right over the top of me.

'The right side of Jeff Horn's face is an absolute mess,' Tessitore continued. 'Swollen. Blood soaked. Blood streaming from the cut. Left hand after left hand after left hand.'

His voice got louder and louder.

'Manny Pacquiao showing prime punching power here in Round Number 9. Oh my.'

CLANG.

The bell mercifully tolled to end the round.

It was the sweetest note I had ever heard.

As I sat down in my corner to recover my senses, the

American referee Mark Nelson came over to me with a grim, mournful face, like a doctor with bad news.

Nelson said that he was there to protect me and he was getting ready to stop the fight and award Pacquiao a victory inside the distance.

My heart sank.

Everyone in my corner yelled back at him that I was fine.

Let me fight. Let me fight. I'm in front. I've just had a rough patch, but I'm fine.

I was starting to look like the Elephant Man with my face horribly disfigured, but I had come too far on my journey to have it end like this.

Nelson repeated that it was his job to protect me and said that I had to fight back hard immediately or he would stop the fight.

What would I do?

This world title shot was a dream opportunity for me. But was it really just a cruel illusion? Was all the hard work, all the planning, all the preparation, all the years of sacrifice, now about to blow up in my face?

My head was buzzing but I was still thinking clearly.

I believed that I was way in front on the scorecards and, even though I'd just gone through a tough round with Pacquiao on top, I felt that I was recovering well in the break between rounds. I knew I could fight back and turn it around.

The fight was a golden opportunity for me to make my name on the world stage but now, as I faced the greatest crisis of my life, it presented me, a schoolteacher, with the opportunity to deliver a lesson in resilience and perseverance.

I could now send kids – and adults – going through a tough time an important message about not giving up, no matter how bad things might seem.

I have been in some nasty scrapes in my life and I have always been the underdog. When I was fifteen, a gang had grabbed a friend and me on our way home from school. Their leader wanted to humiliate us in front of all his mates. He ordered me to get down on my knees in front of him.

In those days I would have had a hard time denting a wet paper bag. But I refused to go down. There was no way I was going to give in.

The bully slapped me hard across the face. But still there was no way I was going down.

Now Manny Pacquiao was trying to force me to my knees too, with hundreds of millions of people watching around the world.

As I got off my stool in the corner and readied myself for Round 10, I resolved in my heart that I would not stop fighting back.

I would not surrender.

I thought about how much this fight meant to me and to Jo, our unborn child, my parents, my family, my friends. I thought about how Glenn had taught me to believe in myself, how like tempering a piece of steel he had shaped me from a nervous kid into a champion boxer through years of patient care and hard work.

I thought about all the people who, before this great sporting contest, had sent me messages of support, all the people who had asked me for an autograph, who had given me a thumbs up in the street or just a smile or a wave.

Every single one of them had helped me reach this point in my life.

As Round 10 began and Manny Pacquiao signalled to me from across the ring to bring it on, I wanted to show the world that if you push through the dark times in your life amazing things can happen.

That's what has happened for me and I want to share this message with you.

2

Once a jolly swagman camped by a billabong
Under the shade of a coolibah tree

– From 'Waltzing Matilda' by Banjo Paterson, first performed publicly in my grandfather's hometown in 1895

BEFORE OUR WORLD TITLE fight at Suncorp Stadium, Manny Pacquiao said there was no way I could ever be as hungry as he was, that I had never known the poverty or lack that he had experienced as a street kid trying to survive in the slums of the Philippines. Although it's true that I have never known the desperate circumstances that Manny experienced, I have my own motivations for fighting as hard as he does. While he was raised in almost unimaginable squalor and dysfunction, I'm grateful that I grew up as part of a big loving family in Brisbane's outer southern suburbs and never had to scrap around the streets for my dinner. I have had tremendous support from my parents, grandparents, siblings, aunts, uncles and cousins for as long as I can remember, and have always enjoyed the huge family get-togethers we have on a regular basis, even if some of them involve plenty of rough and tumble with my male relatives. My family's help has been crucial to my success. One of the big drivers behind my desire to be a world champion was to reward them all for the faith they have shown in me.

Like most Australians, my family journeyed to this country from overseas, and they certainly knew hard times.

I came into this world on 4 February 1988 at Brisbane's Royal Women's Hospital, the third of four children born to Jeff Horn Snr and Liza Dykstra. I did not have my first proper boxing match until I was nearly twenty years and six months, which is late to take up the sport.

My fighting instincts, however, had their gestation many generations earlier on both sides of my family.

'Horn' is a German name. My great-great grandfather, Johan Jacob (John) Horn, was a farm labourer, the son of Peter Horn and Christina Schwab from southern Germany. Like many Germans in the nineteenth century, he fled hard times in his homeland to make a new life for himself on the other side of the world. He arrived in Melbourne in 1865 aged eighteen. He spent most of his life working on bush properties and humping his swag, as he trekked north.

In 1877, at Wallerawang near Lithgow, New South Wales, he married Eva Diehm, a local teenager of German parentage. Together, in 1885, they headed further north towards the great sheep stations of central Queensland as part of a convoy of horses and 21 drays. They settled in Winton, only a short walk from the North Gregory Hotel, which in 1895 staged the first performance of the famous ballad 'Waltzing Matilda'. The poem and song have their origins in the tragic tale of a German swagman, not unlike my great-great grandfather. Banjo Paterson wrote the words a little earlier on a trip to a nearby sheep station. A piano is still used to perform the song at the North Gregory Hotel and my family still makes pilgrimages to the area. One of my cousins has a daughter named Matilda in honour of our family background in the bush.

Johan and Eva opened Winton's first butcher shop and had a son named Bob, my great-grandfather. In the days when wool was one of Australia's most valuable exports, he was a wool presser and drover and spent long periods away from his family, mustering huge flocks of sheep. In a little house in Cork Street, Winton, Bob and his wife, Ruby, raised eleven children. One of their daughters, Jean, became the mother of Graham Quirk, Brisbane's Lord Mayor, who is my second cousin. Among their other children were twin boys, Gordon and Ray. Ray is my grandfather – my Pop – and he has always been one of my greatest supporters. He tells people that when I was a kid he came to see my earliest soccer games and he reckons I ran all over the paddock like a hare. In the last few years, as he was approaching his ninetieth birthday, Ray said that, despite his wavering health and some really heavy knocks he has taken, the prospect of seeing me becoming world champion was one of the things that kept him going.

We don't have much of a boxing background in my family. But when Pop and his twin brother, Gordon, were six years old they used to box in little exhibitions at the race meetings when punters would descend on Winton from the sheep stations all around – from places such as Longreach, Barcaldine, Jericho and Blackall. The best fighters would contest the main events and Pop and Gordon would box preliminary bouts to start off the shows. Their mum, Ruby, would have their boxing kits laid out on the bed, neatly ironed before their fights: white singlets, white shorts and pristine white sandshoes. The twins used to bore into each other – two little kids going hammer and tongs – and all the old bushies would throw a shower of coins into the ring like confetti to celebrate their wholehearted efforts. There would be a towel in the middle of the ring and the twins would collect shilling pieces – a fair bit of money during the Great Depression when times were really tough. They were a pair of crowd-pleasing fighters, something that I have always tried to be in my boxing career.

Pop and Gordon and their brother Mickey were known around the Outback as 'The Fighting Horns'.

They learned boxing from their dad Bob, who had been coached by the famous English war hero Reverend Frederick Hulton-Sams, known throughout the British Empire at the time as 'The Fighting Parson'. Reverend Hulton-Sams joined the Saint Andrew's Bush Brotherhood, a group of travelling Anglican priests, in Longreach in 1908, when he was 27.

Hulton-Sams had been educated at Harrow School and then Trinity College, Cambridge, where he won the University featherweight boxing competitions in 1901, 1902 and 1904, and represented his university successfully in competitions against Oxford.

While in outback Queensland, he mined opals and would ride out to conduct religious services in remote areas. Following his sermon, he would strip to the waist and challenge any of his parishioners to a bout with boxing gloves. He sometimes refereed local boxing matches, too, and if crowds didn't like a decision he rendered he would offer to box any dissenters.

Hulton-Sams enlisted in the English army at the outbreak of World War I and was killed at Hooge, in Flanders, in 1915, while taking water to wounded soldiers. His fiancée had a piece of Jundah opal cut into five oval-shaped pieces and set into the base of a silver chalice to commemorate him and the chalice is still in the Church of England in Longreach.

Mickey Horn's son Mike, who was born in remote Boulia, is still something of an Outback legend for his fighting ability. He once boxed in the travelling tent shows of Roy Bell and Larry Delahunty, where you had to be tough to make a living.

Mike ran a pub at Alpha, between Emerald and Longreach, and then ran the Workers Club in Collinsville, near Bowen, back in the 1980s when he reckoned it was an unruly 'bloodhouse'.

He says in all the places he's ever worked it's the only one where he ever saw 'Santa Claus cop a hiding'. Apparently, one Christmas a very heavy lady sat on the lap of the man hired to play Santa Claus. Santa protested loudly about her weight and the lady's husband became so angry he ripped off Santa's white beard and king hit him, sparking a brawl.

★

In later years Gordon Horn had a few trial bouts at the old Brisbane Stadium which then became the Festival Hall. Gordon and Pop reckoned one of their biggest thrills was going to watch the great Australian welterweight champ Tommy Burns fighting in Brisbane. When I started out on my boxing career Pop hoped that one day I could be as good as old Tommy, who was a real hero to Australian crowds in the 1940s and '50s.

Pop remembers his mum – who raised eleven kids on a low wage – telling him that she sometimes didn't know how she would manage and she would curse being so busy. But when she looked back on her children growing up, doing their hair and making sure their clothes looked neat and buttoned up was the nicest part of her life.

Across the road from the Horn house in Winton there was an Aboriginal lady named Mrs Reid who had a mile of small children of her own. One night, hearing crying that continued into the early hours of the morning, my great-grandmother Ruby went over to investigate.

'Mrs Reid,' she said, 'I could hear the children crying and I came to see what was wrong.'

'Yes, Mrs Horn,' she replied, 'the children are all hungry and I've got nothing to give them.'

So my great-grandmother went home and filled a big plate with sandwiches and took them over. The crying soon stopped. The next morning she took Mrs Reid to the police station to register for 'the sustenance', which was a welfare payment to keep people from starving.

Men tramping the bush looking for work were a common sight during the Great Depression. They were always knocking at Ruby's door asking to chop wood in exchange for a feed. My great-grandmother never had money to give them but she could always rustle up a sandwich. No one ever left the little house in Winton hungry.

In 1936 when he and Pop were eight years old, Gordon started suffering double vision, a loss of balance and bouts of paralysis. While all the other kids could jump puddles, he couldn't. He started to have a hard time just putting on his shirt. Once when my great-grandmother was chasing a cow down a lane, Gordon said he could see 'two mummies and two cows'.

Doctors from distant Rockhampton and Townsville were consulted. Some said it sounded like lead poisoning, others that it was a tumour on the brain. But Gordon had contracted polio, the terrible crippling virus that devastated so many families around the world. Polio proved fatal in many cases or often left its victims with withered limbs. Little Gordon fought the disease with everything that he had. Pop was in his twin brother's corner right through that terrible fight.

The Flying Doctor Service, then still in its infancy and still using bi-planes, flew little Gordon the 1400 kilometres across the vast Queensland interior from Winton to Brisbane for specialist treatment. He was accompanied by his mum and the Inland Mission doctor, who was based even farther out west in Cloncurry. Flying in those days was still pretty hazardous and it took them two days and a replacement plane in Charleville to complete the distance. During the flight Gordon told his mum that he'd like to sit up and she was shocked that when she helped him up he was totally paralysed. The little boy came up in one stiff piece.

He was confined at the Wattlebrae Hospital, a place for patients with infectious diseases within the confines of the Brisbane General Hospital. Even as a little boy Gordon knew he had to fight hard to make a recovery. The nursing staff told my great-grandmother that Gordon was a real little

'Briton' doing all the exercises they prescribed, even though the stretching hurt him badly and he was in terrible pain.

At their school in outback Winton, the teacher gave the students half an hour every morning to write letters of encouragement to Gordon. You can imagine how uplifting those letters from the bush were to that little boy. I guess his joy at opening the mail from all his schoolmates was similar to the feeling I get when people send me messages of support before a big fight. The encouragement worked. Gordon spent six months in hospital and made a complete recovery – 'an amazing one', the newspapers called it. I'm proud that Gordon's son Darren is considered as an uncle.

Gordon and Pop started working in the shearing sheds around Longreach when they were a pair of tiny fourteen year olds. They wanted to help out their mum. They worked up in Queensland's hot dry centre until they were twenty. At every shearing shed they worked they shared a room and Pop says his twin was the best 'womb-mate' he ever had.

Pop loved Winton but the twins eventually moved to Brisbane and Pop worked on the trams and buses for thirty-seven years.

He married my Nana, Betty, in 1955 and they had eight children – Marion, Russel, Jeff, Phil, Carol, Colin, Margaret and Carmel. Jeff is my dad – he's the original Jeff Horn – and in my family I'm known by everyone as Jeffrey to avoid confusion.

My family home for the first few months of my life was in the working-class Brisbane suburb of Inala. My dad is a builder and my parents were determined that they would make do on one wage while Mum stayed home and looked after our growing family. Mum says I was a real 'cry-baby' and when she brought me home from hospital I screamed all day and all night. She couldn't get any sleep and the neighbours would come over and say, 'We heard your baby screaming all night – is everything okay?' My dad, though, could sleep through a nuclear blast and is a very calm person. He would sleep right through the wailing and the next morning wonder what all the fuss was about.

Mum had me up at the doctors all the time because I was losing weight and I wouldn't drink from the bottle or breast. Maybe I was already preparing myself for the sacrifices of boxing training when I would constantly diet to make weight.

When I was a few months old, the family moved from Inala to a 1.6-hectare paddock in the nearby suburb of Pallara, on Brisbane's southwestern fringe. The property came complete with a one-bedroom shack which Dad began turning into our family home. Our neighbours were undisturbed because out in all that space among the horse paddocks no one could hear me scream. Thankfully, I started to calm down when I started eating solid food at the age of about six months.

Our modest home was pretty cramped in the early days. Money did not come easy as we were a one-income family and bills often had to be paid late. Before long there were five of us all sharing the one large bedroom, all sleeping on the floor – Mum and Dad, my sisters, Rebecca and Bianca, who are five and two years older than I am respectively, and me. My brother, Ben, was born eighteen months later.

Now, Rebecca is a schoolteacher who became a stay-at-home mum, Bianca is a lawyer and Ben, who is a talented amateur boxer, works with my dad in the building business. Ben has been in my corner throughout my boxing career and is calm under pressure like me, which is why he makes a good second in the ring. It gives me great pleasure to have Ben in my corner to share in my success.

Mental toughness is one of the most important things a boxer can have and I would say it is my greatest strength. It probably comes from my father, who often faced tough economic times but kept on going regardless and never lost his cool. Dad says that he inherited that toughness from his father – my Pop – who grew up in that little house in Winton and then supported a wife and eight kids on a single income. Pop would never have had more than a few pennies spare from his weekly wage. Although he couldn't provide luxuries for my dad and all his other kids, Pop always took them to Stradbroke Island for school holidays, took them every year to the Royal Brisbane Exhibition and always made sure Nana had a cake for the kids on their birthdays.

While my mental strength comes from the Horn side of my family, I'm sure the physical toughness comes from Mum's family, the Dykstras.

I gave my grandad Jack Dykstra my maroon Queensland amateur boxing team tracksuit a while ago and he's hardly had it off his back since. He's worn it more than I did. He came to Australia from the Netherlands in 1952. Grandma Marie Dykstra's family hails from Toowoomba. They lived in a caravan in their early days of marriage and slept on a home-made fold-out bed.

Grandad was very keen on boxing in his younger days and would ride his Vespa to a gym on Brisbane's southside. He had a couple of amateur fights and would sometimes spar with his mate Merv Litzow, whose brother Rod was the Australian amateur welterweight champion and a silver medallist at the 1954 Commonwealth Games in Vancouver.

Grandad and I have been friendly rivals ever since I can remember. Evidently, when I was a few months old Grandad and his mate Stu were looking after me at our home in Pallara and I created something of a stink by leaving them a present in my nappy. The two men were almost overcome with horror. There was an uncomfortable silence as they looked at each other to see which one would change me. According to reports I've heard, there was plenty of 'you do it' and 'no, you do it' and 'no, I'm not going near it' that went on for ages until my sister Rebecca – who was only six at the time – volunteered for the job no one else wanted.

Grandad escaped from that situation but we have been giving each other a hard time ever since. He has been my chief sparring partner for almost thirty years. From as early as I can remember, I was always wrestling him and his kids – my uncles – and annoying them as much as I could.

Years ago, Grandad would take my mum to the amateur boxing nights at the Acacia Ridge Hall and later he and my father were regulars at the Festival Hall, watching the great Brisbane boxing brothers Brian and Mark Janssen and, on two occasions, the world champ Jeff Fenech in non-title bouts. So even though there were no real fighters of note in our family, there was always an interest in the sport and an appreciation for the skills and toughness needed for boxing.

One of my mum's brothers is the multi-award-winning actor Russell Dykstra, best known these days for his star turn as Barney, in the ABC TV series *Rake*. I know Russell better as the guy who first showed me magic tricks when I was a kid. My love for magic and illusions has stayed with me all my life. I have all kinds of paraphernalia for magic acts:

the fake finger for the hidden handkerchief, the disappearing box of cards, the boxes with the secret compartments.

Illusion is a key to success in boxing. Sleight of hand is paramount. After all, what is a feint or a baulk? What is showing an opponent one punch and delivering another? All through my fight with Manny Pacquiao I was showing him the left and throwing the right, or the other way round. I guess I first learned to trick people as an infant at Pallara.

*

Dad eventually turned our little shack into a comfortable four-bedroom home. I always shared a room with Ben and although my two sisters each had their own room they usually preferred to bunk down together. We were a close-knit unit growing up. I was born into the Catholic faith and as a small child we went to church every Sunday, but eventually I stopped being a practising Catholic although I still believe in the basic Christian principles of human decency and goodwill to others.

To me boxing has never been about hurting someone. It's a sport based on fitness, skill and courage in which two finely conditioned athletes push themselves and test each other to the hilt but can then shake hands and congratulate each other after even the most torrid contest.

My earliest memories of growing up at Pallara are of racing around our paddock with my parents and siblings, playing games with our neighbour's kids outside and then board games on the kitchen table.

I've always been competitive in games – super competitive – whether it's table tennis or Monopoly, but I have always led a pretty sedate life. The bright lights of the high rollers have never been my scene. Even now my idea of a big night out is to go to a friend's house with my wife, Jo, or have friends over to our place to play board games or cards. My cupboards are full of different games. Right now I'm keen on a game called Werewolf that you play just with a deck of cards. I like mental challenges and puzzles as well as the physical challenges.

We usually had animals around. My dad trained a few greyhounds and kept them in our back shed and we also looked after other people's horses. Dad and some relatives now own a pretty good bay mare called Bettyrae Ruby, named after his parents and grandmother. The horse has raced at Flemington, Caulfield and Moonee Valley and won the 1400-metre distance at Pakenham. Dad wanted me to be one of the owners too, but I rarely gamble on animals because you can't talk to them and you can only go on the advice of the trainer. I'd rather gamble on poker, which is largely dependent on the skill of the player and which I love. Even then, though, I only play for a few bucks at a time.

Living on an acreage was pure bliss for an active young kid who loved running around. We had plenty of places to play hide and seek with our neighbours Josh and Michael, or to engage in our little war games with cap guns, and later our toy laser guns, pretending we were snipers or storming our rivals' fortress to take their flag. My brother, Ben, and I spent hours doing that and we fought constantly as kids. Our closeness for more serious battles was forged in those early days. Ben has always had my back and I'm grateful that he has been a big part of my boxing team ever since I started fighting professionally.

I was never a boisterous kid but I had plenty of energy and I have loved sport ever since I could make my legs go fast as a toddler. I suffered the inevitable scrapes and near misses of childhood as well, chasing after my siblings or wrestling with my Dykstra uncles Russell, Gary and Paul. I was always fighting them in a playful way – they were like big brothers to me rather than uncles. Gary is nine years older than I am. As a little kid, he seemed really strong and muscly and I remember saying, 'I want to be just like you when I grow up.'

Once when I was quite young I was chasing my sister Rebecca through the house, going as fast as I could up the hallway. She jumped up on to our parents' bed and I jumped up to get her only to be shoved away in defence. I fell into a cabinet. The door handles were large square knobs and I hit one with full force. It made a deep cut on the side of my head right near the temple. There was blood everywhere and the wound was much worse than those I suffered in the Pacquiao fight. The doctor who stitched me up said a centimetre the other way and I could have died such was the force of the blow.

That close call didn't slow me down though. I have always been a bit of a risk-taker. You have to be prepared to take a chance to make it in boxing. It's a risky business and you don't get anywhere by going with the safe options.

A few years ago I went skydiving with my sister Bianca, a friend Bec and my uncle Gary and the thrill of free-falling through the sky was amazing. I can't wait to go bungee jumping, even though people like my dad say I'd be crazy to do something like that while I'm at the top of my game in boxing.

I'm not much of a drinker and I've never touched drugs but adrenaline is highly addictive. Once at the Dreamworld theme park on the Gold Coast I spent most of a day just riding the Giant Drop. I must have had thirty goes on it, one after the other, and although people are known to throw up on it on a regular basis I never got sick of the rush. The Giant Drop was in the *Guinness Book of World Records* as the 'tallest, vertical drop ride in the world' (it has since lost that title), but even though it stands at 119 metres high, the equivalent of a 39-storey building, I wish it was even higher. You plummet at 135 kilometres per hour towards earth and stop just metres from the ground. I love it.

Of course, the biggest thrill ride for me was fighting for the world welterweight title before more than 51,000 people in a sports stadium where I have been a spectator at State of Origin rugby league and Brisbane Roar soccer games.

When I was a small boy, I would often take a break from running around to sit on the swings in our backyard, stare into space and daydream about becoming a sportsman and being a champion at something.

The man I would one day face for the world welterweight boxing championship had no idea that I existed back then.

Although we were not a wealthy family, my childhood was far more content and comfortable than that of Manny Pacquiao's. While I was growing up in suburban Brisbane, he was fighting to survive in the jungles of his island home and then in the streets of the crowded cities of the Philippines.

*

Senator Emmanuel Dapidran Pacquiao came into this world on 17 December 1978 in a remote corner of Kibawe, a jungle town of around 40,000 people on the southern Philippines island of Mindanao. He was delivered by a midwife in a thatched hut with a dirt floor.

There was no hospital, pharmacy, doctor or nurse within any reasonable distance of where his family lived. The Pacquiao family was the saddest kind of poor and, even if there were modern medical services nearby, his family never had the money to afford such luxuries.

Pacquiao's mother, Dionisia, hoped that one day he would become a Catholic priest. His father, Rosalio, was a farm labourer climbing trees to harvest coconuts, making all of $1.50 for a fourteen-hour shift. Rosalio eventually left home to take up with another woman and, according to Pacquiao's camp, he only came back for a short stay during which in a fit of anger he killed and cooked a pet dog that Pacquiao had adopted.

Manny says he learned to fight as a small boy watching roosters scratch and peck each other to death in cockfights, which are still popular in the Philippines. He says the fighting birds taught him that as a boxer you have to be quick on your feet, that you have to dig deep and that you can never, ever quit. I can vouch for the fact that the birds taught Manny well.

When I was just three years old and enjoying the comforts of a loving home, twelve-year-old Manny had moved with his mother and five siblings to General Santos City, a metropolis of half a million people. While my parents planned out a university education for me, Manny left school before his teens to sell peanuts, doughnuts and cigarettes on street corners to help his family. He imagined a much more exciting future for himself though when he watched the 1990 world heavyweight title match on television between Mike Tyson and underdog James 'Buster' Douglas. As Douglas climbed from the canvas to drive Tyson to the floor with a series of huge blows, Manny recalled thinking, 'This was my first hope in life that I could be something or someone. I was the underdog, and maybe not even big enough to be a fighter. I wasn't from anywhere in the world that mattered. I had nothing to lose.'

Before I started primary school in Brisbane, thirteen-year-old Manny had become an amateur boxer and at only 40 kilograms hit hard enough to break the ribs of other boys. By fifteen, and still sleeping at home on a mattress of cardboard, he was a local hero.

★

I did not know any of the terrors that plagued Manny's childhood and I'm grateful for that. I'm lucky that I have always had close family ties and a lot of support from relatives all around me. But my childhood was certainly not free of stress.

I had my own demons to fight.

For some reason at an early age I developed claustrophobia, which still plagues me. I'm not scared of the dark, but if you combine darkness with a narrow space I can go to pieces.

On chilly nights when I was a kid, Dad would wrap Ben and me in blankets and I would freak out. I hated being tightly constrained and I still do. When I was in the Australian amateur boxing team and we were wrestling around in our room for a laugh, anytime I felt locked up or pinned I would totally go nuts. I'm getting better but being trapped in a small dark place is a fear that haunts my worst nightmares.

I have a constant dread of getting stuck in an elevator and not being able to see where I am. Even on kids' rides in tight, dark places I can feel myself starting to get panicky and I just want to get out of there. Yet falling from thousands of metres with a parachute on my back makes my heart race with excitement.

During one of my overseas boxing trips when I was an amateur – in Prague in the Czech Republic – the handle fell off my toilet door and I couldn't get out. It was a tiny space and instantly my heart rate and blood pressure went off the scale. I was going crazy trying to get someone's attention to get me out of there and thankfully one of my teammates came to the rescue pretty quickly. Much longer and I would have punched a hole through the door.

I don't know why I feel the way I do.

Maybe it's because the Horn family have their roots in the wide open spaces of central Queensland where the sky looks like it goes on forever and at night-time there is what Banjo Paterson called 'the wondrous glory of the everlasting stars'.

In any case, as my sixth birthday drew close at Pallara, I had to pack up my insecurities and start on the road to formal education.

Most boxers are produced in the school of hard knocks but my first classroom was in a pleasant little Catholic primary school. Over the next twelve years, school would teach me some very harsh and unforgettable lessons. It would also put me on an extraordinary path my family had never dreamed that I would take.

3

Most of the important things in the world have been accomplished by people who have kept on trying when there seemed to be no hope at all.

– Dale Carnegie, American writer and lecturer on self-improvement

I EARNED A REPUTATION as something of a knockout artist early in my boxing career but I first made an impression in the classroom as an artist with pencil and paper. I loved drawing things right from my first days at Our Lady of Fatima, the Catholic primary school at Acacia Ridge that my mum and my sisters attended before me.

I spent the first seven years of my school life there and drawing was my favourite activity when I wasn't running around in the playground. I loved to sketch monsters and dinosaurs. I would get my toys and study them before sitting down to try to capture their every detail in portraits the same way I now study opponents, trying to understand them from every angle. I'd get as many relatives as I could to pose for me too – 'stay still, stay still' – as I took pencil or crayon or pen and went to work with all the eagerness of a young Picasso.

Sport was always my real passion at school though.

Dad would throw tennis balls and then cricket balls to me and Ben every chance he got. He'd have us diving left and right to take catches as if we were wicketkeepers in the Australian cricket team. Once when I was playing cricket with my uncle Gary in the park, Dad saw me bowling with a wrist action that he reckons reminded him of Shane Warne. But to be honest I was never all that interested in the game.

Soccer was my great love and I started playing for the local Acacia Ridge club when I was six years old. I played the game for the next twelve years, at striker, right midfield and right back. I was only an average student at school and I directed most of my energies to sport, though I never reached my own lofty expectations in soccer. I was always much keener on playing the game than watching it, but I was a big fan of soccer on my PlayStation. Some of my favourite players were the Socceroos Harry Kewell and Mark Viduka and the great Brazilian, Ronaldo.

I always had a pretty good head for figures at school and learned the value of a dollar at a young age. My family always taunt me about being tight with money but I like to describe myself as a 'careful saver'. I had plenty of practice.

When I was a small boy, Mum would occasionally dole out little packets of Twisties – the crunchy, cheese-flavoured snack treats – from a bulk family pack. The snack-size bags were never big enough to satisfy my taste. I knew from experience that a few mouthfuls and the packet would be empty and I would be looking for more Twisties, which might be days away. So I resolved to practise delayed gratification – something I would get used to years later as a boxer, going without my favourite foods and chocolates for long periods. I decided I would save up all my Twisties packets and hide them under my bed for one grand opening – a gala party with me as the host and the special guest. Over a few weeks I had a really good stash going and I spent time counting the packets, weighing their contents in my hand and imagining myself deep in Twisties heaven. I licked my lips for days in anticipation of the big occasion.

I had a drum roll going on in my head as I snapped open the first packet of what would be many.

They were all stale.

Still, it proved that even at a young age I was developing the willpower and mental strength associated with self-sacrifice.

Even though my family was never flush with cash when I was growing up, Mum would still regularly treat us to a 30-cent ice-cream cone at McDonald's on the way home from school. It was a big deal for us and something a lot of kids around the world don't get to enjoy.

Already, though, I was a student of economics and figured that if I skipped the ice-cream and pocketed the 30 cents I could have a big stockpile of coins by the end of the year.

So at McDonald's, when Mum would go to get the ice-cream for us kids, I'd always say, 'No, I'll take the 30 cents instead, thanks very much.' I exasperated her regularly with my persistence as much as I exasperated Manny Pacquiao with my doggedness at Suncorp Stadium.

'You can't have the 30 cents,' Mum would reply. 'You either eat the ice-cream or you get nothing.'

Mum has a Dutch iron will and I couldn't break her so I never got the cash. At that stage of my young life, I didn't have the negotiating skills to offer a settlement of 20 cents and a win–win for both of us, though in time I would become pretty savvy when it came to fight for contracts and sponsorship deals.

*

Manny Pacquiao never got ice-creams after school or packets of Twisties or too many games of ball with his absent dad.

His family was desperately poor and from his early teens he yearned to make money to help his mother, who was living in dire circumstances in a hovel with a tribe of small children around her.

At sixteen, Manny and his friend Eugene Barutag stowed away on a freighter bound for the boxing arenas of Manila, 1600 kilometres north of their hometown of General Santos City. Manny cried nearly all the way on that long sea voyage because he didn't know if he would ever see his family again.

Manila, with its towering skyscrapers and endless traffic, terrified him. The two teenage boys slept in a park and Manny made $5 a day when he could find work, first scraping off rust at a scrap-metal yard, then toiling as a gardener, construction worker, waiter and tailor. He washed dishes so he could eat restaurant leftovers and bought flowers to sell for a slight profit as a street vendor. He began training in the first real boxing gym he had seen, up four flights of steep stairs in a dilapidated building in a Manila slum. Manny felt at home with the threadbare equipment, dusty floors and the ever-present pong of body odour and the gym owner let him sleep in a tiny room little bigger than a cupboard.

In December 1995 – when I was seven years old – Manny and Barutag appeared on the same fight card, against different opponents, at a small Manila hall. Barutag was winning his fight but faded badly in the later rounds and took one heavy punch after another before collapsing in his corner, unconscious. Chaos ensued as ringside officials tried to revive him.

Manny's eyes well with tears when he tells the story of how he held Barutag in his arms backstage as his friend's life slipped away.

'He was my close friend. I feel so bad,' Manny said. 'I was saying to him, "Come on, you can make it", but his eyes looked straight ahead and he was not breathing anymore.' Eugene Barutag was dead at just sixteen.

But Manny is made of incredibly strong stuff.

Minutes after that numbing tragedy, Manny, baby-faced and weighing just 50 kilograms, climbed into the same ring to beat his opponent by a points decision. He spent the next three days sitting by Barutag's open coffin and he paid for the funeral from the little money he had saved.

The tragedy did not destroy Manny though – it only made him stronger. Three years later in Thailand he won the World Boxing Council flyweight title at 51 kilograms, the first of eleven world championships he has held across eight weight divisions. This was the type of resolute, unshakeable boxer I would confront two decades later.

★

I was ten years old when Manny Pacquiao won his first world boxing title, although I was blissfully unaware of big-time boxing, living in the Brisbane suburbs. Manny would soon become one of the most talked-about boxers in the world but I had absolutely no idea about the sport and never followed it. Even now, having just competed in the biggest Australian fight of all time, I have to admit I am not really a student of boxing and I haven't even seen a lot of the big-name stars – even those who are gunning for me.

In a sense, I've had people gunning for me my whole life.

I don't really know why, but ever since I started school bullies would go after me. Maybe it was because I was small. I have always been polite and a bit shy and some kids took those as signs of weakness rather than as strengths. Maybe it was because I liked playing board games and spending time playing cards outside a classroom on the bag rack, even though I played sports as much as I could. And all through my childhood I got called 'gay' a lot in the days when that was supposed to be an insult.

My time at Our Lady of Fatima wasn't too bad though, despite some kids calling me names and pushing me around from time to time.

Things got much worse when I was thirteen and started at MacGregor High. MacGregor is a good school but sadly when I was there not every student lived up to its motto of 'The Best We Can Be'. Not long after my fight with Pacquiao, MacGregor High principal Liz Foster invited me and Jo back there for the Verge Young Entrepreneurs event, a *Shark Tank*–type initiative where Year 9 students swap innovative business ideas. I was one of five judges on the panel and it was great to be able to go back to my old school and help inspire students to be the best they can be.

The school was an hour-long bus ride during peak hour on the 122 route from my home at Pallara. I only went there because it was my sister Rebecca's old school. I was up every morning at 7 a.m., put on my uniform of white shirt and grey shorts, had a quick piece of toast and then dashed to the bus stop to catch the '7.30 all stops'.

I think I've always been pretty easy-going and easy to get along with, but because MacGregor was a fair way from my neighbourhood in my early years there I didn't have many close friends and wasn't part of any groups. For a long time I was seen as an outsider and my quiet nature didn't help. I became a target.

I would ask my mum, 'Why won't they leave me alone?' as I took comfort in her arms.

One kid gave me a terrible time for ages. He was a lot more confident than I was and he liked to throw his weight around. In the first of many heavy blows I would take, he kneed me in the stomach full force while we were playing soccer during interschool sport at another school. I fell to my knees in agony, as a wave of nausea rushed all over me, and even though I did my best not to look like a weakling, I couldn't stop the tears running down my face.

He laughed. He knew he had my measure and set about niggling me every chance he could.

Once when we were part of a group playing handball on the school courts, he took the bullying to another level. Some of the kids ganged up on me to make sure I was eliminated from the game. When I complained about being treated unfairly, the kid coward-punched me on the side of my head while I wasn't looking.

I was no fighter in those days and getting hit like that was totally alien to me. As my knees went weak, it was like I was on a fast ride in Disneyland with the world spinning around. I was totally disoriented and all I could see was the kid's smirking face distorted and twirling all around like he was in a hall of mirrors. He landed another uppercut on me and another as I did my best to come to my senses while still trying to fight him off. I threw four right hooks at him, but my punching power then wasn't quite what it is today and they were pretty feeble hooks. We both went down to the ground on the handball court and wrestled around until some teachers split us apart.

My head was still woozy as I clambered to my feet with a massive bruise on my chin. To a thirteen year old who wasn't looking it was a devastating punch – as damaging to my equilibrium as the big left hands Pacquiao landed on me in Round 9.

We were sent to the principal's office for fighting. The school treated me fairly and I got out of it. The other kid was punished. He was a dangerous student at thirteen. Another time he punched someone for looking at him funny and he was punished for that too.

I haven't had a chance to catch up with that guy since those days. Some of my friends have suggested I arrange a rematch to show him just how much my right hook has improved. But, honestly, retribution is the last thing on my mind. I'm not a vindictive person.

While I can never excuse the behaviour of bullies, as a schoolteacher myself I understand that their actions often stem from some deep trauma or insecurity. They are often more to be pitied than anything, although that is cold comfort to their victims.

*

At the time, Pacquiao was having much more success in physical confrontations than I was. While I was at MacGregor High he was beating some of the world's best boxers in spectacular fashion, combining speed and power to become one of the sport's big drawcards. Already well known in Asia as a dynamic little world champ, he made his debut in the lucrative American boxing arena in 2001. Raw and exciting he took the chance of challenging the International Boxing Federation (IBF) super-bantamweight (55-kg) champion Lehlo Ledwaba from South Africa on just two weeks' notice and stunned the boxing world with a stoppage victory in the sixth round in the great green edifice of the MGM Grand Garden Arena in Las Vegas.

Before long he was headlining at the massive Alamodome in San Antonio, Texas, battering Marco Antonio Barrera, the conqueror of great fighters such as Prince Naseem Hamed and Érik Morales. There was a huge Mexican crowd to support Barrera that night and the only fans Manny had were the few trainers in his corner. But once again Manny proved that he could win in hostile territory against an army of opposition supporters.

*

Not all the blows I suffered at high school were the result of kids picking on me.

As well as playing club soccer on the weekends for Acacia Ridge and later the Queensland Lions at Richlands, I also became a really good runner and was one of the best in the school at our athletics carnivals. And I played touch rugby league every chance I could in the lunch hours at school.

When I was fourteen a group of us were playing tackle football in the playground, which was against school rules. MacGregor was doing its best to avoid playground injuries and we were defying the edict that said only touch football was allowed in unsupervised competition. In fact, some of us were tackling really hard as though we were Michael Crocker or Gorden Tallis, the State of Origin stars of the time.

In one play, one of my mates was tackling a guy low around the legs while I went for the chest, but my mate's head came up and banged into my nose. It turned into a Vesuvius of blood, gushing everywhere. And you thought Horn–Pacquiao was a bloodbath. It was nothing on this. My teammates managed to stem the blood flow but as I went back to the lunch area one of my friends exclaimed, 'Oh man, your nose is facing the wrong direction.'

It felt like it was at right angles. In the school administration block they quickly determined that my nose was broken and I had to go to hospital.

I was very self-conscious about my looks then and, even though doctors said it wasn't necessary, I pleaded with Mum and Dad to allow me to have plastic surgery and have the bones reset properly. My parents didn't have a lot of money and it was an expense they could have done without. You can imagine that after having to tap into their meagre savings for the sake of my vanity, they were less than thrilled a few years later when I told them I wanted to take up boxing.

My grandad Jack Dykstra still teases me that he never thought I'd be a boxer because I was always scared to mess up my face.

He still ribs me about the time I tried to get Mum and Dad to pay for cosmetic surgery on my pigeon chest. You probably can't even notice it because I've added a fair bit of muscle since my teens – and certainly Manny Pacquiao wasn't focused on it as we were going toe to toe – but as a teenager I was also very self-conscious about my protruding breastbone. I wanted to have it surgically camouflaged.

Mum stood firm and said there was no way I was getting work done on that.

'Don't worry, Jeffrey,' she told me, 'one day some girl will love you, pigeon chest and all.'

She was right.

I met the love of my life at MacGregor High.

*

Joanna Buckley was a fellow student in Year 8, notable for being pretty with a lot of common sense. She's a few weeks older than I am but I felt that she was years ahead of me in maturity and attitude. We didn't really become friends until Year 10 when we were in a few classes together, including maths.

In those days Jo and I were really just friends – and not even that close. She was always a lovely, supportive girl with a very calm temperament, just so sweet-natured. I could talk to her about anything, including about the bullying that I was experiencing. Sometimes we'd even talk about other girls who I liked.

Even though I had rough times at high school, I had plenty of great experiences and made firm friends with a couple of other students, Kiang Lai and Nathan Millington. I also had some good teachers and role models there and loved the classes of the health and physical education teacher Andrew (Drew) Gell. From him, I really learned a lot about human performance that I've been also able to use in my sporting career. Mr Gell probably doesn't even know I thought so highly of him as a teacher. He could be tough on kids if they were a bit naughty. But if you gave him respect, he gave it back to you. I always gave him respect.

A lot of the other students didn't show that much respect for me though.

The worst instance of bullying that I suffered happened when I was fifteen. My friend Jamie was mucking around play-fighting with one of my young cousins and had him up against a wall. Then this other kid, bigger than us and part of a school gang, came up and started menacing Jamie. It was as though the bigger kid just wanted to fight someone and was using Jamie's play-fight as an excuse to start trouble.

'I'm that kid's family, his backup,' the big bloke said, pointing to my little cousin. 'Put him down.'

He wasn't his family at all. The big guy just wanted trouble.

He poked Jamie in the chest and said, 'Three o'clock, after school. I'm going to punch your head in.'

I jumped in to break things up. I always saw myself as the peacemaker in those situations.

I said, 'Leave him alone,' with as much gravitas as I could muster.

The big kid wasn't intimidated. He turned on me instead. 'You're dead too,' he said. 'I'm going to smash both of you after school and I'll bring some mates with me.'

I didn't tell the big kid that I was scared but the blood draining from my face was probably a give-away. 'No worries,' I stammered, trying to kill the butterflies in my stomach. *We're going home a different way today anyway, so you won't see us*, I thought.

We always caught the bus home from the Garden City shopping centre but that day we were planning to visit another mate after school, going a different way home, and we thought we could avoid any confrontations because of that.

Our plan went haywire.

When the school bell clanged at 3 o'clock Jamie and I got ready to make our get-away. We were heading in the opposite direction from our normal route, feeling that we'd dodged a bullet, when one of our friends came running up with news that made us feel faint. 'There are three carloads of guys over at Garden City with weapons,' he told us in a panic.

Weapons? Weapons?

Back then, I was flat out throwing a punch at someone. What could we do?

Before Jamie and I could even think of running, someone in the distance yelled, 'That's them. Get into them,' and about thirty tough-looking young blokes raced across an oval towards us with what seemed like murder in their eyes.

All I could say was, 'Holy crap Jamie, we're in for it now.'

A guy bigger and much older than us, maybe even twenty and I'm guessing a relative of the kid who had threatened us at school, grabbed me and Jamie and put his arm around our shoulders.

He was a bad-looking guy.

'Let's go around the corner from the school, boys,' he said. 'I'm a boxer and I'm going to teach you both a lesson.'

He more or less frogmarched the pair of us out of sight followed by his gang mates, including the big kid who had threatened us earlier in the day, who were almost licking their lips over what was about to occur.

Once we were out of sight of the school yard, the gang leader grabbed Jamie by the front of his shirt and almost lifted him off his feet.

'Now, you little prick, get on your knees.'

Jamie and I gave each other nervous glances and for a moment both of us thought about fighting back. But even if we were good fighters – which we weren't – we were outnumbered fifteen to one. There was no way we could do anything to turn them back.

We would have run but we were surrounded on all sides as the gang formed a ring around us.

Jamie refused to get on the ground.

'I said, get on your knees.'

Jamie again shook his head but some of the others kicked him behind the knees so that his legs collapsed and he went down.

The big guy then hit Jamie hard across the face with his open hand.

Then he turned his attention to me.

'You, get on your knees as well,' he snapped, 'and apologise for what you did at school today.'

I was terrified but I wasn't going to do what he said.

'No way,' I stammered back. 'I did nothing wrong.' The sense of injustice I felt was overwhelming but in this situation I felt hopeless. My throat was tight and my heart was going like crazy. I could feel the sweat running down the back of my neck.

Still, I stared back into the eyes of the bully.

'I said, get on your knees and say sorry,' he snarled again.

'No, I won't. I won't go down.'

I was waiting for his mates to try to knock me to the ground too but instead the leader slapped me hard across the face.

It hurt. The sting sent a shock right through me as the pain spread out in a wave.

I wanted to fight back but what could I do? If I tried to resist he and his mates would have squashed Jamie and me like bugs.

He looked us up and down like we were something he'd stepped in while walking his dog.

'If either of you,' he said, almost spitting at us with contempt, 'ever so much as look at my friend the wrong way again we will come back and kill you.'

With that they let us go and walked back towards their cars laughing.

Jamie and I were utterly humiliated. We had escaped a terrible beating but our pride was badly wounded. Jamie suffered a lot of anxiety and depression over that incident.

He left the school not long after.

I can't say that I fared much better.

I don't swear much but I was muttering under my breath, 'You bastards,' all the way home on the bus. When I got there I retreated to my room. I had my head in my hands and tears in my eyes. Mum knew there was something terribly wrong and came in to give me a cuddle, but I told her to leave me alone. I just wanted to be with my thoughts.

Why was I getting picked on all the time?

It was a really rough period in my life and it was made worse by the fact that a teacher had gone off at me not long before for drawing in my book instead of listening in class. I was only a mediocre student at the best of times and had felt really humiliated by what the teacher said to me in front of the other students.

I had a lot of teenage doubt and angst. In the end I started to think that life sucked and many times when I was alone I would ponder the unfairness of it all.

It was hard for my parents to see me suffering the pain and turmoil. Mum and Dad said they were proud of me for not giving in to the bullies, but they were now genuinely worried about my safety. Every time I got on the 122 bus in the morning they fretted about what lay in store for me that day. My parents didn't really know what to do about the situation – there were not the protocols around bullying that exist today. They were worried that if they went to the school to complain or to point the finger at the culprits, it would only make things worse for me. As it was, some of the bullies didn't even go to the school but were outsiders that MacGregor could not control.

Sometimes, when I felt overwhelmed with all the physical abuse and name calling, I had suicidal thoughts. I was sick of being treated like crap.

I remember many dark days and nights as a teenager when I started to wonder whether it was worth the effort in continuing with life.

It was.

Let me tell you now – things can become better. Much better if you push through and focus on tomorrow.

As my family reflects on those dark days of mine, my life starts to seem like some strange dream, a weird fantasy in which that sad boy crying in his room could one day be centre stage in the biggest boxing match ever seen in Australia.

And as I look back at the most traumatic incident of my childhood, I know those bullies could just as easily have been good kids if their circumstances were different. Just as with the kid who coward-punched me in Year 8, I don't think anything bad of the guys who terrorised Jamie and me in Year 10. As a teacher I now have some idea of what goes into making a bully. It's not just their parents or their upbringing. It's who they're hanging out with and what they're watching on TV and all these things that might add up to building frustration and anger.

Looking back, in a strange way, if it wasn't for those bullies I might never have found the pathway that led me to a world title fight with one of the greatest boxers of all time.

*

Jo was a great friend to me during the whole bullying crisis, the worst trauma of my life. When I told her what had happened with the gang after school she was really shocked, though the worst language she ever uses is 'Oh, my gosh'.

At about the time of the attack on Jamie and me, my uncle Gary Dykstra bought the property across the road from our place and set up a home gym with a few weights. I started training with him and my upper body strength began to increase dramatically. School had taught me that the world can be a pretty dangerous place, especially when some kids have a gang mentality to boost their own feelings of worth and are egged on to behave in aggressive ways. I don't know if my weight training had an effect, but the bullying started to drop off noticeably, even if I was still treated like a bit of an oddball by many of the kids. My reputation wasn't harmed when I became the athletics age champion at sixteen, winning or placed in just about every event I contested at the school carnival. I was a real all-rounder on the track. I became really good at running, especially in the distance events up to the 6-kilometre cross country. I always felt I could push myself harder than everyone else, even when I felt like death. I was never much good at the throwing events, because I wasn't heavy enough to hurl the discus or javelin very far, but in time I would get pretty good at throwing punches.

The strength I'd developed doing weights also helped me playing rugby league for the school and I became a pretty ferocious tackler. The bigger they came, the harder they fell. I wasn't afraid of anyone.

I was scared though when it came to telling Jo the way I felt about her.

We had been friends for a while, but a much deeper connection was developing between us and I could see myself spending a lot more time with her. We have pretty similar personalities, quiet and reserved, and I found myself feeling very calm and relaxed talking to her about anything. Except love.

For the 2005 school formal we had hooked up with different partners but we both felt in our hearts that we should be going together. Just before the big end-of-school celebration, Jo and I both went to an eighteenth birthday party at a friend's place. We bumped into each other accidentally on purpose on more than one occasion and then the mood took over and we started kissing in the pool.

I was still very shy but decided to plumb the depths of her true feelings after the party. Not face to face of course because it was now the twenty-first century. I chatted with her on MSN Messenger, the forerunner of Facebook. We flirted with each other across cyberspace and confessed that we really liked each other.

Unlike Facebook, though, you could never be certain on MSN Messenger that you were actually talking to the person you'd contacted.

I was typing my heartfelt feelings onto the computer screen and sending them to Jo across the airwaves, hoping that my words of devotion were going to her and not some bloke in a chatroom in Russia.

You'll think I'm the ultimate nerd when I tell you this but, to make sure we were both on the same page, we each typed in a message that we would meet up at school the next day. To avoid any embarrassment over our cyber communications, we agreed that if it was really us telling each other of our love we'd confirm it the next day by approaching and shaking hands.

Away from the ice-breaker of the party atmosphere in which we'd first kissed, we were both a bit nervous. But that's what happened. We shook hands. The school formal came and went and it was a little awkward with each of us having a different date on our arms.

The first day of the big schoolies break-up on the Gold Coast was the day that my relationship with Jo started in earnest. It was 19 November 2005.

We drove down to Surfers Paradise where thousands of kids descended for the annual wild holiday that celebrates the end of the twelfth and final year of schooling before they go on to tertiary studies or join the workforce.

Jo and I were staying at different hotels but I went over to hers to hold hands.

'So,' she said.

'So,' I said.

I could normally talk to Jo about anything but revealing my true feelings face to face was very awkward. I felt a lot more comfortable on the keyboard.

'So, why did you come over to the hotel?' she asked.

It was a difficult conversation.

'I guess I really like you,' I said.

'Well, I really like you,' she said.

We looked at each other, looked around at the hotel furnishings for a while as we thought of something more to say and then looked back at each other.

'Well, do you want to go out?' I ventured.

'Okay,' she said.

'Okay,' I said.

Then we kissed.

We've been together ever since.

If we were going to be going out, though, I wanted to be able to protect Jo. The bullying I'd suffered at school made me wary of the perils I might face at pubs and clubs if I didn't know how to look after myself. I didn't want to get into fights, I just wanted to learn the skills to get out of any trouble.

I needed to find someone who could teach me self-defence. I was about to meet the most unique character I'd ever come across. He is a karate champion and a self-made multimillionaire.

Glenn Rushton grew up poor but transformed his mind, body and finances with the power of positive thoughts and relentless determination. These days he makes dreams come true as sort of a cross between Chuck Norris and Tony Robbins, a mix of martial arts moves and motivational speeches.

4

Turn your wounds into wisdom.

– Oprah Winfrey, American talk show host and author

IT WAS THE BIGGEST house I'd ever seen, in the grandest boulevard I'd ever driven along. My old Volvo 240GL rattler, which seemed ready to pass out from fatigue at any time, looked ill at ease among a row of massive homes that reminds some visitors of Canberra's embassy precinct. It was a Thursday night, 20 April 2006. I nervously approached the high mauve-and-cream concrete fence surrounding a mansion in the southern Brisbane suburb of Stretton. Behind it I could see a vast tiled courtyard complete with a massive fountain with what looked like four stone dolphins bursting free. I wasn't sure if I was in the right place. It looked like photographs I'd seen of the Bellagio Hotel in Las Vegas. I would later discover that the mauve, gold and cream–coloured palace before me had seven bedrooms with en-suites, nine bathrooms, an indoor squash court, a tennis court, recording studio, indoor cinema, lap pool and swim-up bar.

It also contained a massive indoor gymnasium.

It was less than a twenty-minute drive from Mum and Dad's place at Pallara to Glenn Rushton's house. Without realising it, I had started a long, arduous journey that would take me to places and experiences and emotions I never imagined were possible. As I drove down Compton Road, I had turned the corner towards a future for myself and my family that really was beyond my wildest imagination. No wonder Glenn calls his gym 'The House of Dreams'.

He was about to give amazing powers of strength and confidence to a shy teenager who at the time did not even know how to throw a punch properly.

Glenn's own story is remarkable.

He was born in Bundaberg in 1957 and has fourteen brothers and five sisters (although, only two are full brothers and two are full sisters).

After his parents split, Glenn lived with his mother and an alcoholic, abusive stepfather for a time in Brisbane before moving with his two brothers to live with their father in Townsville.

In Year 7 at Townsville's Currajong State School he shared a classroom with his future wife, Lillian, and a young sporting all-rounder named Neil Pattel, who went on to become the Australian welterweight champion in the 1970s, fighting some of the Aussie greats of the time such as Hector Thompson, Wally Carr and Steve Dennis.

When he was small, Glenn said, if they happened to pass a nice car or a nice house he used to hear his mother use the well-worn expression, 'that's how the other half live'. He told his mum he wanted to be in that half and not the crappy half his family inhabited, and he set about realising his dreams at a young age.

The year Glenn was eleven, Lionel Rose, a teenage Aboriginal lad from country Victoria, made his first trip outside Australia, upsetting the odds to win the world bantamweight boxing title with a stunning display of speed and power against the mighty Fighting Harada in Tokyo. It was a pivotal moment in Australian sports history and came only a year after Indigenous Australians were first recognised in the census. Lionel inspired Glenn and thousands of others.

Glenn took up boxing the next year after he'd had his head rammed into a brick wall by an usher one night when he was mistaken for a kid who had thrown rocks on the roof of the local cinema. Glenn vowed that it would be the last time he got beaten up by anyone. He'd seen the Jimmy Sharman tent boxing troupe that toured Australia's fairs and country shows and he went off to learn self-defence, like I did almost forty years later. He took boxing lessons from Reggie Kirkham and trained with his classmate Neil Pattel at Townsville's National Fitness Centre on Charters Towers Road. Having learned to look after himself very well, he left home at fourteen with $20 in his pocket to make a new life for himself.

He went fruit picking in Shepparton, Victoria, and worked in the SPC cannery there before setting off to travel around the country. In Brisbane in the early 1970s he got hooked on the Bruce Lee martial arts craze that was spreading throughout the world and became a student of Bob Jones, a karate pioneer. Bob acted as bodyguard to many of the big stars coming to Australia, including the heavyweight boxer

Joe Frazier and rock acts such as the Rolling Stones and Joe Cocker.

Eventually Glenn became a fourth *dan* black belt, formed his own martial-arts style called Scorpion Martial Arts and ran ten karate clubs across Brisbane.

By the time I arrived at his home gym for my first self-defence class, Glenn had also forged careers as a property developer and investment manager.

He is very focused on teaching resilience – the mental and physical toughness that is essential, not just in boxing and martial arts, but in coping with the stresses of everyday life such as financial, relationship and economic pressures. One of the lessons he teaches his fighters is that you might get knocked down in life but you have to keep getting up, the same as in business. Sometimes you get hurt but you have to be tough and fight back. He says maybe one of the reasons we have so much depression in society these days is that people aren't taught resilience. In life you get bullied and in business you can get hurt but, he tells his students, you have to roll with the punches and press on.

*

My family had fallen in love with Jo just like I had and quickly accepted her as one of our own. I had planned on a teaching career to support us if we got married but I'd been hit with a heavy blow with my end-of-school Overall Position (OP) score, my tertiary entrance rank. On a scale of 1 to 25, with 1 being the highest, I was reeling with a 19. I'd been wishing for a 13 but, as Glenn would later tell me again and again in the boxing gym, wishing doesn't get you too far.

My marks hadn't been helped by the fact that I did two health-related subjects in my final year at school – health and physical education, and physical recreation – which weren't heavy hitters when it came to assessing student performances. I just loved sport and, while I had a dream to one day be a professional sportsman, my immediate plan was to become a physical education teacher like Mr Gell from MacGregor High.

My low OP score meant I didn't qualify to study for a degree, so in a sense I went back to school. I enrolled at the Yeronga TAFE in a course to earn an Advanced Diploma of Sport and Recreation, which would improve my OP score and help me get into a teaching course. I knuckled down to improve my prospects. My friend Kiang Lai was going to the TAFE as well and we became great mates there, even though we often needled each other.

For a while it had looked like I had a shot at a soccer career. Dad helped me to get a start training for several weeks in the off-season with the Rochedale Rovers, a semi-professional club. But I was a harsh judge on myself and deep down, even though I was still a teenager training alongside much more mature players, I felt I wasn't on pace to reach the top tier.

I was still playing touch football as often as I could though, as much for fun as fitness, and we formed a mixed team at Mount Gravatt that included my mates Kiang, Cue and Jac Lai, Jason, Michael, Nathan Millington, Josh Peters and my sisters, Bianca and Rebecca. We were called 'The Naked Turtles' and then the 'Unknowns'. I was a pretty good touch football player and had a decent sidestep. Sometimes I was so elusive that I made two opposition players run into each other trying to catch me.

Now that I was going out with Jo to parties and clubs and to the Calamvale Hotel though, I wanted to be able to defend us. When I had been bullied during my days at school, I had escaped some bad situations relatively unscathed. I feared that my luck could run out at any time.

So it was on that April evening in 2006 that I turned into Glenn Rushton's wide, jaw-dropping street, looking to learn some techniques that might get me out of trouble. I found much more – a guiding light who would lead me to a bright new future.

*

Glenn was forty-nine when I met him, though he looked much younger and was as lean and lithe as you would imagine a karate master would be. He still is. I still call him 'Renshi', which is a karate term for 'expert instructor' because that's what he was doing when he first taught me how to fight.

The first time I walked through the front door of Glenn's gym with my cousin Mat Symons, who was eager to learn self-defence as well, I had a lump in my throat as I eyed about twenty other students in martial arts attire ready to start a class.

Glenn says that I appeared to be a 'soft, wimpy sort of a kid ... looking like a mummy's boy', and when I told him I was picked on a lot at school he said he could understand why. He reckons I had one of those choir-boy faces that invites trouble and a hang-dog expression that was all target.

He had been involved in martial arts for thirty years, had won five state and national titles, and he had even been the promoter of a televised competition called the National

Martial Arts League, which staged events in Sydney, Melbourne and Brisbane and featured such fighters as Paul Briggs, Steve Vick, Ian Jacobs and Jimmy Shannon.

Glenn had taught thousands of people self-defence over the years and really enjoyed it, but around the time I arrived to take his classes he had started to become disillusioned with martial arts because, after all the sacrifices and injuries, there was hardly any money for the competitors and no opportunities to compete in global events such as the Olympics or Commonwealth Games. Although he was winding down his involvement in martial arts clubs, he still taught classes from his home because he remained very passionate about the way self-defence could change people's lives, how it could give them confidence which, through the ripple effect, could then benefit the lives of everyone they encountered, including their children in later years.

I signed a form to join his club. One of the first things Glenn told me was that he was glad I was being proactive about my safety and that mulling over being bullied was useless because feeling sorry for yourself got you nowhere. He said that he was a firm believer in people creating their own futures. He promised to show me how.

I lined up with all his other devotees, including a brilliant young kickboxer named Sam Banney, and Adam Partridge, who had become a world champion in Muay Thai kickboxing but found the purses barely covered cab fare to the auditorium.

Glenn and his offsider – his 'sensei' – would stand together and we'd all line up and bow to them. The more experienced guys were at the front of the gym and newcomers like me and

Mat were closest to the door. I used to think it was because it would be easier for us to escape.

We would start the class with fifty push-ups and sit-ups and then he would get us to practise martial arts moves. He taught us what he called the 'four As of self-defence' – Avoidance, Awareness, Assessment and Application – and then over the next few weeks how to break someone's nose.

Glenn said that a palm heel to the nose and a kick to the thigh were the best defences against a bully. You could break someone's nose with the palm heel, he said, and, while it would hurt like hell, you were unlikely to cause them permanent injury the way a punch might if you knocked someone down and their head hit the ground hard. The palm heel was literally a shock tactic that could stop an attack immediately. He taught us other defensive moves too, and we practised all sorts of dangerous scenarios such as someone pulling a knife or a bottle on you. Glenn had simple solutions that could get his students out of dangerous situations without getting into more trouble as a result.

He also taught me how to kick, but I was never that interested in karate or combat sports – at this time I was just concentrating on the self-defence.

I had never been a fighter and I didn't want to be one. But I really enjoyed those first few classes. They were challenging enough to fire up my competitive spirit and kept me going back.

*

A few weeks after Glenn showed me how to make a proper fist and to throw a left jab, I had become interested enough in boxing to watch a telecast of the first proper bout I ever saw. It was a contest that gripped the whole country – Anthony Mundine outpointing Danny Green over twelve rounds at the Sydney Football Stadium on 17 May 2006. There was a crowd of 30,000 and I couldn't imagine the adrenaline rush of fighting before that many people at such a huge venue.

In any case, I wasn't really that interested in boxing as a career for myself. I'd been punched hard enough in the head at school to know that it hurt and I didn't want to get hit again. At the time I was only going to Glenn's classes once a week – on a Thursday night after my TAFE studies. I talked to him about the Mundine–Green fight the next time I was at the gym but I didn't really know much about the sport to speak with any authority. Then, one day after he'd watched me hitting the punching bag for a while, he said that all the soccer and the touch football I'd played had given me good footwork and balance. He reckoned that I had good hand–eye coordination too and that I had some potential as a fighter.

'If you work hard at this,' he said, 'you could become a good boxer.'

'Really?' I asked, genuinely surprised.

'Yeah, really,' he said. 'Stick at it, Jeff. Don't give up.'

*

As I mentioned, Adam Partridge was a Muay Thai world champ but he was getting just $2000 a fight and there was no sign that the purses would get any bigger. As a businessman Glenn knew that return on investment was a waste of time and effort. Just before I joined the gym Melbourne had hosted the 2006 Commonwealth Games and the Australian boxing team – coached by a controversial former East German boxer named Bodo Andreass – had done exceptionally well. Queensland fighters Nathan Di Carlo, Todd Kidd, Brad Hore and Jarrod Fletcher competed and Fletcher took a gold medal. Glenn decided to start teaching boxing as well as self-defence and he guided Adam through two professional fights.

Slowly, the emphasis at the gym switched to boxing and Glenn began training other fighters to compete in the ring. I started to really enjoy the boxing training he gave us, the fitness drills and the bag punching. My confidence was growing gradually as Glenn taught me how to dodge punches, to slip away, get under them and counter-punch. He kept reinforcing the importance of what he calls 'gap control', getting us to stand just out of range of an opponent and then getting in range briefly to fire off punches before escaping in what he calls the 'recovery'.

After a few months of training with him one night a week, Glenn said that he could see 'the spark of something great' in the way I moved and the way I picked up all that he was teaching me. At the time I believed that if I really stuck to the boxing training and learned all the lessons Glenn could teach me, I might do okay in amateur contests because I was getting physically stronger each week and I had good balance. My uncle Gary Dykstra came to the boxing classes as well and encouraged me to push harder and harder.

Glenn started teaching us a style of boxing that he had developed years earlier that he calls 'Broken-Rhythm Pressure Fighting'. He's a student of philosophy and mind power and says the 'Broken-Rhythm' style is built on chaos theory. It makes a fighter who can master it unpredictable and therefore much more dangerous. He explained the style to me many times while shaking his shoulders, wobbling his legs and bobbing his head from side to side.

'I'm constantly coming at you, but you don't know when I'm coming, which way I'm coming,' he'd say. 'You don't know what I'm going to throw at you, where I'm going to hit you, how long I'm going to stay and which way I'll be leaving. There is no rhythm or predictability to it. You just can't work it out. You won't know it because, in fact, the fighter doesn't even know what he's going to throw next. The fighter is just programmed to do so many things, programmed to adjust. The art of deception. It's a completely unpredictable style.'

While Glenn taught us how to fight, his wife, Lillian, taught us that we were now part of their family. Glenn made the Scorpion Martial Arts Club a very tightly knit unit, with both men and women training there, sisters and brothers with a common purpose. Glenn and Lillian became like an extra set of parents to me and before long he told me he loved me like a son. His confidence in me and faith that I could be a boxer made me feel ten feet tall.

From a young age Glenn had immersed himself in self-help books such as Napoleon Hill's *Think and Grow Rich* and they certainly helped him become successful.

He is an extraordinary motivator. As a boy growing up in tough circumstances, he told himself that he was a rich man who'd only been born in a poor man's body. He told me that greatness was a state of mind. 'There are no great people,' he said. 'There are just ordinary people with great dreams.'

One of the things Glenn liked about me was my quiet personality and the fact that I had no idea about boxing when I first went to him. He said I was a good listener, that I was eager to learn because, when it came to fighting, I was a completely blank slate. I didn't think I was a tough guy, he said, I didn't have an ego. I had no mental baggage and he could program me from the outset. All I had to do was box the way he showed me and follow his plans.

Before long Glenn got me to put on a big leather headguard and some gloves and spar with Adam Partridge and Sam Banney. Sure I was nervous, almost as nervous as when the carloads of bullies came after me and my mate Jamie when we were fifteen. And, yes, the punches still hurt even with the headguard and the big padded gloves. But the sense that I was getting somewhere in a tough sport compensated for any short-term pain. That first time, the adrenaline was pumping so fast in me it was like I was stuck on the Giant Drop at Dreamworld.

For a guy who had never sparred before, I thought I went okay and I told Glenn that I'd gladly give it another go.

Glenn told me that I'd boxed well.

'Really?' I asked, surprised.

'Yeah, really,' he said.

*

At the same time that Glenn was teaching me the finer points of boxing, I started making a living in a totally different field – as a childcare worker at the Forest Lake State School, not far from my parents' home. My sister Rebecca was working there and helped me to get a start. Kylee Morris gave me my first job interview. I was now studying for my Bachelor of Education degree, having been accepted to Griffith University, and my friend Nathan Millington was a big help in getting me over the line in one of the subjects on computing.

It was a weird situation – this budding boxer tasked with looking after small children – but I loved it. I loved organising our games of touch football, I loved interacting with the kids, probably because deep down I'm a big kid at heart and I understand what they want and need. I know how kids think. I knew that I would be a hit in the classroom because I had such an affinity with all my young relatives.

*

I had never been to a boxing match but after training with Glenn – still for just one night a week – for twenty months, I finally decided to watch some fighters in a real competition. Dad and Jo came with me and we were all pretty excited to sit in the crowd of about 600 people at the 2007 Australian Amateur Boxing Championships, which were held over three days at Brisbane's Mansfield Tavern from 6 December.

The event was organised by a local boxing stalwart named Allan Nicolson and his wife, Pat, who together have done so much for the sport over so many years. Their son Jamie was a 1992 Olympian but he tragically died with his younger brother, Gavin, in a car accident in 1994. Their sister, Skye, has emerged as a star amateur fighter in her brothers' honour.

There was a stack of good fighters from around Australia competing at those championships: Luke Woods, Kye MacKenzie, Cameron Hammond, Zac Dunn, Joel Brunker, Ibrahim Balla, Luke Jackson, Sam Ah-See, Nathan Di Carlo, Paul Fleming, Anthony Little, Mark Basile, Nathan Carroll and Trent Broadhurst.

My weight division was very fiercely contested between Queenslander Todd Kidd, David Biddle from South

Australia, Angus Hann from Western Australia and Qamil Balla, the eventual winner. Qamil was fast and poised, an eighteen year old from Melbourne's outskirts, who with younger brother Ibrahim was part of a highly regarded boxing family of Albanian heritage. The 64-kilogram final for the Australian championship was fast-paced like one of my sparring sessions at the gym on fast forward, as Balla outpointed Hann for the title.

Even though I'd never had a fight in the ring, Glenn had infused me with an enormous feeling of self-belief, telling me all the time that with hard work anything was possible. Watching the best 64-kilogram fighters in Australia and never actually having had a proper fight in my life, I turned to my dad and Jo and said, 'You know, I reckon with the right training I could beat these guys.'

Jo raised a quizzical eyebrow.

Dad wondered what else I had in my Diet Coke.

'Yeah, right,' Dad said. 'Good on you, son, that's the way to think.'

*

Three months after I attended my very first boxing match, Manny Pacquiao won a thriller over twelve rounds with his great Mexican rival Juan Manuel Márquez at the Mandalay Bay Casino in Las Vegas. Pacquiao took the World Boxing Council's (WBC) super-featherweight title with a close decision in their fight at 59 kilograms. It was a rematch of a 2004 Las Vegas bout in which Márquez climbed from the canvas three times in the opening round to salvage a draw for the world featherweight title at 57 kilograms.

On 28 June 2008, Pacquiao climbed up another division, stopping American David Díaz for the WBC lightweight (61-kg) title at the Mandalay Bay. He was ready to enter the rarefied air of multimillion-dollar purses as one of boxing's most bankable drawcards.

*

Boxing hardly seemed like a viable career for me though, despite my steady progress in Glenn's classes. Anthony Mundine and Danny Green might have made millions from their heavily hyped grudge fight, but for most Australian boxers a purse of peanuts represented a pay rise. To me, there seemed much more lucrative sports I could try, despite being twenty years old and late to be chasing a foothold as a professional athlete.

I thought I might have a chance to make some money from rugby league for a team such as the Broncos, even though I had not played much tackle football beyond school matches and some muck-around games of touch with the team that included my sister. It was worth a shot, even though Dad feared I was too small and too slightly built to have a real crack at the big time.

Dad had some rugby league connections – Phil Hall, who was a leading light in schoolboys' league, and Cyril Connell, a former champion player who as well as being a key talent scout for the Broncos had been Dad's headmaster at Cavendish Road State High School for a year. Phil Hall organised for me to train with Queensland Cup league side the Easts Tigers at Langlands Park in Coorparoo. I went down there and had a few runs with the lower grade players.

It was just big bodies in motion and I knew the only positions I could fill were the playmaking roles behind the scrum. And although I could run, pass, sidestep and tackle, I really didn't understand all the subtleties of the game like a really good halfback does.

I decided to talk to Glenn about really devoting myself to a sport. I said that I wanted to give something a real good crack before I got too old. It was either rugby league or boxing. He had never seen any great desire in me to be a fighter until then.

'Which way do you think I should go?' I asked.

Glenn said something that changed my life. 'Jeff, if you do choose boxing, I believe you have a big future. I can teach you everything you need to know, but I can't make you want it – if you don't want it, there's nothing I can do. Boxing is not an easy road. It is a hard road, it's a difficult journey and most fighters make no money. But some make a fortune and I think you can be one of them.'

Then he said something that gobsmacked me.

'Jeff,' he said, 'if you give me 100 per cent commitment in boxing, I believe that I can take you to the next Olympics in four years.'

I stood there with a stunned look on my face. I couldn't believe what he was saying. But Glenn has a way of making you believe.

'Really?'

'Yeah, really,' he said.

Glenn said he wanted me to go home and think about it very carefully. He wanted me to discuss it with my family because it was not an easy decision to make. I should come back the next week and tell him which direction I wanted to take.

Glenn's words were dancing in my head as I drove the old Volvo home.

I talked it over with Mum and Dad. I said I wanted to devote myself to one sport for a couple of years and see what I could achieve.

Dad said that in rugby league I was on a hiding to nothing. 'You're only 5 foot 9 [175 cm] and 64 kilos,' he said. 'You're going to have to put on a lot of weight to make it in rugby league. You're going to have to play halfback and even if you get to the top – and it's a very big if – you're going to have guys like Willie Mason and Blocker Roach, all 120 kilos of them, hitting you and sometimes two or three guys that same size hitting you all at once.'

Dad still hadn't met Glenn but I said that he was a great trainer and that he believed in me. Dad told me to follow my gut instinct.

The next Thursday night at boxing training I had a heart to heart with Glenn and asked him if he was exaggerating about my potential.

'I mean seriously,' I said, 'I haven't even had one fight yet.'

Glenn repeated that if I gave boxing everything, I could be an Olympian in four years.

'Alright,' I said, 'then I choose boxing. I'll give it everything I've got and we'll see where it takes me.'

Glenn was overjoyed.

He said it was time to get to work. He was about to organise my very first boxing match.

It would be full of surprises.

5

When you take belief and back that up with commitment, that's when the magic happens.

– Glenn Rushton, my trainer and manager

SO IT WAS TIME for me to become a real fighter. I had been training in self-defence and then boxing under Glenn's guidance for two years and four months when I arrived at the Acacia Ridge Hotel with him, Lillian, Jo and most of the people in my extended family for my very first fight on Saturday, 2 August 2008. None of my family really knew that much about boxing and, after the bullying I'd suffered at school, most of them were worried that I would get hurt during a show that promoter Ian Bronson had labelled 'The Rumble at the Ridge'.

Mum had done her best to talk me out of pursuing the sport.

'Don't go down this path,' she said. 'You could get hurt, badly hurt.'

At one stage she even started mimicking the voices of boxers who had gone punchy from too many hits to the head. But in the end I sat down with her and said, 'Mum I'm doing it. You either follow it or not, but I've got the dream of becoming a boxing champion.'

Despite their reservations, my family were willing to support me as I followed my dream. I was now twenty and a half years old and they realised I was a grown man and able to make my own decisions.

Glenn had arranged for me to have an amateur boxing bout on a program of kickboxing fights that would feature my teammate Sam Banney. I would be representing Scorpion Martial Arts. Glenn arrived wearing a jacket bearing the image of our club's No. 1 fighter, Adam Partridge.

Eight months earlier I told Glenn that I had watched the Australian title fights with Dad and Jo and that I thought, with some proper training, I could beat the guys in my weight class. Glenn was stoked and admired that confidence. He said that most blokes would say, 'Oh, those guys are really good,' but I was confident by now that he could teach me the winning ways.

Despite all my training with Glenn and my outward confidence, I was still extremely nervous. This was no longer sparring, this was a real fight, and my opponent, Alex Smith from the Viper Freestyle Club, had a plan to take off my head the first chance I gave him. In boxing you are always just one punch away from disaster. I knew I couldn't afford to make any mistakes or I would suffer badly. Alex was trained by a good teacher named Tyrone

Murphy, who had fought on Glenn's National Martial Arts League.

I was Fight No. 8 on the show. As we waited in our little dressing room for the first seven fights to finish, Glenn went over all the basics that he wanted me to follow, specifically gap control and recovery, using my legs to stay away and then attack. He told me again and again to keep my hands up after an exchange of punches so that I didn't get hit on the way out.

The ring was surrounded by long tables covered in white table linen as patrons ate snacks to go with the knuckle sandwiches the fighters were serving each other.

Alex and I climbed into the ring with our corner teams, me in the blue corner and Alex in the red. He was wearing a pair of Muay Thai boxing shorts, while I had on long blue boxing trunks. Both of us were having our first amateur fight. The bout was set for three rounds, with each round to last just ninety seconds. This was to be a sprint from the opening bell.

The referee was Brad Vocale, a highly respected figure in Australian boxing and a cousin of the great Lionel Rose. Brad had been a handy professional fighter in Melbourne in his younger days but was now better known as a leading referee of professional fights around the world. He had already controlled world title bouts. Once in a charity fight he had got stuck into the Sydney rugby league referee Bill Harrigan, which made him something of a hero throughout Queensland.

When Brad called us over to the centre of the ring to give us a quick recap of the rules, Alex got up in my face, letting me know he wasn't worried about me. Brad told us to shake hands and come out fighting, and Alex slapped my gloves hard as a warning for what was about to come.

As I nervously shuffled my feet in the corner, the first bell clanged. Now I really was a fighter and had to get going. I stuck out my left hand to touch gloves and Alex went after me straight away. He rushed me, grabbed me around the chest and threw me into the ropes. My mum, Liza, and her mum, Marie, covered their faces with their hands. They support me at all my fights, but I learned early on that when things get rough sometimes they're the ones who need the support. They close their eyes but it still hurts them when they hear the punches land.

I could hear Jo, who was holding Mum's hand, yelling support.

'Come on, Jeffrey,' she shouted, words I would hear at every fight. She knew how much this meant to me. Immediately I was into it.

Glenn's training kicked in.

I concentrated on gap control, maintaining my distance and upsetting Alex's rhythm by shifting my attack. As a martial artist, Glenn knew my legs would be the crucial weapons even if I didn't kick with them. By controlling the movement of the fight, I could nullify Alex's attacks and launch my own.

I was jumping in and out like the Energiser Bunny, but even in my raw state I was effective. The first punch I ever landed in a real boxing match was a straight left. A very fast right hand followed. Late in the first round I landed a volley of punches that had Alex staggering and Brad put a standing eight-count on him to give him a respite.

At the bell I went back to my corner and Glenn told me I was doing a great job.

My confidence was now sky high.

In the second round I rocked Alex again with a series of straight, hard punches to the head and body and Brad gave him another standing count. Then, near the end of the round, as Alex was covering up on the ropes, I dug in some body shots. He brought his knee up to his chest instinctively in a Muay Thai protective move. He was badly hurt and Brad jumped in to stop the fight.

I had won my boxing debut with a knockout after less than three minutes of action. My family jumped for joy and Mum had tears in her eyes. In my corner Glenn raised my hand in triumph and Adam Partridge, a fighter I really respected, patted me on the shoulder for a job well done. I felt on top of the world. Straight away I knew I was hooked. That winning feeling is addictive.

*

Over the next nine years Glenn and I have developed the type of bond that can only be forged through this sort of intense combat in such a tough sport. I'm putting my neck on the line in every fight, knowing that he has my back.

Glenn's next move was to register me with Boxing Queensland so that I could compete in the upcoming state titles. Even with just one fight to my name, he reckoned I had a shot at winning the gold medal.

'Really?' I asked.

'Yeah, really.'

I was given a small, blue official book from Boxing Queensland to record all my physical data, medical history and the results of my fights. I had a medical test at Inala on 2 October 2008. The doctor entered my details at the front of the book, listing me as 177 centimetres (out by 2), 63.8 kilograms, with a heart rate of 46 beats a minute and blood pressure of 117/63. He noted I had slight acne, normal heart function, no tremors in my tongue or hands, normal genitalia (hooray) and no psychological problems. I was good to go.

The next day, Friday, 3 October, our team – now called the Stretton Boxing Club – with our friends and families in support, headed south down the M1 motorway to the Beenleigh Arena between Brisbane and the Gold Coast for the 2008 Queensland Amateur Boxing Championships.

With just one bout behind me, and an unofficial one at that, I was matched to face a 27-year-old Brisbane printer named Gerard Le'Gall over four two-minute rounds. Glenn thought Gerard would be the toughest opponent at the titles and I had drawn him first up. I was really edgy and, in his rich Scottish brogue, Allan Nicolson from Boxing Queensland asked Glenn if he was sure about what he was doing – throwing a novice into the deep end where some pretty experienced and savage sharks were lurking.

'It won't be a problem,' Glenn said.

'Really?' Allan asked, with a raised eyebrow.

'Yeah, really,' Glenn said. There were a lot of 'yeah, really' moments in my career at this stage. But I wasn't so sure and, without Glenn knowing, I wolfed down a packet of Twisties in the hope they would crush the butterflies in my stomach.

Le'Gall was a tough, strong guy with a compact defence and he came at me with bad intentions from a crouch. But even though this was just my first official amateur boxing contest, the movement Glenn had taught me allowed me to take a lead and hold onto it, while varying my attack between his body and head.

I dodged most – but not all – of his powerful hooks and right hands. After four rounds the judges gave me a close decision 21–17. It was a nerve-racking time and I vomited up the Twisties in the dressing room.

I was glad to have a day's rest before the final day of competition on Sunday. I was matched with Gary Everuss, a fast, loose-limbed boxer who was getting ready to compete in the Australian Indigenous amateur championships at the Broncos Leagues Club in Brisbane at the end of that month.

At the opening bell, I had a few rushes of blood and was a little wild and overenthusiastic. But with Dad yelling out from the crowd, 'Steady up Jeff, steady. Keep your hands up,' I regained my composure and won comfortably 26–8.

It was a great thrill when Brisbane Olympian Todd Kidd, not long back from the Beijing games, climbed into the ring to present me with my certificate as a state boxing champion and I was delighted to pose with Glenn and Adam Partridge for a team photo.

The memories of being a bullied schoolboy were growing dimmer.

Six weeks later, Glenn and I, with a small team of supporters, travelled down to the Blacktown RSL, a famous boxing venue in Sydney's western suburbs, for my shot at the Australian title.

I had been full of confidence in beating the country's best when I'd seen them the previous year as a spectator, but now I had to match my words with actions.

With just two official fights to my credit, I would face South Australia's David Biddle on 20 November. Biddle had fought the best in the country, including Will Tomlinson, Brendon Wilson, Angus Hann, Cameron Hammond and Todd Kidd. I was sort of an outsider in the Queensland team because I was so new to boxing, and I felt that some of the team hierarchy believed I shouldn't have been at the national titles with such little experience.

Biddle, also, must have wondered who the green kid was opposite him wearing the red singlet.

I simply didn't have the experience to contend with him as he pumped me with some hard shots to open the fight. I was quite good at moving but under his relentless pressure my defence wasn't that great. Early in the first round he shocked me with a wide sweeping right hand and the referee put a standing eight-count on me. Then a minute later Biddle nailed me again with an overhand right and I took another eight-count.

Rather than put me to sleep on the canvas though, his heavy punches woke me up and I fought back hard. It wasn't enough though, and his early lead proved too much. After four frenetic rounds, Biddle beat me 13–7. I was utterly spent as I shook his hand after the fight.

In the dressing room, I had my head over the toilet bowl as I was getting ready to throw up again, sickened by the nausea of nervousness and the bitter taste of my first defeat.

Glenn made me feel much better.

'Let me just say this, Jeff,' Glenn started as my stomach began to settle. 'Firstly, after just a couple of fights, you've managed to have a very competitive fight with one of the very best in the country.'

My ears pricked up

'I thought you did well to get within six points of a vastly more experienced boxer,' Glenn continued. 'He's been fighting at the top level for years. And I guarantee you this, Jeff.'

I stood up now to listen properly.

'I guarantee you, David Biddle will never, ever beat you again.'

'Really?' I asked.

'Yeah, really.'

As usual Glenn was right.

Glenn says that to be a good sporting coach you have to have lived – that all the degrees and teaching doesn't equal life experience. Glenn had come from a broken family and had a fractured relationship with his alcoholic stepfather who used to swing an iron cord at him. Glenn imparts life lessons about resilience to his students from experience. He taught me that anything bad that happened to me had happened to him first and he had coped with it and fought back. Just look at the enormous house he lives in to see how well he fought back.

Glenn told me that I had to learn from the Biddle defeat and use it to make me a better boxer.

He told me all about adopting a poker face – which I knew something about, being an avid poker player – and he taught me ways to bluff opponents when I was hurt, just as he had learned in his days as a bouncer.

Biddle went on to win the Australian title that week, following his victory over me with wins against Qamil Balla and Mark Lucas.

But over the next couple of years I had three more fights with Biddle and I won every time.

*

Two weeks after I bowed out of the Australian championships before a few hundred fans at the Blacktown RSL, Manny Pacquiao scored one of the most astonishing victories in boxing history when he mauled the much bigger Oscar De La Hoya at the MGM Grand in Las Vegas before a global television audience that stretched to hundreds of millions. At the time Pacquiao had held five world titles in five weight divisions and was regarded as the world's best fighter pound-for-pound. De La Hoya, who towered over him, was an Olympic gold medallist who had held ten world championships across six weight divisions. Most boxing experts believed that De La Hoya would be too big for Pacquiao, who was jumping up two weight divisions from lightweight (61 kg) to welterweight (66.5 kg).

I was still driving my old Volvo at the time and hoping Dad would give me his battered Toyota Hilux so I could 'upgrade' my daily ride to university. I thought it would be cool driving a ute and I wanted to drive a manual car. Pacquiao and De La Hoya meanwhile sold more than 1.25 million pay-per-view sales for their fight, generating almost $100 million in television money alone.

De La Hoya had hired Muhammad Ali's old coach Angelo Dundee to prepare him but it didn't help. Contrary to what most experts and bookies thought, Pacquiao destroyed De La Hoya, a little David massacring Goliath. In Round 8, one savage burst of punches after another from the Filipino fireball persuaded De La Hoya to call it quits.

Manny Pacquiao was now the biggest name in world boxing.

*

I had a long break from fighting after losing to Biddle but I did a lot of sparring at different gyms, usually against guys much more experienced. I came off second best a few times sparring at the Boxing Shop, a gym inside Griffith University run by Gareth Williams, who was sometimes in my corner with Glenn when I fought for Queensland.

I celebrated my twenty-first birthday before fighting again. One of my most treasured gifts was a pair of boxing gloves Glenn gave me with the message, 'All it takes to reach the stars is a leap of faith.' He told me that sometimes you have to dig deep to find yourself.

Boxing had certainly given me the confidence not to tolerate being pushed around anymore.

At a twenty-first birthday for one of my school friends, I jumped in to break up a fight that had started on the footpath. This older guy, aged about thirty-five or forty, decided to join in and grabbed me in a headlock. My uncle Gary Dykstra punched him and the guy loosened his grip. I squeezed out of the head lock and dropped him with a a couple of punches. But he wanted to fight on until I told him that he would regret it if I landed another one. He saw common sense and shot through. Even though I had gained the confidence to stick up for others, I learned that even trying to help someone can get you involved in a fight.

It is the only time since I left school that I've had to hit someone outside the ring and I hope it's the last. I hate the idea of fighting on the street and will avoid it at all costs.

Boxing inside the ropes is a different thing and, as 2009 rolled on, I couldn't wait to get in and have another go, to get back on the winning track.

At the end of February, we travelled to Maroochydore for

a fight but I couldn't get matched. It wasn't until 7 March at Allan Nicolson's Albert Boxing Club at Yatala that I returned, with a win over Dylan Dhamu, who had recently represented South Australia at the national Under-19 titles. I was again suffering a lot from nerves because I knew he was a good fighter and I didn't want back-to-back defeats. I won but was sick again after the fight.

Then, for just my fifth official bout, Glenn and I headed to Port Adelaide for the selection trials to pick an Australian team to compete in the world amateur championships in Milan, Italy. Jo, Mum and Dad, and Lillian Rushton joined us to give me support. A shot at the world championships was pretty audacious but Glenn's philosophy has always been to bite off more than you can chew and then chew like mad. We'd made great progress in a short time and figured that I had a good chance to beat anyone there.

In the opening fight, on 27 March, I won a close decision over Ryan Stinson, then scored a huge personal triumph by winning a close one on a countback over David Biddle. Glenn's prediction was coming true. I was so happy with myself for winning because it was a reminder of just how competitive I am, whether it's in boxing, playing poker or trying to take over everything at Monopoly.

For the eighth fight of my career, I squared off against the vastly experienced Qamil Balla over three three-minute rounds for the right to represent Australia on the world stage. The Balla brothers, Qamil and Ibrahim, were red-hot on the national amateur scene in those days and I think the scoring in our fight reflected that the judges saw him as the golden boy of the time. He smashed me in the first round but, even though I was taught a defensive lesson, the score shouldn't have been as one-sided as it was – it was something like 18–0 his way. They had electronic scoreboards on the side of the ring and every time I'd cover up the judges were hitting their buzzers to record punches, even though I felt I was blocking most of them. That fight taught me that I couldn't just cover up and counter because the body shots Qamil was banging into my elbows were all going onto the scoreboard as legal punches. The scoreboard was going ding, ding, ding, and my chances of winning were going down, down, down.

Glenn was ropable in the corner.

The judges were scoring the fight like I didn't exist.

After two rounds, when it was obvious I needed a knockout to win, Glenn told me just to go out and batter Qamil as much as I could – not to worry about the score but just serve notice to him that I was going to be a force to be reckoned with in the future. I went after Qamil in the third and final round and forced a standing eight-count on him with a big body shot.

Qamil's father came over after the fight and said to me, 'You're one tough boy.' That might have been the case but I felt like crap because I had lost. Because of the score – 21–2 for Qamil – Mum and Jo were really worried that I'd been knocked around. But only my pride had been badly hurt, and foolishly I carried that emotional baggage into my next fight, against Luke Howlett at Caboolture, north of Brisbane.

The Howlett fight was on 30 May and I was certain I had the measure of my opponent, who had been in the Queensland team with me at the Australian championships, but in the lighter division at 60 kilograms. I didn't think there was any way I could lose, but I was silly to think it would be easy. Luke was a big puncher and he got me with a lot of big shots. In the second round he dropped me twice, the second time, while I was face first on the canvas, the ladies in my family were crying their eyes out. Luke finished the round by knocking my head back again and almost stopped me. It was the worst serve I'd ever copped.

One of the things Glenn always liked about me though was my physical toughness and my burning competitive desire.

I fought back in the final round.

Luke won the fight 22–8, but sometimes you learn more from a loss than a win. I learned a painful lesson about never underestimating an opponent.

Luke didn't get too long to celebrate his victory. I stopped him in the first round of a rematch later in the year. In June that year, I outpointed an Inala boxer named Alberto Ortiz at Deception Bay and in July I made a quick trip with an Australian invitational team to New Zealand for a win against Kiwi Dane Williams and a loss against Josh Diab of New South Wales.

After my first twelve amateur fights, my record stood at nine wins against three losses. It was about to get worse.

*

My next opponent, Todd Kidd, was one of the most brilliant Australian amateur fighters of recent times and, with more than a century of tradition behind him, why wouldn't he be?

He is less than three years older than I am but had a lifetime more experience, having started boxing at age eleven with Don Tindall at Caboolture. His 158 amateur bouts included wins over an Olympic gold medallist and world amateur champion as well as Commonwealth Games and Olympic appearances.

When he was just fifteen, Todd competed in Russia with Kostya Tszyu as his mentor. And he had a sporting pedigree that includes some of the greatest fighters in history. Todd was trained by Steve Deller, who in turn was trained by John Burke, who learned many of his skills from Reg Layton at Brisbane's Lang Park Police Citizens Youth Club in the early 1960s. Layton had been taught boxing in the 1930s by Tod Morgan, a visiting American world champ, whose skills had been passed down from Jack Blackburn, who had worked the corner of world heavyweight champion Joe Louis and sparred with the mighty Texan, Jack Johnson, the first black man to win the world heavyweight title.

So Todd certainly had a proud boxing tradition stretching back to the legends of the sport. As I prepared to face him on 31 July in a big amateur event promoted by Deller at Brisbane's Hilton Hotel, I was understandably wary. Jo and I watched a video of him and I thought his jab and speed were sensational.

Jo was nervous for me and it showed in her frown. Sitting on the couch, she looked over at me and asked, 'Are you really sure you want to do this?'

'I'm sure.'

'But he looks so fast. He's really, really good.'

He was too.

As the bout started and Todd's left hand came at me like a bullet, all I could think was, *Holy moly, how fast is this guy?*

Fighting him was a whole new experience.

I made the fight competitive, but Todd's quickness and ring-smarts were too much and he outpointed me at the Hilton. He repeated the victory at the Golden Gloves tournament at Caboolture the following month, winning 28–12.

Todd was a great fighter and is a terrific bloke, too, one of the nicest guys you could meet. In the years since I have done a lot of sparring with him. He turned professional but unfortunately his skin cuts like tissue paper and he could not scale the same heights that he had in the amateurs.

I was still climbing hard though, despite the occasional setback. Glenn kept telling me to 'hold the dream' and focus on the finish line.

*

Manny Pacquiao closed out 2009 by being named the Fighter of the Decade by the Boxing Writers Association of America, which had previously bestowed that honour on Muhammad Ali and Evander Holyfield. In November Pacquiao capped off a remarkable ten-year spell at the top of the sport by stopping welterweight Miguel Cotto in the final round to win a title in a record-setting seventh weight division.

Forbes magazine listed Pacquiao as one of the world's highest paid athletes, having earned A$50 million in the twelve months to June 2009.

*

Glenn and I planned a great Christmas for 2009 and the biggest gift we wanted to give each other was an Australian title. Having lost to Biddle the year before we were determined to turn things around at the national championships held at the Australian Institute of Sport (AIS) in Canberra. We caught the train out to and back from the venue – Mum said after years of feeling so sorry for me getting bullied she now felt as safe as Fort Knox when I was with her, even late at night on the trains. That's because of the confidence boxing had given me.

That confidence translated into victory over New South Wales fighter Chris Reidy on Friday, 4 December, which set up a Sunday showdown with Biddle for the 64-kilogram title. I had learned a lot from my loss to him the previous year and was now ahead of Biddle in our three match-ups, two to one, having also edged him two months earlier at the Golden Gloves. Now, in Canberra, my movement and defence had improved markedly and after three rounds, again I was the winner 9–1. As Biddle scowled over the decision, I let out a war whoop of victory.

I was the new Australian champion and it was an enormous honour, even though my name was recorded on the official list as 'Jeff Horne'. (I tell people who misspell my name that I'm not 'Horny' at the moment.) Glenn and I knew that I was now a hot favourite to win a place at the 2010 Commonwealth Games in Delhi.

The trials were set for March 2010 at the historic Esplanade Hotel in Fremantle, just outside Perth. I wanted to make my own slice of history. On 18 March I outpointed fellow Queenslander Michael Tapua but the following day suffered a controversial loss to a local fighter named Callum Cassidy. The judges scored it 3–1. In those days boxing scoring worked on a synchronisation method. The judges had to push a red or blue button for either boxer when they reckoned they had landed a punch. Two of the three judges had to hit their respective buttons within a second of each other for the punch to register – if they didn't, you didn't score. Callum had a real cover-up style and after you'd launched an attack at his arms and gloves, he'd spring on you to land one clean punch. Obviously the judges clicked his sporadic punches and not mine, even though I thought I was much busier. Actually, the judges registered more of my punches but because they were not synchronised their clicks didn't count. Callum won against me, but lost in the final against Tasmanian southpaw (left-hander) Luke Woods, who went to Delhi but was eliminated in his second fight by the eventual bronze medallist.

I came home from Fremantle dejected.

Missing out on the Commonwealth Games was a major disappointment.

I was the Australian champ but the loss to Cassidy was disheartening and it contributed to subsequent defeats in quick succession in Queensland – one at Nerang against the Gold Coast fighter Jesse Ross, who towered over me, and another to my mate Ozan Craddock at the Tattersalls Club in Brisbane. The fight with Ozan was close but the judges saw it Ozan's way.

I refused to stay down though. Glenn again told me that boxing is a great lesson in resilience. You get knocked off course but you have to get back on track. We could either focus on what had happened or focus on the Olympics for 2012.

I said we'd concentrate on the Olympics.

'Good. Let them go and celebrate,' Glenn said, 'while we go back to work.'

6

Do not be embarrassed by your failures, learn from them and start again.

– Richard Branson, British entrepreneur

IN MAY 2010, MANNY Pacquiao, who had long been the most celebrated sports hero in his nation of (at the time) over 90 million people, was elected to the House of Representatives, the lower house of the Philippines Congress. A noted philanthropist who has given away millions of dollars to the poor, Pacquiao was re-elected in 2013 and three years later became a senator, elected for a six-year term.

A few months before his 2010 election, Pacquiao had dominated Ghana's rugged Joshua Clottey in their world welterweight title fight, winning every round before a crowd of more than 50,000 at the Cowboys Stadium in Arlington, Texas, and a massive pay-per-view television audience that contributed A$45 million to the coffers of promoter Bob Arum.

By contrast, in May 2010, I outpointed Elliott Balk before a few dozen fight fans at the Inala Police Citizens Youth Club in Brisbane. My brother, Ben, also won on the same card, competing at 69 kilograms.

Boxing hadn't made me rich or famous like it had Pacquiao but the sport was certainly turning my life around.

Since I had started training with him four years earlier, Glenn had been moulding me into his vision of a samurai warrior – a boxer with a detached personality, who was a different person in the ring from the person outside of it and one who could compete completely devoid of emotion.

Glenn was always telling his fighters not to get angry in the ring because the anger actually drains your energy and you can't sustain that deep emotion over the course of a long fight. He also taught us not to acknowledge the other fighter's punches which, he said, eventually breaks their spirit. He wanted us to be like cyborgs, like the Terminator, showing no sympathy or pain.

Boxing certainly had given me the confidence to deal with difficult situations.

Not that long after I started fighting as an amateur, I was with Jo, my sister Bianca and a group of friends playing cricket and touch football and having a barbecue at a park near our home. Some guys were hanging around one of our friend's cars and they eventually got into a fight. My friends chased them off but the other guys threatened to come back with weapons. We weren't going to wait around to see if they were all talk. Jo and Bianca had started rushing around getting all our things together so we could get out of there, when this carload of jerks pulled up and they come running towards us with hammers in their hands.

Holy crap.

I grabbed a cricket bat from Jo's hands and, as the invaders charged over at us, I used Glenn's advice in the gym to stay calm and think logically. I showed the pitch invaders the cricket bat and that I wasn't scared. As cool as I could, I said, 'Are you guys really sure you want to do this?'

They backed off straight away. I knew they would. Only cowards would arm themselves with hammers in the first place.

Glenn always says that you don't have to look tough to be tough. That real toughness isn't tattoos or swearing or a bad attitude, it's an inner courage to do the right thing and to stand up for your principles.

⋆

I may not have been drawing as many fans to my fights as Manny Pacquiao had done filling the Dallas Cowboys' home ground, but I was returning to a winning run. I scored two back-to-back victories over a rising star from Tamworth named Kye 'Mr Frenzy' MacKenzie. Kye was being talked about as a 'killer' – a fighter to be feared – but I defused him at Souths Juniors in Sydney in June 2010 and then two months later at the Golden Gloves at Caboolture, winning the second fight 24–6. It was weird fighting Kye because he wouldn't shut up, whispering in my ear all the time. I would hit him and he'd say, 'Is that all you got?' Or he'd be saying, 'Oh, good shot, Jeff, good shot.' There were so many fights at Caboolture that year that Kye and I ended up fighting at about 2 o'clock in the morning.

For most fans, the highlight of the Caboolture fights was an appearance by the former world champ Kostya Tszyu, who was there to watch his son Tim win a gold medal. I've never been a big autograph hunter and Kostya had people surrounding him the whole time, wanting to talk about his career, so I left him alone. But it was cool seeing one of Australia's greatest.

Straight after the win at Caboolture, I headed to Kostya's homeland of Russia, as part of the Queensland team for an invitational event. It was October and freezing cold there, but I won my bout in a small auditorium that was like a lecture theatre. It was another step in my education as a boxer.

★

The London Olympic Games were less than eighteen months away and Glenn had promised that he could get me there. I was doing everything I could to help him keep that promise. My studies at Griffith University were progressing, but gaining my teaching degree was taking a lot longer than the usual four years because of all the time I was taking off to compete at major boxing tournaments.

The 2011 national championships were set for Melbourne in March, at the Reggio Calabria Club in Brunswick, and I would be going in as the defending champ. It was also my chance to settle some old scores. On 3 March, I outpointed Ryan Hampton 9–1 and the following day I beat Kye MacKenzie 13–2. The day after that I scored my revenge over Callum Cassidy, the kid who had kept me out of the Commonwealth Games. The score was 7–2.

I was set to face Commonwealth Games representative Luke Woods for the Australian title on 6 March 2011. Glenn devised a brilliant strategy for the fight. Luke was fast and cocky and had good range. He knew how to use his southpaw style to great effect. Glenn wanted me to concentrate on sniping with my straight right, which is the best punch against a left-handed fighter and the punch that I would later rely on heavily against Manny Pacquiao. Because Luke was an evasive southpaw, Glenn felt that if he got in front on the scorecards he would stay away – clinch and run – to preserve his lead. So he wanted me to be super-aggressive from the opening bell.

So it was me who got away to a 4–0 lead early. This made Luke come to me, rather than fight on the back move. In the end I busted Luke up and won 8–0, to take my second Australian 64-kilogram title and gain some feeling of satisfaction after the disappointment of the previous year in Fremantle. Victory meant I would represent Australia at the 2011 world titles.

There were some other impressive performances at that event.

My fellow Queenslander Damien Hooper won the 81-kilogram light-heavyweight gold medal after a stirring come-from-behind 9–8 win over Victorian fighter Jake Carr. The capacity crowd was roaring as Carr got out of the blocks fast, with former IBF world super-featherweight champion Barry Michael calling the shots from the corner. Carr established a three-point buffer, but Hooper stormed forward, decking his opponent in the second round for an eight-count from referee Steve Donkin. Hooper forged ahead before Carr made a late rally despite an eye injury.

Kostya Tszyu's thirteen-year-old son Nikita won the Under-15 38-kilogram paperweight gold medal, but sixteen-year-old Tim Tszyu, who was unbeaten coming into the championships with twenty straight victories, lost on a countback to Sydney's Daniel Lewis in the 64-kilogram Under-19 semi-final. Daniel would go on to fight for Australia at the 2016 Rio Olympics. Both Tszyu boys had their uncle, Igor Goloubev from Sydney's Tszyu Boxing Academy, in their corners, giving advice in Russian.

★

With the Olympics just sixteen months away but with no guarantee that I would be selected, Glenn wanted me to gain as much international competition experience as I could. He didn't care who I fought because he believed that on my night I could beat anyone in the world. He wanted me to become used to fighting out of a suitcase – getting off a plane and boxing the next day – because he saw it as making me tougher and more resilient, even if I needed compression stockings to stop the fluid build-up that I sometimes suffered on long flights. First, my legs ballooned and then I had cankles.

Less than two weeks after winning in Melbourne I was in Halle, Germany, for the 2011 Chemistry Cup with Aussie teammates Luke Jackson, Jesse Ross, Damien Hooper and the first Aussie female boxing Olympian Naomi Fischer-Rasmussen. I lost 9–2 to the Englishman Scott Cardle. A few days later we were in Usti nad Labem in the Czech Republic, where I lost 3–0 to an Armenian named Hrachik Javakhyan.

The following week the team hit Helsinki for the prestigious GeeBee tournament that started on 8 April and included some crack international fighters such as the Irishman Michael Conlan and England's Luke Campbell. I won my first two fights on points – against Arturs Ahmetovs of Latvia and local star Alex Vasiljev – but dipped out 12–2 in the final against the talented, tall and rangy Englishman Thomas Stalker, an experienced 26 year old whose curriculum vitae included gold medals at the 2008 European titles and the 2010 Commonwealth Games.

At this stage of 2011 it was non-stop fighting. I was hardly off the plane from Europe when I headed to Darwin to compete with some of the best fighters from the South Pacific in the Arafura Games. Starting on 9 May, I beat Hobart's Glenn McKeown 21–10 and then Stanley Emmanuel from Papua New Guinea 17–5. Next up I outpointed Western Australian Mark Pevinsky 25–15 to reach the final of the prestigious event. Winners at the games included Ibrahim Balla, Cameron Hammond, Luke Jackson, Jason Whateley and, in the super-heavyweight division, my mate Joseph Parker, a quiet young Kiwi who would one day win the world heavyweight title.

My opponent for the 64-kilogram final was Qamil Balla. The last time I'd fought him he'd given me a boxing lesson early. With the Olympics beckoning, I knew I had to win this one – and win big.

And I did. Qamil told Brisbane's *Courier-Mail* that I won the rematch 'fair and square' in taking a 29–15 decision, nullifying his speed with my movement and then striking when it was my time.

I followed that tournament victory by beating Brisbane fighter Joseph Nicholls 32–12 in August at Caboolture.

*

I was in a winning groove, but the middle of 2011 was a sad time for the Horn family.

My pop, Ray Horn, lost his two lifelong mates.

In July, Pop's twin brother, Gordon, who had survived polio, had sparred with him more than seventy years earlier in Winton and had been his buddy through the good times and bad, passed away at the age of eighty-three.

Then, less than two months later, Ray's wife of fifty-six years, my Nana, Betty Horn, died after a long illness.

Ray had now seen all his siblings and then his wife go over the years and he could have been very depressed and buckled over by grief. Yet he decided to live the best life he could and inspire the rest of us. He has been one of my great supporters at ringside and his lessons in perseverance have been truly inspiring.

Sadly, also in the lead-up to the London Olympics, my mum and dad decided to split.

Glenn and Lillian were really worried that it could blow my games preparation out of the water but by then I was old enough and tough enough to cope. I'm very lucky that they have remained friends. I have tried to evenly divide my time between both the Horns and the Dykstras, enjoying Grandma Marie Dykstra's lemon meringue and caramel tarts as often as my diet will allow and spending as much time with all my relatives as possible. I love going to uncle Russell Dykstra's place at Umina on the New South Wales central coast and he still shows me new magic tricks when I occasionally visit. Just like Mum's family, Dad's brothers and sisters have backed my boxing career from the day dot.

Not that I don't annoy them. A lot.

For as long as I can remember I've been into fancy dress and costume parties. I even set up a haunted house downstairs in my garage. We get right into the spirit of it, so to speak, and I've always been a big pranker.

Once, when I was much younger, I staged a terrible prank on some of Dad's building workers at his place at Pallara. They usually park their cars just inside the yard. I got dressed up with a fake wig and a hat – the disguise was so good that when I checked myself in the mirror I really looked like another person. I went to one of the worker's cars, which was open, making sure they all saw me. I slammed the car door and jumped over the fence, which was pretty high. They gave chase. One of the guys was swearing at me in the distance and then they were all running after me. Looking back, it was pretty stupid because one of them could have thrown a hammer into my back. Then they got into their cars and started driving around looking for the bloke who was breaking into cars.

I saw Ben while I was hiding out down the back of our property and told him what had happened. I followed his advice to stay low until it all blew over, especially when I saw police cars turning up.

*

My boxing was much more serious. My Olympic quest next took me to the world championships in the exotic city of Baku, Azerbaijan, on the Caspian Sea. I didn't get much time to go sightseeing there as I was focused on becoming Australia's first-ever world amateur champion.

I got off to a terrific start in the tournament on 30 September, outboxing a Bolivian named Elias Roca and winning by a whopping 42–5. But I found the jump up in international class to my next opponent too big to bridge. The fact that half our hotel, including me, had gone down with dysentery didn't help. Brazil's Éverton dos Santos Lopes was a slick boxer in the Floyd Mayweather mould, incredibly skilful, and I faced him washed out with dehydration.

I really didn't stand a chance.

Under amateur rules for major international events, Glenn couldn't be in my corner so he stayed home, researching my opponents and emailing me battle plans. Even watching from a distance, he thought I could go deep into the event.

He watched the fight on the internet in Stretton with Lillian and knew straight away I wasn't feeling well. The judges preferred the slick moves of Lopes rather than my aggression and the Brazilian was up 5–0 after the first round and way ahead after the second. The damage was done and I couldn't make up the leeway. Lopes won 22–10. But Glenn has always taught me to learn from my defeat and Lopes taught me a lot about counter-punching and defence that I could use in later fights.

In the world championship final, Lopes outpointed Ukraine's Denys Berinchyk 26–23 for the title at 64 kilograms. Berinchyk's teammate, the 2008 Olympic gold medallist Vasyl Lomachenko, won the 60 kilograms title with his almost ghostly moves, proving harder to hit than smoke, while a huge Englishman named Anthony Joshua took silver at super-heavyweight.

The following month in London, in a test event for the 2012 Olympics, I dropped a close decision, 13–11, to Scotland's Josh Taylor.

Being in London and seeing the buzz ahead of the games, fuelled me with the determination to compete at the real thing the following year. I rang home to tell Jo and Glenn that nothing would stop me now.

*

I was getting fights fast and furious. Straight after the worlds, I travelled to Perth for a State of Origin boxing event with Glenn and my Stretton Boxing Club teammate Joe Goodall, a gentle giant outside the ring with incredible natural talent.

Joe had trained with us since 2009 when he turned to boxing after suffering hip injuries playing Aussie rules for Brisbane's Western Taipans. His father, Leigh, had played for Port Adelaide before the club joined the AFL and he starred in the Solo soft drink commercials of the 1980s. Like me, Joe had never boxed until meeting Glenn and, while I took a few months to master the basics, he was a natural from his first night in the ring.

Joe beat the Australian champ Sam Blyth in Perth but I was a bit flat for the tournament after the excitement of the world titles. I won two fights there – against Callum Cassidy and Victoria's Jake Perrins, a tattooed tough guy – but dropped a decision to Val Borg, the fast-moving, high-volume puncher from Sydney.

A month later I won my fourth Queensland title, stopping Matthew Dowdle from the Rebels Boxing Club at Walloon near Ipswich and then Patrick Clarke, an Indigenous sensation from Palm Island. Patrick was the star boxer in the highly successful team of fighters guided by the old master coach Ray Dennis on the tropical island off the coast north of Townsville.

Ray, eighty at the time of writing, moved to Palm in 1999 and is known as 'Uncle Ray' to the inhabitants of the settlement. He has been inducted into the Queensland Boxing Hall of Fame for his work helping the Aboriginal community and has trained more than fifty champions over the years on Palm, giving hope and a hand to a community that not long ago was described as the most violent place on earth outside of a war zone.

Ray says the discipline of boxing can keep kids off the streets and away from drugs and drink and, like Glenn, he is one of the great ambassadors for the benefits that boxing can have on society.

Glenn has always wanted me to be a role model and spokesperson for the sport and he says that the confidence boxing instils and the health benefits it can create through training make devotees better people.

If all fights in the world took place in the boxing ring, the world would be a better place. Often people lash out because they are afraid. Confident people don't lash out and they generally have better ways of coping with stress.

*

The next step on my Olympic journey was the 2012 Australian championships starting on 1 February and spread over five days of high pressure. They were held at the Aurora Sports Stadium in the Hobart suburb of New Town. Sam Banney and Joe Goodall, my teammates from Stretton, were also members of the Queensland side and we had huge hopes for a hat-trick of titles.

But there was a shock early on. Big Joe was leading Jason Whateley 14–13, but right on the final bell Whateley was awarded a point and they finished 14–all. We all thought Joe would get the decision but Whateley won on a countback. He lost to Jai Opetaia in the final but eventually represented Australia at the Rio Olympics four years later.

Sam had beaten Jesse Ross in Queensland and was favourite for the Australian title in the 75-kilogram division. In Hobart he was dominating his fights. In the semi-final he was ahead against Canberra's David Toussaint when the referee inexplicably stopped the fight in Toussaint's favour with just thirty seconds remaining. Sam's Olympic dream was shattered. It was a cruel blow for us because we had both started in Glenn's self-defence classes six years earlier and had the plan to go to the Olympics together. In a turn-up Jesse Ross then beat Toussaint to take the Australian title and virtually guarantee himself an Olympic berth.

As it was, Sam was named the best boxer of the national titles the following year.

In Hobart I had three good fighters standing between me and a third Australian title. I stopped Abe Archibald from Sydney and then took an 11–8 win over Jake Perrins. Finally, it was me and Qamil Balla again going toe to toe for the national crown. It was a terrific battle but I emerged with the win 24–19, shattering his Olympic dream and preserving my own. Qamil's brother Ibrahim made the team in the 56-kilogram division. Light-heavyweight Damien Hooper did not compete at the event because he had already qualified for the Olympics. Our Australian coach, Don Abnett, told reporters the national team would go to London with more than just Hooper as a medal chance. He nominated me, Luke Jackson and Cameron Hammond as all capable of springing upsets.

I still had some work to do to earn my ticket to the games. The final selection trial was the Oceania qualifying event at the AIS in Canberra in March 2012. I wasn't going to let my Olympic hopes rest with the judges and went on the attack right from the start, dropping Kiwi Harry Scaife in the third round and then Samoa's Livai Hinoma in the first.

The sense of joy at becoming part of the Olympic team was almost overwhelming and I told reporters after the event that, 'in my dreams I wanted to be standing here, so I am just stoked that I am now'.

Our Olympic team was:

Light-flyweight (49 kg): Billy Ward
Flyweight (52 kg): Jackson Woods
Bantamweight (56 kg): Ibrahim Balla
Lightweight (60 kg): Luke Jackson
Light-welterweight (64 kg): Jeff Horn
Welterweight (69 kg): Cameron Hammond
Middleweight (75 kg): Jesse Ross
Light-heavyweight (81 kg): Damien Hooper
Heavyweight (91 kg): Jai Opetaia
Super-heavyweight (91^{+} kg): Johan Linde

Australia had filled all ten of the Oceania region's allotted Olympic places for the first time ever, and while Abnett and most of the experts tipped Hooper to be our best chance to end a 24-year medal drought in the sport, the rest of us on the team had our own aspirations of coming home with gold.

Despite producing many great professional champions, Australia had never won a gold medal in Olympic boxing and the last Australian to win any medal – Spike Cheney – won his silver way back in 1988, the year I was born.

We were an interesting mix of fighters.

The heavily tattooed Hooper, from Dalby in country Queensland, was considered the wild child of the team and was an explosive puncher.

My good mate Luke Jackson was named team captain. He had fought off the heartbreak of previous defeats, severe anxiety problems and a career-threatening stress fracture in his back to earn his place. 'It is just amazing. I have been busting my arse for six years for this moment,' he told reporters. 'After missing out on Beijing, the last four years I haven't not thought about this for one day.' Luke was a two-time Commonwealth Games representative and was agonisingly close to selection for the Beijing Olympics, but fell at the final hurdle after losing at the Oceania qualifying event in Samoa to Paul Fleming, a man he had previously beaten three times. 'It was the worst feeling of my life and I went home to Tasmania with nothing,' Luke said. 'I had to see a doctor after missing out on Beijing because I couldn't sleep for the ten days I was over there [in Samoa]. I probably had seven hours' sleep and I suffered from anxiety and I never knew that before.'

The 91-kilogram Jai Opetaia was just sixteen but the heavy-fisted, fleet-footed southpaw from the New South Wales central coast had already sparred many rounds with Anthony Mundine and Danny Green. At the time Jai was selling shoes part-time at Rebel Sport. His bloodlines suggested he was born to be an athlete. One cousin is Socceroos star Tim

Cahill, another is star rugby league five-eighth Ben Roberts. At the previous year's World Youth Boxing championship in Kazakhstan he had beaten a German, Turk and Russian on his way to winning the light-heavyweight crown. Jai's grandfather, Billy Opetaia, was a tough middleweight who fought such foes as Tony Mundine and Kahu Mahanga in the 1960s. Jai had been trained by his father, Tapu, since the age of eight.

Queensland provided four of the ten members of the squad, with me, Hooper, Jesse Ross and Gladstone's flame-haired Billy Ward, who was greeted at his home airport by a cheer squad with red wigs to celebrate his inclusion. A former gymnast, little Billy had to overcome a bout of Ross River Fever in 2008 on his way to establishing himself as one of Australia's best young talents.

At the other end of the size spectrum was another of my great mates Johan Linde, a super-heavyweight giant from Adelaide. He was embarking on his Olympic dream with a political heavyweight in his corner – South Australian treasurer Jack Snelling, who was a big fan. Johan had a commerce degree from the University of Adelaide and worked in the revenue section at the South Australia Treasury and Finance Department. 'I'm a calm person and I enjoy studying and things like that,' Johan said in an interview after his selection, echoing my thoughts. 'People have this image of boxers as big meatheads, but all the guys I know in boxing are probably some of the nicest guys in the world.'

It could have been me speaking.

My mum reckons one of the reasons for my success in boxing is the calmness that is in my genes. Fighting is not really in my nature and I have always seen the sport as a battle of skills rather than a test of toughness, even though physical courage and tenacity are essential.

These are the things that Glenn Rushton taught me from Day 1 in his gym. And in 2008 he told me that if I committed myself to boxing he could take me to the Olympics within four years. After so much hard work and riding the highs and lows of the sport together, we had honoured our promises to each other and now it was time to get busy again.

We were going for gold.

7

The most important thing in the Olympic Games is not winning but taking part; the essential thing in life is not conquering but fighting well.

– Pierre de Coubertin, father of the modern Olympic Games

I HAD HOPED I could stay in Brisbane and train with Glenn in the lead-up to the Olympic Games, but that was never going to happen with the national boxing team based at the Australian Institute of Sport (AIS) and then on tour for the four months leading into London. Our squad was set to train in China and Thailand, with competitions in Serbia, Lithuania and Belarus to follow, before we headed to Belfast in Northern Ireland for the final games preparation.

The best part of staying at the AIS was the food hall, which was sensational, and I was also able to spar with the best boxers in the country. Luke Jackson was a regular sparring partner and, even though we slugged it out many times, Jacko and I became great friends. Some of the toughest sparring I've ever had was with Cameron Hammond, who is still working hard to gain the confidence to fight in the ring the way he does in the gym.

The worst part of the national team environment was the feeling I was being treated like a child by some of the officials.

I have my father's easy-going temperament and I always try to stay calm no matter the situation. On international trips my teammates constantly would try to rile me up – without success. And rather than blow up outside the ring, I tend to give people the silent treatment if I'm upset. That was the case with some of the officials in charge of our team.

For example, Don Abnett, the Australian head coach, sometimes gave me the craps. We get on okay now, but didn't back then.

I always thought I was one of the hardest workers in the national team, but Don would line us up after training and he'd stare right at me and say things like, 'That was not a good effort on the track today, boys. I expect better.' I was annoyed because I worked hard and always finished the runs at the top.

By this stage, I was a 24-year-old university graduate, but I felt like I was being treated like a kid. Maybe because of my quiet nature Don thought I was soft and not a real fighter, and it frustrated the hell out of me at the time. I planned on showing him how tough I was, not by answering back but by performing well in competition.

When we went to China in April 2012 and were all getting ready for the biggest moment any of us had faced, we trained with the local fighters, and paired off and sparred against them in a giant sports hall. We also had what they called 'competitive spars' – unofficial fights – but they were scored and the Chinese came at me like they were fighting for their lives. I went 1–1 in those two battles. But we were in total tourist mode as we climbed the multitude of stairs to pose for a team photo atop the Great Wall.

Then we went to Thailand to train with their best fighters at a place a couple of hours outside Bangkok. I wasn't meant to have a fight there, but on short notice I got the call-up to tackle the army champion at a kickboxing stadium. It was such short notice that I hadn't had anything to eat and, because I didn't want to chance the street food, my pre-fight meal was an ice-cream at the venue. It was a reminder of the days when I'd chow down on Twisties because of my nerves, but thankfully I didn't throw up after I won my bout.

Travelling with the team for weeks at a time meant lifelong friendships were formed and two guys, Jacko and Johan Linde, became my great pals. We were three amigos and often roomed together and went off sightseeing whenever the opportunity came up. Even with fights on, we could go out and have a pizza in China now and then or go touring on the back of a ute in the pouring rain in Thailand. My mates cheered loudly when a local table tennis champion, a little kid about a metre high, belted me off the table in China.

Jacko and Johan, about 30 centimetres apart in height, were united in their attempts to rattle me for a laugh. I could set them off pretty quickly so that they would 'chuck a nana' and tell me to get stuffed. They could never rattle me though, never make me yell or swear no matter what they tried. I'd just say, 'I'm fine, guys, you're not annoying me,' and mentally switch off from whatever they were doing.

I must have supreme patience, which is probably why I work well with kids. Ever since the day I told Glenn I wanted to get serious about boxing, he had been telling everyone he spoke to that I had the talent to be something special.

In 2010 he sent the following letter to Griffith University and potential sponsors:

> Jeff Horn commenced boxing with me on 20 April 2006, although it was only in mid 2008 that he decided to take the sport seriously. He entered the 2008 State titles with just one bout under his belt. Jeff won the State title convincingly, and has progressed rapidly ever since.
>
> Allan Nicolson, the secretary of Boxing Queensland, stated that in all of his many years in boxing he had never seen anyone achieve so much as quickly as Jeff.
>
> I have been involved in boxing/self-defence/martial arts for approximately 40 years and have coached some of the very best. I have no doubt that Jeff has the ability to go all the way in boxing. He is extremely fast, has great footwork, excellent defence and he punches well above his weight. This is a wonderful and necessary foundation, but his greatest attribute is his attitude. He is a quiet, respectful, well-mannered young man, who is a great ambassador for Australia and an excellent role model.
>
> Sport is a huge part of the Australian ethos. Australia's first entry into Olympic boxing was in 1908 yet, in over 100 years, Australia has still not achieved the holy grail of boxing – an Olympic gold medal. Jeff has the ability to make this dream come true.

There was no point in Glenn coming overseas with me because my training for the Games would be overseen by the Australian team management. But he did an analysis on all twenty-eight fighters in my weight division based on footage and news reports he gleaned from the internet.

He thought Denys Berinchyk from Ukraine would be the man to beat, even though he had lost to my foe Éverton dos Santos Lopes in the final of the world titles in Baku the preceding year. I knew many of the fighters in my weight class and believed that I was a good chance against them.

Before I got to test out Glenn's theory in London I had to compete in three pre-Olympic tournaments in Europe. By now I had my Bachelor of Education in health/physical education and computing from Griffith University but was still working as an assistant at the Forest Lake Outside School Care at the local state school and also doing some bookkeeping for my dad's building business.

The Beogradski Pobednik tournament began on 2 May in the gorgeous city of Belgrade, Serbia. I was off to a flyer against Lewis Benson, a Scottish boxer known as 'Kid Caramel', and I took the decision 11–4. Next was a 9–8 decision over Frenchman Abdel-Malik Ladjali, the eighteen-year-old son of North African migrants. Then I was in the final against a quality Russian teenager, Radzhab Butaev. He won a close 12–8 decision that I felt could have swung the other way. Radzhab has since turned professional and moved to New York where he is the North American light-middleweight champion.

Damien Hooper was our only gold medallist at the tournament, but Johan held Joseph Parker to a draw 11–11 before losing the super-heavyweight final on a countback.

A week later our travelling boxing troupe was in Kaunas, Lithuania, for the Algirdas Socikas Tournament, where we had more success. I outpointed the local star Deividas Kliucakas 13–9 in my first fight and then beat Irishman Philip Sutcliffe Jnr 14–9, outboxing him and slowly increasing my lead each round. Philip's dad was a two-time Olympian, who had fought at the 1980 and 1984 games. I lost the final to seventeen-year-old Lithuanian Eimantas Stanionis, who got the nod over me 24–16. Stanionis now trains in California with Manny Pacquiao's coach, Freddie Roach.

Lithuania was a happy place for Cameron Hammond and Damien Hooper who both won gold, while big Englishman Anthony Joshua grabbed the super-heavyweight title, having beaten Johan in the semis.

Our final pre-Olympic event took place in the city of Minsk in Belarus. I beat local Denis Yutskevich 10–7 in my opening fight. I was stoked because he had an awkward style and I didn't feel I performed anywhere near my best. Two days later, Sabit Telepbergenov of Kazakhstan eliminated me in the semi-finals 15–13. I thought I did enough to win, and Jacko reckoned I was robbed, but I had to be content with bronze. It was not what I was hoping for with the Olympic Games beckoning. Damien Hooper was unstoppable on this trip, winning his third consecutive gold medal.

My long-time supporter Allan Nicolson told the press back home that, although Damien carried 'the most expectation' for the games, 'fellow Queenslander Jeff Horn was "a tricky customer" who could also do well'.

Before the games the underwear company aussieBum produced a motivational video for me featuring Glenn,

Mum and Dad and my pop, Ray Horn. Ray told an interviewer, 'I heard a saying a long time ago when I was very young that the big, loudmouth fella talking about who he beat isn't worth two bob – it's the quiet ones like Jeff you have to watch. There'll be no prouder people in the world than those of us who love him dearly if he's standing on the dais.'

The interviewer asked me if I was going to win gold and I promised him that I would do my best.

*

We returned to Canberra for some final training with seven weeks to go until the opening bell at London. The kids at Forest Lake Outside School Care – with some help from their mums and dads – made a wonderful sign that said 'JEFF 4 GOLD' and I was rapt. We finished off with some final sparring at the No Contest Academy in western Sydney on a weekend when my uncle Russell Dykstra was unfortunately out of town. We've been verbal sparring partners ever since I was born. Russell, who was starring in *Rake*, sent me a message saying, 'That'd be right! Come to Sydney when I'm not there!! You know I'd kick ur arse. SOOOOO gutless!!!'

I guess Sydney was never big enough for both of us.

The team finished off the preparations for London with a week's training in Belfast. It rained most of the time we were there but the surroundings were lovely and green and the locals were super-friendly. Almost as friendly as my supporters back home, who kept me supplied with 'hero messages'. They meant the world to me.

★

At the same time as the Aussie team was getting ready for our shot at glory, the boxing world was rocked when Manny Pacquiao, riding a wave of success – seven years without defeat – came unstuck against a slick American muscleman named Timothy Bradley. The American had held world titles since 2008 at super-lightweight, the division below Pacquiao, but it was still a major upset when he won a close decision over twelve rounds at the MGM Grand in Las Vegas to take Pacquiao's WBO welterweight title. Bradley was a seven-to-two underdog. He made the biggest purse of his career to that time, A$6.5 million, but that was overshadowed by Pacquiao's whopping $32 million.

Two American judges scored the fight 115–113 for Bradley but a third American judge scored 115–113 for Pacquiao. The now ex-world champ and his team were furious at the result and protested to the WBO, which organised a re-score. Five new officials, drawn from around the world, sat down and viewed a video of the fight two months later. The panel re-scored the fight for Pacquiao, by a landslide. Their scores were 115–111, 116–112, 117–111, 118–110 and 117–111 all for the Filipino congressman. Under its rules though, the WBO was not able to overturn the official result. Bradley remained the world champ and Pacquiao would go through hell trying to regain the title.

★

We headed to the London Olympic village on 24 July. I received an enormous boost when Jo came over to watch the greatest moment of my sporting career and was joined by my mum and my sister Bianca. The village had such an uplifting atmosphere and I was living a dream. I posed for photos with Olympic mentors such as Laurie Lawrence, Kieren Perkins and the towering John Eales, who made me look like a midget.

I wore the green Australian blazer with immense pride as we marched into the stadium illuminated by huge flames shooting up into the sky at the opening ceremony. Feeling the heat from those flames was a powerful moment and even years later I still get a buzz when I think about it.

I reflected often on how much boxing – and a great coach – had done for my life and my career. What a journey Glenn and I had been on together in a few short years as he moulded a total novice into someone ready to face the world's best on the greatest sporting stage. My room in the village looked right out onto the vast Olympic Stadium.

I believed Glenn when he said I could beat anyone at the games, but I suspected some of the guys who made the Australian team felt that their job was complete just getting on the plane for London. They didn't have the confidence to go on and win the big fights. A lot were worried about the draw, fearing they might snag an opponent from the powerful Cuban, American or former Soviet bloc sides.

Some of the guys got Olympic tattoos but I didn't. I've never been into tattoos and can't see the point.

My first fight in the light-welterweight division was set for 31 July at the ExCeL Arena against an unheralded twenty-year-old Zambian named Gilbert Choombe. Gilbert told a Zambian news agency that, 'These boxers are not as tough as I thought. I can handle them.' He said he was prepared to 'die a little' for Zambia and that he was not intimidated, even though he was the only boxer from his country at the Olympics.

While I was eating well in London, I was still hungry to win.

I came out for my first fight with my game face on. Don Abnett and Mick Daly followed me to the ring in readiness to work my corner. Some sections of the crowd booed when I was introduced and I put that down to the old sporting rivalry the English have with Aussies. I didn't know much about Choombe but I wanted to put him on the defensive from the start. He was quite flat-footed and I hurt him with a body shot midway through the first round and rocked him with a big right. I was ahead 6–1 after the opening round and 10–3 after the second. One of the television commentators, the former world champ Richie Woodhall, said Choombe couldn't cope with my speed and angles and he was surprised hearing Don telling me in the corner that I was 'too sloppy' and that I shouldn't trade punches with my opponent. To make sure there were no scoring anomalies, which are all too common in amateur boxing, I put my foot down on the accelerator and punched non-stop in Round 3, firing a lot of lead right hands – my shock punch – to take the decision 19–5. The press said it was the most dominant display by any of the Australians.

After the fight I told a reporter for Australia's ABC network that, despite my confidence, I still got nervous before every fight.

'But I need those nerves to help me produce my best,' I said. 'I tried to relax. I slowed down a bit in the second round. Overall, I moved when I needed to move and I came forward when I needed to come forward.'

I felt that Choombe, as the underdog, had the backing of the crowd and I told the ABC, 'I fully expected the crowd to cheer for the opposition. The crowd is always on the opposite side to the Aussies, but it's all good.'

Already some of our team were out of the competition. In Olympic boxing you only get one chance to impress. Ibrahim Balla, Cameron Hammond and Damien Hooper had won their opening fights, but Billy Ward, Jackson Wood, Luke Jackson and Jesse Ross were already out. Damien fought especially well to beat the American champ Marcus Browne and was living up to the accolades that had been heaped upon him. He had sparked an international controversy though by walking to the ring wearing a T-shirt featuring the Aboriginal flag, in violation of Olympic rules that ban demonstrations or political, religious or racial propaganda.

'I was not really thinking about any fallout,' Damien said after the fight. 'I was thinking about my family and all that. It made my whole performance better.'

None of that controversy worried me. I was only concentrating on lanky 25-year-old Abderrazak Houya, a Tunisian All-Africa Games silver medallist, who also boasted a win over Choombe in Casablanca. A victory over Houya and I was into the Olympic quarter-finals.

Beating Houya was a tougher task than my first Olympic fight. He was a dangerous counter-puncher with heavy hands and he really tried to dig in the body shots. But my movement was better and my attack more varied. I out-boxed him in the first round, keeping my composure and digging in a big left to the body near the end of the round. I was up 5–3 at the first bell. I kept up the pace in Round 2 and was ahead 12–7. Houya started throwing a lot more in the third, although I managed to dodge the majority of them and dropped him with a body shot. I was constantly on the move using the Broken-Rhythm Pressure Fighting style. The judges gave me the win 17–11.

It was a fantastic feeling knowing that I was now just one win from becoming Australia's first boxing medallist since the year I was born. As it was, I was the first Aussie to win back-to-back Olympic fights since Robbie Peden in Barcelona in 1992. Peden had also competed in Atlanta four years later, in the same division as young American bronze medallist Floyd Mayweather.

On the same night I beat Houya, there was another cracking fight in my weight class when Cuba's Roniel Iglesias Sotolongo beat world champ Éverton dos Santos Lopes 18–15 in a battle of southpaws. Both had been world amateur champs. Lopes was the gold-medal favourite but was going home empty handed.

Despite a good start by some of our fighters, by 4 August I was the last of the Australian men left in the competition. 'Super' Hooper lost on points in his second fight, against Egor Mekhontsev who went on to win Russia's only gold medal. Cameron Hammond bowed out against Canada's Custio Clayton. At 49 kilograms, Billy Ward was out-boxed by Cuba's Yosbany Veitía Soto but said the experience would help him build towards the Commonwealth Games in two years' time. Billy was the life of the team, a jovial little redhead who was always buzzing.

As the last man standing, I was interviewed by an American video journalist. I was pretty shy and nervous – being interviewed was something very new to me and I still wasn't quite comfortable doing it. I told the journalist that

Denys Berinchyk, my opponent for the quarter-final, was a tough boy who kept coming forward. I said I felt 'awesome' and couldn't wait to get in there and out-work him. 'I like that type of style, so hopefully I can beat him up,' I said. 'I just want to do Australia proud and hopefully I can fight to the best of my ability on the day.'

When the journalist asked me who I thought were the best boxers in the world, I said I didn't follow boxing as closely as I should, but that Floyd Mayweather and Manny Pacquiao were my idols.

If they ever fought though, I said, Mayweather would outbox Manny.

*

Jacko and I became huge fans of Vasyl Lomachenko, who was on his way to a second gold medal. We even practised some of his moves and I had a combination of punches that we called 'the Lomachenko' which involved throwing half a dozen hooks to the body to open up the arms to deliver a devastating uppercut.

Berinchyk, Lomachenko's teammate and the world silver medallist, was unlikely to let me throw too many of those combinations. I was ready for the toughest fight of my life. He just scraped into the quarter-finals though, with a 24–23 win over Sweden's Anthony Yigit, and I thought I could tip the scoreboard my way.

Glenn did his best to coach me over the phone before the fight and I received goodwill messages from right around Australia. All of them were much appreciated.

Like his big Ukraine teammate Oleksandr Usyk, who went on to win gold at 91 kilograms, Berinchyk had a radical haircut, with a close-cropped skull decorated by a thick mop of hair hanging to the left side. In that moment of silence before the roar of the fight began, I thought *how bizarre*. I had not even had an official bout at the time of the previous Olympics in Beijing and here I was taking on one of the world's best for a medal.

Berinchyk was the world silver medallist but I took the fight to him straight away. I had him backing up early in the first round. A minute into the fight though, he nailed me with a hard left hook while he was briefly in the southpaw stance. According to television commentator Richie Woodhall, the Ukraine champion was struggling as he tried to work out my unorthodox movement. 'All Horn has to do is bring him on to a right uppercut,' Woodhall told viewers. 'This Ukraine fighter makes so many mistakes when he's coming forward. He relies on his strength and just barges forward recklessly at times. But his sheer persistence and sustained pressure always seems to work.'

Berinchyk tried to wrestle me around and he caught me with a pair of solid rights just before the end of the first round.

I was behind 5–3 at the break.

In the second round, Berinchyk kept bustling forward and I failed to move well enough to stop him. In hindsight I should have tried to fight fire with fire. Berinchyk was fighting like an aggressive pro with a high volume of punches. I should have stayed on the attack rather than trying to out-box him on the back move. My hands were way too low. He was ahead 12–7 after Round 2.

In the third round we went toe to toe, me in red, him in blue, slugging away with everything we had. 'There's not many boxers who will put Berinchyk on the back foot but Horn is doing that,' Woodhall said. 'What a performance in the last round from this young Aussie.'

But there was no doubt Berinchyk deserved the decision and he went into the semi-finals with a 21–13 victory.

We shook hands and embraced and then I waved goodbye to the crowd.

Just like that my Olympic dream – the mission Glenn and I had worked tirelessly on – was over.

I had wanted a medal so badly. I was gutted.

I was also realistic. Before long I was able to console myself that, after just four years in boxing, I had competed in the greatest sporting spectacle on the planet and given the world No. 2 a hell of a contest.

I believed that with Glenn back in my corner I could one day be world No. 1. And make some money along the way.

But now it was time to party.

Jo and I went out on the town with Jacko and Johan Linde and some of our other mates. The food hall at the Olympic village offered free McDonald's and I've never eaten so many burgers in my life and I've never enjoyed putting on weight like I did for the few days after my Olympic career had ended. I would load up on cookies, taking handfuls out to eat in the park with Mum and Jo – so many in fact that we soon had cookie overload. When you've had to watch your weight for years it was an unusual and very welcome freedom. Not that I get too stressed about food these days. I've learned that eating chocolate while plonked in front of the TV late at night can be a disaster, but I can still eat a little bit around my training times and get away with it because it burns off quickly. This is good news for anyone in my area who sells Cadbury's Caramello, Snack, Creations – the Popping Candy one – Maltesers, Tim Tams or Oreos.

Although I wish I had still been in the competition on the final day, I could put my feet up and watch some of the other guys fight for the gold medal. Roniel Iglesias Sotolonogo won the final in my weight class, outpointing Berinchyk. Vasyl Lomachenko took the gold as expected at featherweight, and in the heavier divisions Oleksandr Usyk and Anthony Joshua came away victors. Joshua would soon be one of the biggest names in the sport.

I caught some other magic moments in London, including seeing Sally Pearson win gold in the hurdles and Usain Bolt take out the 200 metres. I went to the swimming and the table tennis events as well. At the table tennis I picked up pointers on how to wipe out my mate Kiang Lai back home. Kiang has since bought a $100 racquet in the hope of beating me, but he will need more than that.

Having family members with me had been a terrific shock absorber. The closing ceremony, in which I marched with Jacko, Johan, Sally Pearson, Natalie Cook and so many other friends I'd made in London, capped off a wonderful couple of weeks during a phenomenal time in my life.

After flying back into Sydney, where there was a street parade for the Olympians, I returned to Brisbane on 22 August for another street parade down the Queen Street Mall. Even though I was sorry I didn't have a medal around my neck I still couldn't wipe the smile from my face. After the years of hard work, I was glad to finally give my body a rest.

Then it was a bit of a whirlwind. Ethan Warren, an Olympic diver, took me to try the 7-metre high board. I had a go but decided to stick with boxing because it was my area of expertise. I did the rounds of a few schools – at Springfield, Park Ridge and Calamvale – talking to the kids about my Olympic experience, and at Brassall I acted as a reading mentor and judge for the kids' fancy dress. It was special going back to see the kids at Forest Lake Outside School Care to talk about London 2012 and to see their excitement. I'd now worked there for a few years and had a real rapport with a lot of the kids and parents.

I organised a fantastic fancy-dress Halloween party in which Jo and I dressed as zombies but my grandad, Jack Dykstra, frightened the hell out of me when he feigned a collapse midway through the haunted house when I jumped out at him. I was petrified and yelled out for someone to turn on the lights. He got up laughing. I know where I get my love for practical jokes.

I went to watch some of the kids at the Golden Gloves boxing tournament and thought of how much sporting talent there was in Australia just waiting to blossom. I tell young athletes to follow Glenn's mantra that the key to success is believing you can be successful.

I put out some feelers to find work as a personal trainer. I was planning to turn professional and I ran a contest among my Facebook friends to come up with a nickname for my fighting career. I had suggestions such as Jeff 'The Jawbreaker' Horn, Jeff 'The Jackal' Horn, Hurricane Horn, Hardcore Horn, Battle Worn Horn, 'Horny Horn (!)', Jeff 'Has a Raging (!!)' Horn, Enormous (!!!) Horn, Hit Man Horn, Henchman Horn, Hard-hitting Horn, Beeping Horn, The Babyface Assassin and

'The Storm' Jeff Horn. Someone even came up with Jeff 'The Dentist' Horn because everyone is scared of the dentist.

From September, I began getting some work as a relief teacher and was constantly challenged to arm wrestles by six to sixteen year olds. Some of the other nickname suggestions were 'The Students' Nightmare' to the simple but true Jeff 'The Guy Who Is Now Teaching at My School' Horn.

Lochie Gould submitted 'The Hornet' and on 1 November I let everyone know via Facebook that my fighting name would be Jeff 'The Hornet' Horn.

I sent Lochie an Olympic uniform as a prize but he's not getting any royalties. I had thought of that name already, but it stood out to me in front of the others.

*

Undoubtedly 2012 had been a remarkable year for me. But the best was yet to come.

On 10 November Jo and I headed to the Gold Coast for a short break in a room at the Hilton Hotel lent to us by Natalie Cook, my friend from the Olympics. My sisters, Rebecca and Bianca, had arrived at the hotel before us and decorated the room with dozens of roses. Jo was amazed at the colourful, fragrant display.

On the CD system I had a song playing called 'More Than Words' by the American band Extreme, a song we both really liked. The music wafted on the gentle breeze coming from outside.

Out on the hotel balcony, as Jo wondered what was going on, I went down on bended knee and asked the best person I've ever known if she'd marry me.

She said, 'Yes.'

It was my real gold-medal moment.

Jo is the most important person in my life. And that day was the start of our most exhilarating journey together.

For us, the good times had only just begun.

8

Boxing is show-business with blood

– David Belasco, an American theatre producer and playwright

NOT LONG AFTER I came home from the Olympics, Glenn sat me down to tell me some exciting news. I was no longer just a fighter, he said. I was now an entertainer and he wanted me to be an all-action hero. I was going to become a professional boxer and it was my choice whether I became a rich and famous one or a poor, anonymous battler.

'Jeff, there are world champions who fight for $100,000,' he said, 'and there are world champions who fight for $100 million. Which do you want to be?'

Hmmm. Decisions. Decisions. I thought about it for about a nanosecond.

'I'll go with the big money,' I said.

'Well, if you want to be the sort of boxer who earns the

big bucks, you have to entertain the crowd,' he said. 'You have to be exciting, you have to be a thriller. You can never be in a dull fight. Every time you get into the boxing ring you have to set hearts racing in the crowd and your wins have to be spectacular.'

'Okay. Suits me. Let's do it, Glenn. Let's win a world title.'

*

Amateur boxing is a sort of rugged version of fencing, score a point and get away. Professional boxing is a far more brutal and exacting test of strength, stamina and physical and mental toughness.

I was ready to be tested to the limit, to take on anyone toe to toe, but I was a far different person outside the ring than between the ropes. I was still playing all-night Monopoly games with my old school friends, still trying to take the shirts off their backs at poker and still racing them on the go-kart track.

I was also still swooning after Jo accepted my marriage proposal.

Before the serious business of fighting for a living began, Jo and I headed to Patong Beach in Thailand for a few days to celebrate our engagement. Back home, I played in a celebrity baseball game with the Brisbane Bandits, and was honoured to receive the Jamie Nicolson trophy as the best international boxer in Queensland, a tremendous gift from a family who have done so much for the sport and whose son was a brilliant Olympic boxer. Seven fighters from my gym won state titles that December – Glenn's daughter Angel

Rushton, as well as Sam Banney, Bon Cos, Simon Cooper, Zach Bacigalupo, Joe Goodall and Adam Copland. Bon Cos and his brother Bee are sparring partners of mine, and Bon also played another crucial role in my boxing career when he and Nathan Millington worked on my logo – an angry hornet blasting away with boxing gloves. For their designs they used 'Hornet Orange', the colour of my old soccer club, the Queensland Lions – and of the Netherlands. It's my favourite colour.

*

Manny Pacquiao was not enjoying life as much as I was at this time. On 8 December 2012, at the MGM Grand in Las Vegas – his home away from home – Pacquiao faced his arch foe, Juan Manuel Márquez, a tremendously tough and aggressive Mexican who two years earlier had climbed from the canvas to beat Toowoomba boxer Michael Katsidis. Pacquiao and Márquez had previously fought each other three times, with the first bout being scored a draw and the other two going to Pacquiao by razor-thin decisions. Márquez claimed he should have been given the verdict in all three fights and he set about proving it in 2012. In Round 3, he used a humungous, looping right hand to drop Pacquiao for the first time in their epic battles. In the next round Márquez landed some more hard right hands, but Pacquiao roared back behind his devastating straight left in the fifth to send Márquez to the canvas for a flash knockdown. A follow-up left hand broke the Mexican's nose. Then right on the bell to end Round 6, as Pacquiao looked to land another finishing left hand, a bloodied and hurt Márquez ducked under a jab and hit Pacquiao in the mouth with a pounding right hand. Pacquiao's head snapped back and he fell face first, stone-cold unconscious to the canvas, where he lay for two minutes. It was the worst loss of Pacquiao's career.

I filed the memory of that right hand into my brain for future reference. I might need it some time.

*

The Pallara State School was the first school where I taught on a regular basis. I was there for two years on a contract, which gave me work for three days a week. I was qualified to teach both primary and secondary and I also picked up other work as a relief teacher at various schools around southern Brisbane. I have to tell you that it felt extremely weird teaching small children at school while, at the same time, learning how to knock men unconscious. Each morning I would sit on the carpet with the kids and take the roll call, then read them a story about the cat in the hat, or the wolf and the girl in the red riding hood, or ones that I could more easily relate to, like that diary of a wimpy kid, which I had been once.

My 2012 New Year's resolution had been to make the Olympics and to have Jo accept my marriage proposal. Happily, I had succeeded in both. My resolution for 2013 was to start my career as a professional boxer and secure an Australian title. Glenn and I began working towards those goals.

To avoid injuries, I started off nice and slow when I returned to the Stretton gym, but it wasn't long before I regained my hunger for victory and my appetite for combat.

Glenn planned to give me a few easy fights to build a solid professional foundation. Given my performances at the Olympics, we were offered promotional contracts from around the world. One was from the former world champ Ricky Hatton, who was signing up a lot of promising fighters in Australia, including Cameron Hammond. Dad and Glenn looked at all the offers and thought they were rubbish, the basic premise being that the boxer did all the bleeding and the promoters made the money.

We elected to remain free agents and to take fights wherever we could, even if the purses were small change.

There are plenty of stories about boxers making millions of dollars, but boxing is like any other field of entertainment – only the very top of the iceberg is in the cash. Most fighters get little reward for their efforts. Promoter Adam Wilcock offered me $1500 to make my professional debut in Melbourne against a stocky Kiwi named Jody Allen, who at the time had two wins from nine fights. He was a few kilos heavier than I was, but my punches carried more weight.

At twenty-five, I was fairly old in boxing terms to be making my debut. But I had all the enthusiasm of a teenager when Glenn and I arrived for the fight at a wedding venue, the Grand Star Receptions lounge, in the suburb of Altona North on 1 March. I had finished my amateur career with a record of forty-eight wins and eighteen losses, but as a pro I planned on remaining undefeated.

I wore the Australian colours of green and gold into the ring.

My pro debut was scheduled for four rounds, although I planned to finish long before that. I hit Jody early with some wicked head and body shots. His corner tossed in the white towel of surrender a split second before the referee, Tony Marretta, waved it off at two minutes and twenty-two seconds of the second round.

Immediately after the fight, veteran ring announcer Howard Leigh interviewed me and I told the crowd, 'It was great to get back in the ring after an eight-month break following the Olympics. I'm really excited about becoming a professional boxer.'

My fight was only a preliminary bout to the main event of the evening, when Australian light-heavyweight champion, Blake Caparello, outpointed a showboating Ayitey Powers of Ghana. Also on the card a veteran New South Wales welterweight named Alex AhTong boxed a draw with a Japanese whirlwind, Charlie Sugiura. Adam Wilcock wanted to match me and Alex next, but Alex told Glenn there was no way he was getting into the ring with me.

The following month Jo and I had a huge family gathering for our engagement party. I had an engagement of a different kind on 27 April when my team, now known as the Hornet Swarm, were at Steve Deller's gym in Newstead, Brisbane – which goes by the grandiose title of the Fortitude Stadium – for my second pro fight against Kiwi Torin Rophia, a late replacement who had gone the distance with the undefeated 80-kilogram Steve Lovett from New South Wales in his previous bout.

I dropped Torin three times and the referee, Tony Kettlewell, stopped the fight after just ninety-three seconds. I was still an undercard fighter though, and my next bout was down the card on a show topped by world-ranked heavyweight Alex Leapai at the Royal International

Convention Centre inside Brisbane's Showgrounds. The program was being televised by Fox Sports.

Alex was due to fight the hulking John Napari of Ghana, but the big African withdrew at the last minute and a Melbourne fighter named Joe Lloyd made a frantic dash to the airport as a replacement. He was putting on his hand-wraps in the cab on the way from Brisbane airport and virtually jogged from the cab into centre ring. Predictably he didn't make it beyond the first round as Alex ran over him on his way towards a world-title shot with Wladimir Klitschko.

My fight lasted just 162 seconds. I dropped a Thai kickboxer named Rangson Poonsang twice in the opening round for a quick stoppage. That meant a hat-trick of quick knockout wins to start my pro career.

Damien Hooper was just as sharp on the undercard, scoring a first-round knockout, while Jarrod Fletcher, the Beijing Olympian, took six rounds to stop Philip Kotey from Ghana.

My three wins, coupled with the fact that I was now working as a schoolteacher, started to attract considerable media attention and on 1 June *The Courier-Mail*, the major daily newspaper in Brisbane, ran the first big feature on my budding career. Photographer Peter Wallis came to the Pallara State School where I was teaching Years 4 and 5 and took some cracking shots of me with the kids. There were some very happy children and a few tears from the ones who weren't at school that day and missed having their photo in the paper. Some of the kids were a little overenthusiastic when it came to posing with me. Peter asked one little girl to put on a boxing glove and rest it against my chin to highlight my status as 'The Fighting Schoolteacher'. Let me just say that little girl had an uppercut that would have done Manny Pacquiao proud as she let fly with a couple right on the button. I gritted my teeth and said, 'Gentle, gentle.'

The article made a big spread in the sports section. I was quoted as saying, 'I'm pretty softly spoken and mild most of the time, but I love the competition of boxing. When I get in the ring I'm a different person. You have to be ruthless and get rid of your opponent as quickly as possible. I had a very good teacher in boxing right from the start in Glenn Rushton. He not only taught me the skills of boxing but he taught me to believe in myself and that with hard work anything is possible.'

It wasn't just me gaining media attention. My brother, Ben, busy helping me get ready for the next fight, also made our local paper around that time for winning a Queensland Novice Title.

The same weekend I featured in *The Courier-Mail*, Jo and I flew down to Sydney to see my uncle Russell starring in *The Addams Family* musical at the Capitol Theatre. It was a sensational production and Russell was brilliant as the odd-looking Uncle Fester, a role I tell him that he was born to play. The fact that he needed very little make-up helped (ha ha).

A few days later Glenn and I signed a contract for my fourth professional fight, against Leti Leti, a brilliant young Samoan fighter living in Queensland. He had just suffered the only loss of his career – a decision to the world-class Samuel Colomban – and was eager to get back on the winning list with a victory over me. Leti had a record of eight wins in nine fights and a lot of experts said he would be too advanced for me at that stage of my career. But Glenn and I were confident I could do it.

I sparred with some tough guys, including Jarrod Fletcher, Dennis Hogan, Liam Hutchinson, Clay Waterman, Paddy Murphy and Hone Huni, but on 28 June we had to announce that Leti Leti had pulled out of the fight and that I had gone up another gear or two in my choice of opponents.

I was matched with former IBF world super-featherweight champion Gairy 'Superman' St Clair, one of the six men the great Sydney trainer Johnny Lewis had guided to world titles. Gairy was a veteran of sixty pro fights, had gone the distance with the likes of Lovemore Ndou and Amir Khan, and had spent years as a sparring partner of Kostya Tszyu. Still, we were ready, and every day after reading the kids a story and going through the Education Queensland syllabus in my lessons, I got ready for trench warfare with a man said to be harder to catch with a clean punch than greased lightning. I loved teaching but, given a choice then, I would have preferred to concentrate full time on boxing. Still, I had to work to pay the bills and save to buy a house. I was very happy that Joel Brunker, a good fighter from the amateurs who was now a world-rated pro, was singing my praises in the media as a future star. Maybe Gairy St Clair read Joel's comments or heard how hard I was training because he called it a day on his career and I was left to find another opponent.

Finally, promoter Jamie Myer announced that Rivan Cesaire had signed to fight me on a Fox Sports card at the Southport RSL on 8 August. Rivan is a slick fighter from Cameroon and had a record of eleven wins in fourteen pro fights, having recently beaten good-quality opposition, including my old nemesis Todd Kidd. His manager, Matt Clark, said that with less than four completed rounds of experience behind me, I had gone too hard, too early, in challenging Rivan who had fought seventy-five rounds.

'If I was Jeff Horn's manager I wouldn't have taken this fight,' he told reporters. 'Jeff is a good fighter but this is going to be a huge step up for him. Rivan has already beaten some of Australia's best in Tim Hunt, Todd Kidd, Alex AhTong, Jason Kanofski, Ben Costello and Steven Maxwell. He's very confident about beating Jeff Horn as well.'

I was taken aback in the days before the fight when I learned that our little mate from the Olympics, Billy Ward, had taken his own life at just twenty years of age. Billy was a nice guy, a tiny dynamo with a mop of curly red hair and a cheeky grin that endeared him to all the other fighters on the Australian Olympic team.

I went into the ring at the Southport RSL wearing a black armband in tribute to him. Glenn, his daughter Angel Rushton and my brother, Ben, were in my corner.

Rivan was a big step up from my previous opponents but, even though he is fast and extremely hard to hit, I won the first two rounds with superior footwork, walking him down and putting him under relentless pressure. Unless you have good footwork against Rivan you will struggle big time. In the third round, our heads banged together during an exchange of punches and he emerged with a deep wound over his left eyebrow and blood gushing into his eye. The ringside doctor stopped the fight but, because the bout had not gone three complete rounds, it was ruled a technical draw. It still makes me angry that on my record I have a 'technical draw'. I think the rule should be changed and those sorts of endings be ruled 'no contest'. It wasn't a 'draw' – I was dominating –

but the 'draw' is a blemish that will stay on my record no matter how much I complain.

The fight earned me a shot on Fox Sports against the Australian welterweight champ Samuel Colomban, a tall, awkward fighter who had been in Australia since representing Cameroon at the 2006 Commonwealth Games. In 2011 Sam had gone twelve rounds for the Commonwealth welterweight title in Oldham in the United Kingdom and he would come into our fight at the Melbourne Pavilion in Kensington on 12 September with a record of twenty-one wins in twenty-six pro bouts. One of his victories was against the South African former world champ Philip Holiday, who now lives in Brisbane. Sam was a tall order for me in every sense, enjoying a 7-centimetre height advantage and 10 centimetres in reach that he planned to exploit.

I prepared for the fight by sparring with tall middleweights Reagan Dessaix and Nathan Carroll. I felt that since half of my sixty-six amateur fights were international bouts against some of the world's best, I had the background to cope with Sam's greater pro experience. I was ready to back my skill level and physical strength. Glenn and I studied the way Sam moved his head when he was fighting, the patterns he used in attack and defence and we practised again and again the ways to catch him.

A few days before the fight Peter Wallis took another great photo of me and my pop, Ray Horn, for *The Sunday Mail*, in which Pop talked about my nana and his brother Gordon and the fact that he hoped I could emulate his hero Tommy Burns and win the Australian welterweight title. I told the paper that I would do my best, even though some commentators were saying it was a mismatch.

The fight card in Melbourne was huge for a local show, with Kye MacKenzie and Qamil and Ibrahim Balla all winning their fights and a tough Filipino southpaw named Czar Amonsot stopping rugged Steven Wills. Despite all the training I'd done in preparation to land my power shots on Sam, I was expecting a tough gruelling ten-round fight. At the opening bell he came at me with a fast, long left jab, trying to blast through for an opportunity. I managed to dodge him and with just over a minute gone saw the opening Glenn and I had prepared for. As Sam dipped low to my left, I sent a straight right screaming down after him and it landed flush on his chin. There was a loud crack that could be heard ringside. Sam pitched face first towards the canvas. Before he even hit the floor, commentator Chris McCullen had started to exclaim, 'He's out cold.' It was the sweetest right hand I ever landed and, although some critics reckoned it was a lucky punch, it was what Glenn calls 'a well-rehearsed ad-lib line', a lucky punch we'd practised hundreds of times.

As soon as Sam went down, the referee, Tony Marretta, knew he wasn't getting up any time soon and waved the fight off without a count. Peter Lewis, the ringside doctor, jumped in to offer assistance to the unconscious former Australian champ. In Brisbane all the boys from my Stretton gym, who were watching the fight together, jumped around like school kids who'd been let home early.

The fight had lasted just seventy-eight seconds. Thankfully Sam recovered after a few minutes, even though he still had no memory of what had happened. It was the first time he had been stopped in twenty-seven fights.

'Wow, I'm shocked,' I said after the fight. 'I never thought it would end like that. I was expecting to go ten rounds.

I'm feeling stoked. Some people thought I was being rushed because this was just my fifth pro fight but I feel I've already fought the best in the world in the amateurs. If you can box, you can box. I want to keep fighting every few weeks. I've only got a few rounds under my belt at the moment so I want to keep improving and gaining that experience against good fighters. People tell me I have a pro style so hopefully one day it will take me all the way to a world championship. Right now, I'm going back to school to show the kids this Australian title belt.'

*

The teachers and kids at Pallara surprised me with a chocolate cake when I arrived home from Melbourne. Immediately I was faced with another challenge.

Anthony Mundine.

Australia's most outspoken and controversial sports star was in Brisbane preparing to face America's former world champ Shane Mosley, who two years earlier at the MGM Grand in Las Vegas had struggled to win a round when losing on points against Manny Pacquiao. Anthony was the first real fighter I ever watched on TV and a lot had happened for both of us in the seven years since I'd seen him outpoint Danny Green. He was looking for sparring partners and I put my hand up – both of them actually as I went after him. We did six solid rounds at a boxing gym near Brisbane's Story Bridge and, although 'The Man' landed some good punches, *The Courier-Mail* ran a terrific photo by Annette Dew of me piercing his defence with a straight left, right on the nose. The paper's headline was 'Welcome to Brisbane, Man

WHACK'. Mundine told me after our spar, 'Man, you're an awkward guy. You're making me work hard.' Anthony was the fastest professional fighter I had faced at that stage, but I'd fought a lot of top amateurs who were even quicker than him. I felt that if we were having a real fight rather than just a spar, I would have Anthony covered, even though he had a few kilos on me.

Jo and I headed to Sydney for another short holiday. If you think it's scary taking on heavy punchers like Manny Pacquiao in the boxing ring, that's nothing compared with Luna Park's Hollywood Horrors, a haunted house–style thriller where movie monsters – one with a chainsaw – chase you down dark and eerie corridors. Jo had shivers down her spine and I have to admit it was entertaining to see her so frightened.

Facing Rivan Cesaire in a rematch on 16 November at the Royal International Convention Centre did not hold anywhere near the same terrors for me. But he withdrew at the last minute and I ended up facing a replacement opponent, Aswin Cabuy, an Indonesian living in Sydney. Aswin had become a journeyman opponent in recent years, fighting anyone he could on short notice, but he boasted a win over Samuel Colomban and was a very experienced southpaw. And very tough and awkward.

I wanted to stop him quickly but I rushed too much and was messy in the attack. I wasn't happy with my performance. I got clipped a couple of times, but we knew that Aswin used a lot of rough tactics and I wanted to get him out of there as quickly as I could. Despite making a few mistakes, I battered him in the first round and stopped him in the second when he couldn't recover from a big body shot.

After six pro fights I was yet to go beyond three rounds.

*

Jo and I were just moving into our first house together, a renovator's delight we bought in the suburb of Acacia Ridge. The house had everything we needed. It was only a few minutes from Glenn's gym, it was close to the Pallara school where I was working and there was a McDonald's going in nearby for the brief times when I wasn't training. Jo and I put up our first Christmas tree in our own house. Now we just had to pay the mortgage. Jo was working in the city at Sarina Russo Apprenticeships, matching apprentices with potential employers, and I wanted to match opponents with my right hand as quickly as I could.

After the Aswin Cabuy fight, Glenn received a call from Danny Green's trainer, Angelo Hyder, who was promoting a show in Perth. The main event was a world featherweight title fight and once again I was needed to fill a spot on the undercard, fighting two-time world-title challenger Naoufel Ben Rabeh on just two weeks' notice. The wiry veteran had a huge reputation but I wasn't worried. While the details were being sorted out, I played a little bit of golf with my mates and went ten-pin bowling. I try to have a relaxed, normal life with my friends when I'm not fighting. But I knew that this would be the toughest bout of my life and an even bigger challenge than the Olympics. Ben Rabeh had been an Olympian for Tunisia at the 2000 Sydney games and had settled in Australia after that. He was thirty-six years old and had a record of thirty-seven wins in forty fights. One loss was early in his career on points against another Olympian, Fred Kinuthia, and the other two were against world champions Juan Urango and Lovemore Ndou. A lot of people thought Ben Rabeh had deserved the decision against Urango in their fight in Florida.

My purse was just $4000 for six rounds. It was hardly a fortune to face a dangerous guy who had gone within a point or two of being world champion. But when Glenn asked me what I thought, I said, 'Take it, straight away.'

About an hour later, Angelo Hyder rings Glenn back and says Ben Rabeh wants one last condition – winner takes all.

So there you go. Welcome to the glamour of big-time boxing – fighting a tough, dangerous guy on two weeks' notice, flying all the way to Perth at the back of the plane, fighting the local star in his adopted hometown, and then having a big chance of flying home not just with a loss on my record but nothing in my pocket.

I told Glenn to take it. If Ben Rabeh wanted winner takes all, he was about to do his dough and I'd be going home with the best part of $8000 – less Glenn's 25 per cent – to knock off the mortgage.

I finished the last of the school reports I was working on and on 6 December headed across the Nullarbor for a massive step up the boxing ladder.

At London 2012 my Tunisian opponent was tough and a hard puncher. But Ben Rabeh was even more dangerous – extremely quick, especially so since my distance was a bit off early. I had my hands down way too low in the first round and Ben Rabeh used my nose for target practice. He hit me with four or five hard straight lefts in a row as I was trying to figure out just where they were coming from. After a minute he was also unloading with fast chopping combinations from both hands. In the last seconds of the round though, I started to connect with my own big punches and near the bell I used my old trick of turning southpaw to hit him with a straight right hand on the button.

Still, I was a bit of a mess when I went back to the corner with blood spurting from my nose. Dad was in my corner for the first time and he found it confronting.

Glenn immediately went to work on my face and my mind. He knows I don't mind a dollar and he said, 'Jeff, this is winner takes all. Winner takes all. We didn't come all this way to go home with nothing. Now get out there and move your head more. Extend the gap. Make sure you're just a little further back to dodge his punches. But when you attack, attack hard. You're giving him too much respect.'

I started moving more and attacking harder and I won the next round and the next, and the pattern continued.

After six rounds, Ben Rabeh looked like he'd been smacked over the head with a shovel and I was the winner by a six-round decision. If the fight had been ten rounds, I don't think he would have lasted the distance. He hasn't fought since.

The Courier-Mail reported:

> Brisbane schoolteacher Jeff Horn is likely to burst into the International Boxing Federation [IBF] world welterweight rankings after his upset points decision over two-time world title challenger Naoufel Ben Rabeh in Perth on Friday night. Horn, a London Olympian and cousin of Brisbane Lord Mayor Graham Quirk, dominated the six-round bout. Australia's IBF representative Ray Wheatley says he will push for Horn to be included as a contender for the world crown. Wheatley, a former IBF vice-president who was

inducted into the Australian Boxing Hall of Fame last year, still has a major influence on the world standings.

The upset victory in Perth aroused the interest of the Auckland-based promotional firm Duco Events, which was guiding the career of my old amateur pal Joseph Parker and was about to kick off with a new concept in rugby league called the NRL Auckland Nines.

Stuart Duncan, the company's matchmaker and the former manager of the top Melbourne middleweight Sam Soliman, rang Glenn and said Duco was interested in signing me to a promotional deal as it saw me as the best prospect in Australia. He said one of Duco's directors, Dean Lonergan, a former New Zealand rugby league test forward, was planning to come to Jupiters Casino on the Gold Coast to watch my rematch with Rivan Cesaire, which was now scheduled for 19 March 2014.

First though I had some important down time. I went ten-pin bowling and go-karting with some of my old schoolmates for my twenty-sixth birthday and had a few days at Surfers Paradise with Jo. Then I did some hard sparring with super-quick Cameron Hammond and Dennis Hogan because Glenn and I wanted to right the wrong of the 'technical draw' against Rivan Cesaire by combating his speed.

Things went exactly to plan. Rivan is a very good boxer with fast counter-punches off both sides, but I was able to apply pressure with my jab in the early stages and dropped him with a straight left in the first round. He gave me a good fight through the middle rounds, but after the midway point I was wearing him down. I was intent on stepping up the pressure after the eighth round and was starting to land some good right hands when one cannoned off his left shoulder blade as he rolled forward and he suffered a dislocation. The judges had me way out in front by Round 9, when the referee, Paul Tapley, stopped the fight after Rivan slumped to his knees clutching at his shoulder in agony.

The next morning Glenn and Dad sat down for breakfast with Dean Lonergan and Stuart Duncan at Spinnaker's Café inside Jupiters. They talked about me becoming Duco's star Australian fighter. The company planned to make boxing a major mainstream sport in Australia again, as it was in the 1960s and '70s when Lionel Rose and Johnny Famechon ushered in hit programs such as *TV Ringside*.

Glenn had reservations about the deal. 'Dean, I don't know if you're the right fit for us,' he said. 'I see Jeff Horn filling Suncorp Stadium in Brisbane for a world-title fight – 50,000 seats.'

Dean almost spilled his coffee. This was a bit more than the former test footballer was expecting – there had only been a few hundred fight fans watching me at Jupiters. But Glenn is persistent.

'Do you see Jeff filling Suncorp Stadium, Dean? Because if you don't, then there's probably not much point in us talking.'

Dean was a bit tentative but warily replied, 'Suncorp? Well … yeah, maybe, yeah, eventually.'

'Well, let's keep talking,' Glenn said, glad that Dean didn't go right off the idea. Most other promoters had, using the old line, 'Tell him he's dreaming'.

Glenn said that if Dean wanted to do something, we all had to move quickly because I was now twenty-six. Glenn wanted me to fight only guys in the world rankings and all with the aim to get me a world-title fight as quickly as possible.

Dean said he was willing to invest in my future.

Glenn phoned me to say Duco Events wanted to make me a world champion.

'Really?'

'Yeah, really,' he said.

9

Friendship … is not something you learn in school. But if you haven't learned the meaning of friendship, you really haven't learned anything.

– Muhammad Ali, three-time world heavyweight champion

TO BE A WORLD champion you need a terrific team in your corner and terrific people backing you up outside the ring. Glenn has always fostered a spirit of teamwork at the Stretton gym and we support each other totally, whether it's someone fighting Manny Pacquiao for the world welterweight title or a novice making their boxing debut. I put my faith in Glenn and in turn he put his faith in me and I've had terrific support from so many other friends and family members.

After my sparring session with Anthony Mundine, I was contacted by a gym owner and fitness guru named Dundee Kim. He said he wanted to be involved in my career because he saw me as a potential champion who could do great things for the image of the sport, given my job as a schoolteacher. He became crucial to my team as a strength and conditioning coach, and in the years leading up to the Manny Pacquiao fight I trained twice a week with him. He became a key figure in my pro career.

Dundee came to Australia from Korea two decades ago with a new wife and not much else. Grateful for every opportunity his new country has given him, Dundee has helped many people lead better and healthier lives. Born Deuk-Rae Kim in the late 1960s, he arrived in Australia on a student visa and then decided he needed a proper Aussie name if he was going to be a proper Aussie. He chose 'Dundee' after the movie *Crocodile Dundee*. When he was a boy, his life was very poor and he wasn't confident. Like me, he was bullied at school and took up boxing to defend himself. Not only did Dundee build up his body but he also built up his mind, as a soldier in the South Korean army and then as a migrant to Australia who was eager to learn and work. His popular gym is in West End and he is branching out with new gyms at Yeronga and Bowen Hills. The father of three became the regional director of international relations at James Cook University, speaks four languages and has a Master of Business Administration degree. He has also helped Glenn with a lot of other fighters at the Stretton gym as we powered ahead with victories in major tournaments.

A few weeks after my win over Rivan Cesaire, my Stretton teammate Joe Goodall outpointed my Olympic buddy Johan Linde and then the big Sydney rugby league player Willis Meehan to win the Australian amateur super-heavyweight title. Joe is a super talent who went on to win a silver medal at the 2014 Commonwealth Games in Glasgow. At the same time Joe was also helping Alex Leapai with sparring.

It was a busy time for big fights.

On 9 April 2014 in Newcastle, Anthony Mundine showed enormous heart in climbing from the canvas an astonishing five times to survive twelve rounds with Joshua Clottey, a former victim of Manny Pacquiao. Three days after that mauling, Pacquiao returned to the world-title picture with a revenge win over Timothy Bradley. The Pac-Man was world champion again and *The Courier-Mail* began trumpeting my chances against him.

Glenn told the paper that, 'Hopefully by the end of next year Jeff will have worked his way up to become the No. 1 contender just as Alex Leapai has done in the heavyweights. That's our business plan. Jeff will now only be fighting top rated guys. A fight with Pacquiao would be a huge, worldwide event and Jeff has already shown that he has the potential to be a world champion before long.' Glenn told the paper that he wanted me to have three more fights before my wedding to Jo on 6 September.

Duco Events was promising to back my career to the hilt but, before we committed to its contract, there was a lot of toing and froing across the Tasman as Glenn and Dad refined aspects of the deal. Eventually Duco agreed to pay me a wage so that I could concentrate on boxing, but I still got in six months of secondary teaching at Springwood High and other schools before focusing full-time on the fighting.

Glenn continued strengthening my mind and body, with the plan to continually step me up against world-class fighters – better, tougher opponents with each victory. He wanted me to be the complete package when I fought for a world title, not just an over-hyped contender with a record padded against easy beats. Matchmaker Stuart Duncan went looking for guys in the world top fifteen who had 90 per cent winning records. Glenn said we'd need a few of them, one after the other.

Duco was already backing Joseph Parker and had a lucrative TV deal in place to showcase him in New Zealand. I started fighting on his undercards as he marched towards a world heavyweight title shot.

First up for me under the Duco banner was a lanky Brazilian, Fernando Ferreira da Silva, on 5 July in Manukau City, Auckland. He was the No. 13 contender for Floyd Mayweather's World Boxing Association (WBA) welterweight title and had just three losses in thirty-five fights. He had won twenty-four by knockouts, so he was a heavy puncher as well.

The fight was to be the chief support bout to Parker's battle with American slugger Brian Minto. Even though we had agreed to fight for Duco, I hadn't met Dean Lonergan until I arrived in Auckland for the fight. He would become one of the driving forces of my career.

In interviews before the bout, I said that I would be ready to fight Pacquiao within eighteen months and that I just needed the right fights to prepare me.

Da Silva was the perfect opponent at that stage of my career, tough and cagey. Glenn told me when I first started out boxing that it was all very well to believe you could be a world champion, but belief in itself wouldn't do it. 'You've got to be sensible and realistic,' he said. 'You've got to put the work in, to craft a good plan. Blind faith is no use. You have to back that up with science and hard work.'

Over the previous few years that's what we had been doing. The da Silva fight was a great opportunity for me to gain international exposure, being my first international pro bout and first on pay-per-view, even if I was still a support act. The fight was broadcast by SKY Arena in New Zealand and Main Event in Australia. I saw it as representing the beginning of the next phase in my career as I built towards a world-title opportunity.

Da Silva was hard to hit because he was tall and rangy and knew how to use his distance. I busted him up with body shots while also busting a ligament in my right hand.

During the minute's rest after the eighth round, I told Glenn I thought I'd broken my fist.

'Don't worry,' Glenn said. 'The other bloke doesn't know that and you're not going to let him know. You're just going to have to throw it sparingly. Just tap it now and then. Still throw the right occasionally otherwise he'll know it's broken. But you're winning the fight and you can win it with one hand.'

The injury almost certainly saved da Silva from a knockout, but I still dominated. I dropped him in the twelfth and final round to win 120–107 on all three scorecards, which meant I won the first eleven rounds 10–9, with a 10–8 round in the finale. It was da Silva's first defeat in four years. I finished the fight with a big smile on my face. But back in the dressing room I shoved my busted hand in a bucket of ice as Jo held a cold compress against a swelling under my right eye and Ben held another against the left side of my face.

On that same night, in his hometown of Moree, New South Wales, Cameron Hammond won the biggest fight of his career, outpointing Argentina's Alfredo Rodolfo Blanco.

Cameron's promoter, British boxing hero Ricky Hatton, was at ringside. There was talk in the press that Cameron and I could meet down the track, but instead Dean Lonergan sparked something of a sensation by suggesting he could stage a fight between me and Anthony Mundine in November in a deal that would pay The Man a fortune.

'With pay TV money from Australia and New Zealand the deal will be worth more than $1 million for Mundine,' Dean said. 'We believe that Jeff is a future world champion and we were absolutely thrilled with his win. He showed power, skill and personality. He is a wonderful clean-cut kid and a great ambassador for the sport and we want to give him the platform to become a real sporting hero in Australia and New Zealand. We think he will beat Anthony Mundine and that the fight would be the perfect launching pad for Jeff to then take on the world. With the amount of interest it would generate, there would be more than $1 million on the table for Mundine to fight a kid who has had just nine pro fights. Jeff wants the Mundine fight and so does his trainer Glenn Rushton. They both believe he has the power and the speed to overwhelm Mundine. All that has to happen to make the fight is for Anthony Mundine to say "yes".'

I told the press, 'I know I can beat Mundine. Bring it on.'

The fight didn't happen. Mundine wanted to get back into the world-title picture immediately and he targeted one of Hatton's fighters, Siarhei Rabchanka. It was a gutsy move after the beating Mundine had taken against Clottey.

I had a much more important meeting ahead of me.

*

I married Jo Buckley, the love of my life, on 6 September 2014 at the Boulevard Gardens in the Brisbane suburb of Indooroopilly. Our life together since we became an item at schoolies nine years earlier had been bliss.

I prepared for married life with a round of Paintball at Skirmish on the Gold Coast as part of my bucks party. If you haven't done it before, Paintball is like a military game in which you fire bullets made of paint. I played it with more than a dozen of my mates, including my brother, Ben, Josh Peters, Jason Balke, Nathan Millington and Kiang and Cue Lai. I play it every year or so and it's great fun. I reckon I'm pretty good at it, even though I always end up covered in bruises – I've faced some of the heaviest punching welterweights in the world, but those paint bullets really hurt. I usually go a bit crazy too. I get caught up in the moment. When it's over, if I have any bullets remaining I've be known to shoot my own teammates in the back, just to make sure I 'get' someone – and my money's worth. When you're a professional fighter, even if you're billed as a mild-mannered one like I am, you can still do some pretty crazy stuff. I also make my own 'tasers' out of mosquito zappers. You never know when you might have to do something really shocking to someone.

Our wedding was lovely, with 108 of our family and friends there. Jo's sister Melissa said that although she'd given her plenty of opportunities to run, Jo seemed happy enough to live a life of finding bobble heads in letterboxes and putting up with my practical jokes. We didn't have a lot of money and the wedding probably cost us about $25,000, but our parents helped out. I had Ben, Nathan and Kiang as my best men. It was a really beautiful day. Mum's parents gave Jo and me a wonderful wedding present, a little Staffordshire terrier we call Lexi and who is the third member of our household. We honeymooned for ten days, swimming and scuba diving on the island of Ko Pha Ngan in Thailand. Then we returned to Lexi and my life as a professional fighter. It's weird when I look back at the photos of me on the beach with Jo – we look like a happy quiet, unassuming couple from the suburbs – and I contrast that with the fighting machine Glenn has programmed to search and destroy.

By the time we got home, Duco were lining up some great fighters for me to knock down.

*

My right hand was still giving me a lot of grief long after the da Silva fight and I needed cortisone injections. Glenn put me on a martial arts program to strengthen my hands against future damage. Three days a week I would go through intense bone-strengthening exercises under the principles of Wolff's law – that bones grow stronger under heavy loads. I'd do dozens of push-ups on my knuckles and hit hard surfaces hundreds of times to make my hands as hard as house bricks. But it would still take a long time for them to grow stronger and they would cop a flogging for a while yet.

My next fight was set for 6 December in Hamilton, New Zealand, against unbeaten southpaw Robson Assis, who had a 14–0 record with eight knockouts and held the interim WBO Latino title as well as the Brazilian belt. A couple of great Aussie fighters – Daniel Geale and Jarrod Fletcher – had just lost world-title fights and Danny Green endorsed me as Australia's best boxing prospect.

'Horn's a great talent,' Green said, 'and a good kid. He's from a good family, has a great work ethic and has his head screwed on right. He came to Perth and beat a really good fighter named Naoufel Ben Rabeh. I was really impressed.'

I sparred with Fletcher, Lenny Zappavigna, Dennis Hogan, Shannon 'Shaggy' King, Clay Waterman and Miles Zalewski in preparation for the Assis fight and put in nearly as much work for the Halloween costumes for our 2014 party, the first one in the haunted house we put together at our place. Dad used his skills as a builder to erect narrow hallways for the haunted house. On the internet I found ways to replicate flesh wounds much worse than I've seen in boxing by using cardboard and paint.

My corner man and mate Stephen Edwards flew me and Joe Goodall to Melbourne to sit ringside for Mundine's fight with Siarhei Rabchanka on 12 November. It was there I met the great Jeff Fenech, who won the third of his three world championships in the year that I was born.

I had hoped that Duco might be able to sign a fight between me and Mundine but, after he won a close decision over Rabchanka, Anthony became the No. 1 contender for Floyd Mayweather's WBC super-welterweight title at 70 kilograms. He now wanted to concentrate on an unlikely challenge against Mayweather and showed no interest in the million-dollar offer to fight me. I could only dream of what a million bucks was like. Duco were helping me financially, but I was still only making $15,000 a fight, rising to $20,000 if the opponent was high up in the world ratings or if I cracked the world top five.

My bout with Assis was set for Hamilton's Claudelands Arena. I was unbeaten in nine pro fights, but felt much more seasoned as the level of my competition was quite high. Assis had a reputation as a solid boxer, strong and a pretty good puncher. He looked dangerous, but the fact he came to fight and was aggressive suited me. I always prefer guys who attack because they're more predictable than those who are slippery and loose limbed.

It was a tremendous show in New Zealand. In the main event Joseph Parker scored a stunning fourth-round knockout of Brazilian slugger Irineu Beato Costa Jnr, the former Warriors rugby league captain Monty Betham proved too much for All Blacks great Carlos Spencer, and rugby league's Willie Mason scored a hard-fought three-round split decision over the Chiefs rugby prop Ben Tameifuna.

I was now ranked the No. 11 contender for Pacquiao's WBO welterweight title and Assis was one place below. But I knew an impressive victory could push me into the list of top ten contenders. A week earlier, Pacquiao earned A$25 million retaining his crown with a one-sided decision against American Chris Algieri in Macau and I wanted a slice, even a small slice, of that cash pie.

I wore a black armband into the ring on my right arm in honour of Philip Hughes, the test cricketer who was my age and had just died tragically on the pitch. The referee for the fight was Brad Vocale, the guy who had officiated at my very first amateur bout in 2008 at Acacia Ridge. After hurting my left hand early, I had to concentrate on hitting Assis with right-hand leads and banging him with body shots. I stopped him in five rounds, handing him his first defeat.

The Courier-Mail reported:

> The mild-mannered and newly married 26 year old, a qualified child care worker and primary school teacher,

> fights like a bigger version of Jeff Fenech and he tore the Brazilian southpaw apart, cutting him in the first round, dropping him twice in the fourth and finishing him off in the fifth. Horn set a scorching exam, mixing a brutal body attack with razor sharp head shots and finally Assis, 29, sunk to the canvas for the third and final time in Round 5, a battered, bruised and broken Brazilian. Horn's performance was reminiscent of Fenech at his most destructive. He is now undefeated in 10 one-sided fights. It wasn't so much a fight as a back alley mugging by a boxer who looks like a choirboy. With both hands swollen from the pounding he gave them, Horn was cheered for the fight by his grandfather Ray Horn, 86, who was allowed a brief visit back to his Brisbane home after a heart operation to watch the big win – one of the best by an Australian this year.
>
> 'To fight Manny Pacquiao would be a dream come true,' Horn said. 'My plan is to work my way to the No. 1 position and secure a fight with him as the mandatory challenger. That was my best performance ever and I really wanted to put on a show.'

After I pulled off my gloves at the end of the fight there was a deep bruise on the palm of my left hand. Back in Brisbane, I received confirmation that I'd broken my hand on Robson's head. The broken bone didn't hurt as much as the ligament damage on my right hand from the previous fight against da Silva. My surgeon said I broke the hand early in the fight and kept grinding down the metacarpal by continuing to punch with it. The original plan was to insert a titanium plate in the hand but in the end my surgeon used wires.

Jeff Fenech described my win as 'absolutely brilliant'. 'Jeff Horn has all the talent in the world,' he said, 'and if he stays focused he has an enormous future.' My old Olympic teammate Luke Jackson also gave an interview around this time and I was so happy when he said, 'Jeff is one of the quietest, most humble guys I have ever met but he has a style that is quite hard to combat. He gets in and gets out very quickly and has knockout power. He's a very tricky customer and I can see him giving quite a few out there real problems. We pushed each other a lot in the amateur days and as a result we bonded. His work ethic is second to none.'

New Zealand became my home away from home as Dean Lonergan tackled the task of pushing me up the world ratings, in the same way he had relished tackling the toughest guys in the NRL. I was starting to make news around the world too, and threw out a challenge to Britain's former world champ Amir Khan when he was chasing a new opponent.

The broken hand kept me sidelined for a few months before my next fight, booked for Palmerston North, New Zealand, against Richmond Djarbeng, the WBA Pan African welterweight champion from Ghana, who was now the No. 13 contender for Floyd Mayweather's WBA welterweight title. Djarbeng, who had had twenty-two fights for nineteen wins, one draw and two losses, had never been stopped. He had won nineteen in a row and his last defeat was in 2006.

First though, I had a much bigger fight to think about.

*

My friend and sponsor Steve Scanlan from Recon Solutions bought me a ticket to watch the most hyped fight of all time,

Manny Pacquiao versus Floyd Mayweather, on 2 May 2015 at Pacquiao's favourite venue, the MGM Grand in Las Vegas.

Steve and I flew over together and stayed at the Venetian. The fight was the most lucrative ever in boxing history, with *Forbes* magazine estimating that Mayweather pulled more than US$200 million from the deal and Pacquiao more than $160 million. The amounts are staggering but I'm not surprised. Steve paid $15,000 each for our tickets in the bleachers. The atmosphere was electric. I had never seen anything like it, with all the hoo-haa about. I had never seen Manny Pacquiao in the flesh before and, to be honest, I didn't think that I would ever see him close up. As spectators, we didn't get anywhere near him or Mayweather before the fight and we were a long way from the action when the bell went.

From where I was sitting, I thought Pacquiao won the fight. He was certainly the aggressor and throwing more combinations, but without the benefit of TV replays I didn't get to see all the really clean shots Mayweather was landing on the inside. Mayweather ended up winning a clear-cut decision and Pacquiao went back to the drawing board.

After that fight I told *The Courier-Mail*, 'I'd love the chance to fight either Mayweather or Pacquiao. Even if I lost the fight at this stage I don't think my career would suffer because I believe I could still put up a great fight on the world stage and my name would be out there. My career has always been about high risk, high reward – taking on big challenges. I was fighting world-rated guys after just a few pro fights and I'll fight anyone anywhere to push my career along.'

At that stage I didn't think I'd ever get to fight Pacquiao or anyone of that standing, even though Dean Lonergan and Stuart Duncan were working hard at propelling me to the top of boxing. I went to Las Vegas to soak up the atmosphere of a world-title bout. I believed that one day I would get my title opportunity, but not in Australia and not against Pacquiao – most likely fighting one of the lesser American champions in Las Vegas.

★

Back in Brisbane I returned to my odd double life. I went to the races with friends for a fun day out and had a little first birthday party for our dog, Lexi. I resumed sparring in gym wars with Sam Banney, Adam Copland, Nathan Webber, Luke Travers and a former European champion, Kerry Hope, as I prepared to stop Djarbeng from scoring his twentieth straight victory at my expense.

The only thing I really knew about Djarbeng was that he was a lanky big puncher and he had promised his fans in Ghana that he would knock me out. Tall, rangy guys are always awkward to fight because you have to change your distance, and when you try to get in close there's always headbutts and their wild loopy shots. We heard that Joshua Clottey, who had mauled Anthony Mundine, was helping Djarbeng with sparring. We could find no decent footage of him to study, but that was okay. In the amateurs I had to fight guys I'd never seen before all the time, so I was prepared for anything. We arrived in Palmerston North four days before the fight. Djarbeng now sported a Mohawk haircut dyed yellow. My mate Dave Letele, a cult hero in New Zealand after having lost 70 kilograms, started the fight night with a bang, calling out football stars Paul Gallen and Sonny Bill Williams after knocking out two opponents within a few hours.

I started my fight fast, rocking Djarbeng with a hard lead right in the first round and then shaking him later in the round with a left hook. He was an awkward guy with a long left hand and he was trying to bring me on to his right cross. I wanted to pressure him from the start, but I was careful about jumping in too quickly in case we bumped heads. I knew when I shook him early that he couldn't take my big shots. With half a minute left in Round 2, I dropped Djarbeng with a left-hook, right-hand combination. He hung on for dear life until the bell. In Round 3, he simply couldn't handle my punching power anymore and after two knockdowns referee Brad Vocale stopped the fight.

The win elevated me to No. 10 in the world. Six months out of the ring is a long time when boxing is your livelihood and I told the crowd I had a long list of people to thank after the fight: '... my sponsors Recon Solutions, Dan Burley from Sommer & Staff Constructions, Everlast, Barrier Reef Pools, Morinda Bioactive and of course my wife Joanna Horn for keeping me calm and putting up with me during my pre-fight temperament.'

Immediately, Dean Lonergan organised a return trip to New Zealand, this time against the world No. 12 Viktor Plotnikov of Ukraine, the same country that produced my Olympic nemesis Denys Berinchyk. The fight would take place on 1 August in chilly Invercargill on a night when the Jeff Fenech–trained heavyweight Bowie Tupou challenged Joseph Parker.

At 180 centimetres, Plotnikov had a height and reach advantage over me and, with thirty-four professional fights dating back to 2002, had more than three times my professional experience.

Glenn told me, 'We are going to Invercargill to win the fight emphatically, but don't be under any illusions about the opponent. It is going to be a tough, tough night. Jeff, you will need to win the fight with your legs more than your hands because Plotnikov is a master at dominating the distance. He's able to hit going back, he puts his left jab constantly in the face of his opponents and he has a very dangerous right hand. He's tough too and knows how to hold in close.'

Glenn worked on building my explosive leg strength so I could cut the ring off and restrict Plotnikov's movement, and he had me doing thousands of step-ups using a weighted vest.

I did ten-round sparring sessions every second day and constantly practised shutting down Plotnikov's savage straight right, which he could land on the back-move. I worked on my feint, my right-hand lead, my weave and switching from orthodox to southpaw stances midway through combinations. I sparred a lot of tall, rangy fighters in preparation – Reagan Dessaix, Hone Huni, Sam Banney and Adam Copland.

Plotnikov was thirty-seven but he had just scored the biggest win of his long career in his previous fight, dominating Britain's former Commonwealth welterweight champion Denton Vassell over twelve rounds in Belfast.

Three weeks before the fight, I was at Suncorp Stadium to see Johnathan Thurston's man-of-the-match performance as Queensland romped home 52–6 in the 2015 State of Origin decider. I wondered what it was like to play sport in such a huge stadium in front of such a huge crowd. It was a freezing night and Jo and I were rugged up with scarves as we sat cheering in the stands. But Brisbane's winter is nothing like Invercargill's and, when Glenn told me to be careful against Plotnikov or I could get iced, I wasn't sure if he meant knocked out or frozen.

When we finally met at the weigh-in, Plotnikov had a face like an axe and a sniper's deadly focus. I had the bigger guns when we started punching it out though and, although he was tough and wily, I attacked relentlessly with power shots from both hands and from both the orthodox and southpaw stances. He was crowding me when he could to nullify my power. In the sixth round, we clashed heads during a fierce exchange in close and I emerged with a terrible cut over my left eye. The fight was halted a round later and, since I had dominated the scoring, I was declared the winner on points.

In boxing, not all the pain is administered in the ring. In fact I find the action is usually so frenetic, and sometimes even chaotic, that while you can feel a shock when you get hit, you usually don't have time to feel the actual pain of a punch landing. It's different after a fight though, and I have become used to cut eyes and even surgery. As Joseph Parker was blowing away Bowie Tupou inside a round in the main event under the blazing lights, I was propped up against a cold white wall in my austere dressing room in the bowels of Stadium Southland. Local doctor Nick Terpstra went to work in New Zealand's coldest city, sewing my eyebrow back together with six stitches. As the needle dug into the side of my forehead, a hot rush of adrenaline surged through me and, despite the torrid fight I'd just come through, I flinched for the first time that night. I later posted the footage onto my Facebook page, but warned people not to watch if they were squeamish.

*

Manny Pacquiao had taken a break from boxing after his loss to Floyd Mayweather. Timothy Bradley was back as world champion, having won the interim WBO welterweight title with a commanding decision over California's Jessie Vargas, although 'Desert Storm', as Bradley is known, had to weather some heavy thunder in the closing stages. I was now rated the No. 7 contender for the title.

The world's leading boxing commentator, Las Vegas–based Bob Sheridan, who travelled to Invercargill to call the fight for worldwide television, said I was a future world champ. Bob had begun his career calling Muhammad Ali fights fifty years earlier and has called over a thousand world title bouts. He told the TV audience I was 'the real deal'.

'Plotnikov came into the fight with a great record – thirty-two wins in thirty-four bouts – but Horn totally dominated the bout and was a step ahead of him right from the opening bell,' Bob said. 'Horn is such a nice kid but he's a baby-faced assassin. In the ring he's a real destroyer.'

In another interview, Australia's new world middleweight champion, Sam Soliman, said I punched like a super-middleweight and moved like a lightweight. 'The world needs to watch out for this gun,' he said.

Glenn gave me two weeks off following the biggest win of my career. Then it was back to work, though no sparring for a few weeks while my cut eyebrow healed.

My next opponent would be Argentina's Alfredo Rodolfo Blanco on 15 October in Auckland. Blanco had lost to Cameron Hammond in Moree, but had never been stopped in eighteen fights. I thought I could end the fight inside the distance, but the slippery 25 year old managed to preserve his record for endurance even though I dished out a lot of punishment. I was aggressive from the opening bell and walked through his wild looping punches, but I was surprised how well he stood up to my shots. It was hard to get my range a lot of the time because he was going backwards and then throwing wild punches. He has a long reach and he's a good fighter. I was happy to go through ten rounds without hurting my hands, and I decided late in the fight not to risk the type of infighting that resulted in the cut against Plotnikov. All three judges scored the fight 99–91, giving me nine of the ten rounds.

The opponent I was up against next was even slicker, one of the fastest and best guys I've faced. He was the 25-year-old Moroccan-born Frenchman Ahmed El Mousaoui, who held a European championship and had just beaten England's former world champ Junior Witter. He had lost just once – by a close decision – in twenty-four starts and was full of confidence that he could handle someone with my limited experience.

The fight was set for 5 December at the Claudelands Arena in Hamilton, again on the undercard of a Joseph Parker fight. My eye was right by then. In preparation, I sparred many rounds with Reagan Dessaix and Les Sherrington, and I helped Dennis Hogan in the lead-up to his WBA title fight with Jack Culcay-Keth in Germany. Unfortunately, Dennis didn't come home with the title, although he did last twelve rounds with the champ.

I was more successful in my bout. Dean had just signed a deal with Fox Sports and I was keen to impress.

Mousaoui came from Saint-Denis in Paris, scene of the recent terror attacks, and I presented him with a French flag as a show of solidarity before the opening bell. But that's where the friendship ended. At 182 centimetres, he had a

7-centimetre height and reach advantage over me and I was glad my pressure tactics never allowed him to use them. It came down to a battle of my aggression against his quick hands and movement. I set the tone of the fight with a solid right cross in Round 2 and then turned southpaw, using my right hand as my jab. By Round 3 I was breaking his rhythm and outworking him, forcing him to cover up on the ropes with his gloves held high. By the sixth round I sensed Mousaoui no longer thought he could win and was fighting for survival as I tattooed him with volleys of leather. His face was marking up badly, but he tried sporadic fightbacks, clipping me with a lightning right in Round 7. In the next round he landed a solid body shot. He came out in the ninth full of confidence and by the end of the round I had another cut over my left eye. But I was never in any real danger and I finished the fight strongly in Round 10. All three judges had me winning by big margins.

That victory marked my sixth win in a row over a boxer rated in the world top fifteen. Duco now had a TV deal with Fox and I had a sponsorship with South City Mazda to drive a Mazda to replace a rattling 2004 Toyota Camry that had become my daily drive. I was also named Australia's Fighter of the Year by the website Aus-Boxing.com.

Yet storm clouds were moving towards me at a great pace.

The perfect world I was creating was about to fracture. Soon all around me was growing dark and I started to feel numb everywhere.

One punch was all it took.

Before long, I was afraid that I would never fight again.

Worse. I was afraid that I would die.

10

Our greatest glory is not in never falling, but in rising every time we fall.

– Confucius, Chinese philosopher

ARE FIGHTERS BORN OR made? Through years of patience and hard work, Glenn Rushton was able to take me from a bullied schoolboy to a world-class boxer, drawing a fighting instinct from me that had previously been dormant. In the years since I joined his gym I have come to believe that you can train the body and mind as much as you want, but that fighting spark has to be there in the first place – a boxing champion has to have that burning desire not to surrender which pushes him beyond what he might think are his absolute limits. It's not so much a question of talent but of grit. Glenn was the man who sparked my competitive desire into a fire. But that iron will to never give up, which I have carried into the ring since I started in boxing, was sorely tested in 2016.

The year began sedately enough. Jo and I drove the new Mazda to the beach for some fun outings with Kiang and other friends, and I became a supporter of Danny Green's campaign to wipe out the coward-punch. I donated $1500 from the sale of a painting of me to the family of Cole Miller, who had died as a result of random street violence.

I went with sponsors to the Gabba test match between Australia and India, and Steve Scanlan took me to see the final of the Brisbane International Tennis where I saw one of my sporting idols, Roger Federer, get towelled up by a Canadian named Milos Raonic. I filed the victory of the bigger, younger, stronger man over the ageing legend for future reference. You never know when you might need that sort of reference point.

Early in the year I signed a sponsorship deal with an amazingly passionate character named Phil Murphy, whose $4 million stake in the Brisbane Broncos gives him a 19 per cent share of the club and makes him its biggest private owner. He is a land developer who helped Alex Leapai in his world-title quest against Klitschko, but he has his own astonishing sporting background.

As a jockey Phil rode more than a hundred winners before a fall at Mount Isa in 1968 when he was seventeen. A horse called Little Dignity fell at full gallop at the winning post during trackwork. The horse smashed both front legs and sent Phil somersaulting for 40 metres. He spent five months in a plaster cast.

These days Phil leads a section of the cheer squad for me and is at some of my sparring sessions. I don't know how he finds time because his company, Oxmar Properties, has twenty projects under way around Queensland, 1000 building blocks worth $250 million in a carve-up at Narangba and a kilometre of beachfront at Burrum Heads.

A decade ago Phil was running a charity auction for his daughter's school, Living Faith, at Murrumba Downs. He had seen the Broncos on TV but never taken much notice until he rocked up to a game with two footballs and two jerseys, hoping some players might sign them for the auction. He was standing outside the dressing room a bit flustered when the great forward Shane Webcke came up and said, 'You look like you're doing it tough, mate.' Shane took Phil's things and got them all signed. It was the start of a great friendship with Shane and with the Broncos club.

Phil was at a Broncos charity fight night in 2008, scratching his head over how Andrew Gee didn't get the decision against former Knights player Tony Butterfield. Fighting the main event was Alex Leapai, then an unknown Logan truck driver, who told Phil he was so broke he could only train occasionally. Phil promised to sponsor him. Six years later the pair were together in Germany as Alex fought for the heavyweight championship of the world.

Then in 2016 Phil read about my boxing career, thought that I looked a decent sort of a bloke, and offered to help me towards a world title fight too.

While training at Dundee's gym I also met a Brisbane lawyer named Mark Briggs, who became a great mate. Mark introduced me to the team at the leading legal firm Hannay Lawyers – Chris, Daniel and Shaun – who have given me no end of support in backing me as a professional boxer.

Randall Bailey was not offering me the same assistance.

Late in January, Duco organised a press conference at the Brisbane Convention Centre where my second cousin, Lord Mayor Graham Quirk, announced that I would be fighting Bailey there on 2 March. As I continued to climb the ladder of dangerous opponents, this promised to be the most telling test of my career.

At the time Graham was involved in a pretty tough fight of his own with the Brisbane City Council elections looming, and at the press conference he tossed a friendly arm around my shoulder and declared, 'Mate, we're both looking for a knockout but we'll settle for a points decision.'

He told the media, 'This is a great opportunity for Brisbane to get out and support Jeff. While he is not yet a household name, that is going to change very rapidly. This is a young man on his way to becoming Australia's sporting hero. They call him Jeff "The Hornet" Horn, but they could just as easily call him Jeff "The Gentleman" Horn. He is a guy who has great humility but a lot of flair.'

Bailey had a lot of power. He was a lean, mean fighting machine who called himself 'The Knockout King' – and with good reason. The veteran American slugger had won his first twenty-one fights all by knockout before losing a split decision in a world-title bout. He had diabolical power in either hand and he talked a good fight as well.

'I think [Horn] is going to try to come forward until I hit him,' Bailey told the website ringsidereport.com. 'If I hit him and catch him good, it's over. I expect Horn to come out and try to put a lot of pressure on me. We're fighting in front of his home crowd, he's going to have all the pressure on him, he's looking to try to impress. I know once I touch him, it's going to be devastating.'

In a battle between two fighters with heavy artillery, Bailey said he would leave me shell-shocked.

I got the message.

Bailey was a three-time world title holder from Miami, who had become a specialist in knocking out rising stars, and he said it would be no different when he faced me. He was forty-one but had lost just once in the previous six years – a points decision to slick American Devon Alexander in a world-title fight. His forty-six wins included thirty-nine knockouts.

Glenn and I studied footage of him carefully. He had a big uppercut that came out of nowhere and a heavy left hook and right cross. He looked very relaxed and patient when he fought, to go along with the slow southern drawl when he spoke. But he was like a striking cobra when he saw an opening. In a fight he would wait, and wait patiently, for that one mistake and then the fangs would come out.

Thirteen years after his first world-title victory in 1999, Bailey was a mile behind on points against the previously unbeaten American Mike Jones when he struck with a right uppercut of tremendous force to score another one-punch knockout. The win gave him the IBF world welterweight title. Jones was left a bloodied mess. After the fight Bailey said, 'I hit his nose, and it felt like meat coming out.'

Bailey said he specialised in destroying boxers in front of their fan base and to back that up, in his last bout before hitting Brisbane, he battered Japanese prospect Shusaku Fujinaka in Incheon, South Korea.

In media interviews, Glenn described this fight as 'an irresistible force against an immovable object'. 'Bailey is a massive shock puncher and Jeff has a granite chin,' Glenn said. 'Bailey is a patient fighter who stalks opponents and he's like a crocodile just waiting for that one mistake so he can strike. He's knocked out a lot of guys with one punch, so our focus is for Jeff to maintain a high work rate and not get careless; to make sure he lands his own shots and gets away before Bailey can counter. Jeff also has a lot of power so it will be an explosive night.'

Jeff Fenech came out and said that if there was one fighter in the world he'd pay to watch it was me because I throw 'punches in bunches', while Dan Rafael, the boxing writer from the ESPN network, described Bailey as 'one of boxing's best pure punchers'.

I was now ranked No. 6 in the world by the IBF and took the opportunity of a weekend off before the start of heavy training to visit Duco's Auckland Nines at Eden Park, where I caught up with some great rugby league players such as Wally Lewis, Johnathan Thurston, Alfie Langer and Andrew Johns. I enjoyed the experience and some exciting rugby league but I was a bit flat after the trip. On 11 February I posted onto my Facebook account a promotional video about the fight and ticket information and then I went to Glenn's gym that afternoon to work out. Glenn was out of town on a quick business trip but left instructions about the guys I was to spar. Instead, while the teacher was away, the students misbehaved.

I ended up in the ring with one of our very experienced amateur fighters, Simon Cooper, who is about 85 kilograms and a southpaw, which was not the ideal preparation when you're facing a 67-kilogram orthodox fighter such as Bailey. I had done plenty of rounds with Simon before and I needed to get some more rounds for the fight. I needed to get the work done and just like the time I pranked the workers at Dad's place and had them chasing me in their cars, it seemed like a good idea at the time.

What happened over the next few minutes threatened to end my career.

Simon caught me in the throat with a good shot. It hurt but I didn't think about it too much – I didn't have time to because the punches were coming so fast. It's rare to get hit in the throat at any time, but that day with Glenn out of town, I must have been extra careless. As I was leaning away from another of his attacks, Simon got me in the throat again with a looping southpaw left hook. Something in my windpipe didn't feel right, my throat felt displaced and uncomfortable. I stopped boxing to tell Simon I'd been punched in the throat, but no sound came out of my mouth. I took my headguard off straight away. Eventually I was able to speak but my voice was feeble. I kept trying to talk but it was just a croak.

The last punch had fractured the thyroid cartilage over my larynx. I didn't know what the hell was going on, but over the next few days doctors told me that it was a career-threatening injury. I was stunned. I knew my unlikely singing career was over, but I still hoped to one day dance with the likes of Manny Pacquiao and Floyd Mayweather in centre ring.

Three ear, nose and throat specialists examined me. They told me if I got punched on the same spot again there was the real possibility I could die.

My jaw just about hit the floor.

They said there was a loose flap that could cover my airwaves if I got hit on the throat. It would instantly shut down my breathing and basically I would suffocate on the spot. I would need someone nearby to perform a tracheostomy so that I could breathe through my neck and not my blocked throat.

Not exactly the news you want to hear when you're trying to make a career as a fighter.

But finally, after several examinations, my surgeon, Dr Scott Coman, decided that inserting a titanium plate in my throat was the best option, making the whole area 'armour plated'. There were thoughts that I might have a croaky voice permanently, like the rugby league great Darren Lockyer who had suffered a similar injury playing football, but I could live with that. Dr Coman said I'd be able to start sparring again in six weeks without complications.

Duco rescheduled the fight for 27 April. It was amazing that Bailey, the guy who was training in Miami to tear my head off, sent me Facebook messages of support.

On 18 February, a week after the injury, I was prepped for surgery at Brisbane Private Hospital. My claustrophobia was starting to really play up – the idea of being trapped and confined on the operating table frightened me more than any opponent. Someone was going to knock me out with anaesthetic and I would have no control over what was happening to me. Then I started to worry about the surgery on my throat. I started to run through a long list of things that could go wrong. This was my throat after all, not a leg or a hand. If there were complications – well, let's just say I was especially miserable as I said my goodbyes to Jo and the rest of the family. I felt very panicky but, before I could start to freak out, the anaesthetic went to work and I began growing sleepy. I thought rather grimly, *I hope I wake up from this because you just never know.* I started to wonder what was on the other side of the bright lights. Then my eyes closed and everything grew dark. I was gone.

*

Guess what? There was nothing to worry about. The surgery was a complete success. I had a 1-centimetre piece of expensive metal inserted in my throat to guard my larynx and my voice returned to normal. This may or may not be a good thing since I always think I sound like a twelve-year-old kid when I hear some of my interviews played back. I wouldn't have minded a bit of sandpaper in the tone.

Bailey told American reporters that he was coming to Australia to knock me out and suggested I was more Milky Bar Kid than Mike Tyson. He said it was business and not personal and that, while we might be Facebook friends, he would be a deadly enemy in the ring. As much as I didn't like to dwell on the piece of titanium sitting under the purple horizontal scar on my windpipe, I knew it would be like a flashing bullseye for Bailey, who was being billed as one of the most dangerous fighters ever to hit Brisbane.

The training for the fight now began in earnest, although Glenn insisted that I was never to spar again without him being there. I was only able to resume sparring on 1 April and would have liked an extra week of hard work to prepare, although Matt Burgoyne, Mark Gadaleta, Todd Kidd, Ben Kite and Richard Smith all gave me hard sparring. I received a boost for the fight when the IBF bumped me up to No. 5 in the world behind their welterweight champ, Kell Brook of England.

Bailey arrived in Brisbane with a head of steam. Six days before we were due to fight, we held separate training sessions in a specially erected ring in the Queen Street Mall. When we were asked to pose for the camera together, he got right up in my face and held his big fist against my chin. I didn't say anything to him because I wanted my fists to do the talking. Jeff Fenech warned me that I risked disaster and that I had to fight 'smart, not brave', that a toe-to-toe firefight could blow up in my face. Or my throat. Fenech told an interviewer, 'Jeff Horn is a fantastic prospect. He likes to mix it up with his opponents and that makes for exciting fights but he doesn't need to take those risks to win big. He's a very intelligent boxer, he has a great eye, great reflexes, fantastic timing. I'd hate to see him come undone by making a mistake against a guy who can really punch.'

Glenn and I knew that controlling the distance against Bailey was the key, that I had to stay busy in the ring, keep him off balance, and that when I finished an exchange I couldn't give him a single opportunity to counter.

On the eve of the fight Bailey gave an interview to *The Courier-Mail*. Small beads of sweat snaked down his long, straggly goatee as 'The Knockout King' talked about drugs, guns, prison and a manic life far removed from the suburban niceties that cosseted my upbringing. He told the newspaper that the only big guns he had now were the ones encased in his Everlast boxing gloves, but he admitted that he had shot at people and been shot at in return. He said that as a youth he spent time in prison for carrying weapons. 'Where I grew up you needed a gun just to protect yourself,' he said. As a teenager he made drug deals – 'not marijuana, the big stuff' – and said many times he had to fight for his life.

'Jeff Horn's background is very different to mine,' he told the paper. 'He's a schoolteacher and I'm from the streets. But coming up that way has helped me as a fighter because there's no fear in me. I grew up fighting on the street – boxing is easy compared to that life. When I was little the older guys in my neighbourhood would make the little kids fight for entertainment. When I started getting older and got into fights you were liable to get shot. That's why I carried a gun.'

In Brisbane Bailey fulfilled a life's ambition by seeing a kangaroo hopping about at the Lone Pine Koala Sanctuary – an experience he said was 'awesome' – but he still had the goal of leaving a winner against me. His diminutive trainer, Javiel Centeno, was happier than anyone that the hard work was done because he'd been nursing bruised hands for weeks. Holding the punching pads for Bailey, he said, was like being hit with a baseball bat.

At the time Bailey was ranked No. 11 in the world and said he was grateful for the opportunity to fight me because many of the big-name Americans were dodging him, and my No. 5 world ranking was something he coveted as a springboard to another world-title shot. Bailey said he didn't expect me to come out against him 'at full blaze', like I'd done in other fights, 'but I hope he does because I have something for him'.

At the weigh-in the day before the fight, Bailey said that as soon as he hit me with a big shot the fight would be over.

But Glenn fired back. 'No, as soon as you hit Jeff, that's when the fight starts,' he said. 'Because Jeff has a jaw of granite and getting hit will only make him fight harder.'

Bailey looked like trouble as soon as the opening bell clanged. He circled me, brooding and patient, just waiting for me to put a foot wrong as I tried to outmanoeuvre him. In Round 2 I dropped him with a left hook on the side of the head and, in the tangle of feet that followed, I fell onto him,

My grandpop and his twin brother, Gordon (at the front), pictured with some of their siblings. The twins boxed exhibition bouts at outback Queensland horseracing carnivals in places such as Longreach, Barcaldine, Jericho and Blackall.

Me as a baby at the beach with Mum, Liza, and my grandma Marie Dykstra.

Soccer was my first love and I had dreams of being the next Harry Kewell while playing for Acacia Ridge.

MacGregor State High School was not always a happy place for me, but I met the love of my life, Jo Buckley, there. That's us in the middle.

It was a double celebration for Dad and Mum when Ben and I both won at an amateur boxing tournament early in our careers.

I won my first fight at the Olympics with a points decision over Zambia's Gilbert Choombe.

Jo and I were married in Brisbane in 2014. Here we are with (from left) my dad, Jeff Snr; sister Rebecca and her husband, Michael; my mum, Liza Dykstra; my brother, Ben; and sister Bianca.

In Brisbane in 2016, I overpowered American Randall Bailey, a heavy punching former world champ.

Dean Lonergan (left) and Bob Arum were the promoters of the Pacquiao fight at Suncorp. Dean played rugby league for New Zealand and backed me to the hilt from the time I was a relatively unknown professional boxer from across the Tasman. Bob Arum has been the most important promoter in world boxing since he started arranging fights for Muhammad Ali in 1966.

illian Rushton has been a huge help ever since I walked into Glenn's gym to learn self-defence in 006. That's Lillian (left) with Glenn, my cornerman Adam Copland, me and Jo in New Zealand.

Ready to rumble: My team, just before we marched out onto Suncorp Stadium to face Manny Pacquiao. Back row: Ben, Joe Goodall, Adam Copland, Dundee Kim, Steve Scanlan and Sam Banney. Front row: Me, Glenn and my cutman and great mate Stephen Edwards.

Manny Pacquiao and I turned on an intense and gruelling fight. My jab and right hand kept Manny on the defensive for much of the fight, and we both bled from deep wounds.

Oh, what a feeling! When ring announcer Michael Buffer declared me the new world champion, Glenn and I and my team hollered to the heavens.

Three generations and one all-important belt. Me with my pop, Ray Horn, and Dad. Pop, who learned boxing in the Queensland outback, had just seen his grandson claim the World Boxing Organisation welterweight belt.

I caught London's Gary Corcoran with some big shots, but he was hard to rattle in our Brisbane world title fight, 13 December 2017.

My wife, Jo, and daughter, Isabelle, have made me a very proud husband and father. Our second child is on the way.

Fast and cocky Terence Crawford took my world title in Las Vegas, on 9 June 2018, and I would love a rematch.

In the lead-up to our bout on 30 November 2018, Anthony Mundine talked a good game, but he had no answer to my power punches – I stopped him in 96 seconds.

my knee hitting him in the groin. Accident, I promise. But he really squawked and I could tell straight away that, while he liked dishing it out, he wasn't so keen on taking punishment. I followed up that knockdown with some big body shots and I could feel them taking effect immediately. They weren't totally debilitating though.

In Round 3, as I shuffled my feet trying to feint him into a mistake and speared out two fast left jabs, Bailey stepped a little to the side and threw a big looping right hand that crashed into the side of my skull and perforated my ear drum. As I started falling towards the canvas, I instinctively stuck out my left hand to break my fall. The glove touched the canvas and referee Danrex Tapdasan, a Filipino lawyer from Manila, immediately put a standing eight-count on me while I stood there grinning at him like an idiot and bouncing on my legs to get my balance back. It was the hardest punch I've ever taken. Bailey went on the attack, a savage old lion after his prey, but my head was clear enough to tell my legs to keep moving and I made him miss with the big shots. I went back to Glenn's plan not to stand in mid-range. It was deflating to Bailey that I took his best punch and was still standing.

Commentator Bob Sheridan was fired up. 'This is where we find out,' he told the audience, 'just how tough Jeff Horn is – Bailey is very, very dangerous.'

Up close, I could see deep into Bailey's eyes and the hunger he had to be a world champion again. He was hunting me, looking for that one big finishing punch. But he was loading up his power punches. I could see them coming and I would not let him catch me. My future and the future of my family hung on staying out of danger. I dodged and ducked for most of the round and by the end of it I felt I was back in charge.

I always try to drain the confidence of opponents by making them feel that their punches are having no effect. I want them to doubt their own 'power'. My fightback eventually broke Bailey's heart. Then, over the next four rounds, I broke his body with a sustained attack. I could feel him grunting and starting to keel over every time I dug punches into his ribs. By Round 6 he had started to wilt and his legs had lost all their strength. At the end of Round 7 Glenn told me that he could see from Bailey's eyes that he had taken enough punishment and that he did not want to be there any longer. Glenn had warned Bailey before the fight that if he hit me hard it would only galvanise me to fight harder and that's what had happened. As Bailey slumped in his corner after Round 7, his trainer, Javiel Centeno, stopped the fight.

A few days later *The Courier-Mail* said I showed 'recuperative powers worthy of Lazarus' and that Bailey had decided to retire from boxing, heartbroken.

That fight night proved a double celebration because my mate Sam Banney won a thriller over a rugged super-middleweight named Nicholas Reiter on the undercard.

Dean Lonergan now wanted to launch me immediately at another world-rated international fighter. But I had other plans.

*

Jo and I had booked a six-week trip to America long before the Bailey fight. We eventually planned on having a family and I knew, with the level of competition in my boxing career getting tougher and tougher, time was running out for us to have a great overseas holiday as a couple.

Duco was now my employer and I was doing everything to reward the company's faith in me, even giving up touch football for fear I might twist an ankle and damage its investment. But nothing was going to stop Jo and me from enjoying our big American vacation.

And what a holiday we had. A week in Waikiki, hamburger joints in Times Square, a Yankees baseball game, the top of the Empire State Building, Walt Disney World and Universal in Orlando, a cruise to the Bahamas, sightseeing in LA and San Francisco, seeing the tame whales at SeaWorld in San Diego and of, course fabulous Las Vegas.

I checked out Floyd Mayweather's gym there but Floyd wasn't around – maybe he'd heard I was gunning for him. We saw Human Nature and the David Copperfield magic show and we met up with Jo's parents, who were also in Vegas on a holiday. We all went to see a Cirque du Soleil show called *Zumanity*, without realising it was a sex-themed program. It was all very funny and embarrassing at the same time, and none of us knew where to look.

Much more watchable was the Grand Canyon. We took a helicopter ride through it. Jo was beside herself at the grandeur and majesty of one of the world's great natural wonders. She asked me what I thought.

'Yeah, not bad,' I said.

'Not bad? Jeffrey, it's the Grand Canyon. Don't you like anything?'

'Yeah, I like it,' I replied. 'I just don't get overawed by anything.'

I guess that sort of sums me up. It's a good approach when you're tackling some of the toughest fighters in the world. None of them overawes me.

★

I remained Facebook friends with Randall Bailey and found a new friend in a German welterweight named Rico Mueller. Duco matched us to fight at the Sleeman Sports Complex in Brisbane on 21 October. Victory over Mueller was likely to elevate me to No. 2 in the world. The momentum was building for an even bigger fight. With Manny Pacquiao.

After Pacquiao had lost to Mayweather in 2015, he had climbed back to the top of boxing and was now set to fight the WBA's new champ, Jessie Vargas, on 5 November in Las Vegas.

Another title opportunity presented itself to me though, as England's Kell Brook was likely to vacate the IBF welterweight championship following his loss to middleweight Gennady Golovkin. That could mean I would fight Texan Errol Spence for the vacant crown. Spence is a heavy-hitting southpaw who, like me, had lost in the quarter-finals at the London Olympics, but in the heavier 69-kilogram division.

First, though, there was the clear and present danger of Mueller. He promised to be a solid test, with just one loss in twenty-two fights and an unbeaten run since 2010. He lacked the knockout power of Bailey, but he was tough, resolute and had a tight defence that Glenn and I called the Berlin Wall. We knew that to beat him I would have to feign and baulk to get him to open up.

I received a big boost for the fight from Graham Quirk, who told the press just before the bout:

> I really love the fact that Jeff is such a humble, down to earth, clean-cut guy. He is a tight family member;

> the whole Horn family have always been close and supportive of each other. I took a great interest in Jeff's fights at the London Olympics where he made the quarter-finals but his boxing career really came out of the blue. A lot of us didn't appreciate how deeply he was going into the world of boxing until he started making headlines. Jeff was a late starter. He didn't even start boxing until he left high school and for any sports person who makes it to the elite level that's very late. But he is really doing a great job. He's unbeaten and getting close to a world title fight and as a family we couldn't be prouder of his success in the ring and the image he portrays out of it. He is a young man who is all about hard work, determination and showing respect for everyone he meets.

Glenn had me muzzled in training. I wore a special protective mask constructed by Madison Sport to protect against any last-minute injuries as I sparred with Cameron Hammond, Adrian Rodriguez, Mark Gadaleta and former Australian amateur champion Nathan Webber. While the mask made me look like a cross between Hannibal Lecter and Darth Vader, it gave me a relatively worry-free campaign in the lead-up to the most important fight of my career.

Rico Mueller is such a strong walk-up fighter and has had such a solid defence that Glenn and I did a lot of training with Glenn wearing a body shield and me punching into it incessantly. We wanted to pierce that defence again and again. If I could stop Glenn walking forward behind the shield we knew we could stop Mueller. I had to get the timing right to use Mueller's movement against him, force him to keep turning. My fight plan revolved around slowing him down, breaking him down and then ripping him apart.

Mueller has bright, piercing blue eyes and for our fight had a confidence bordering on aristocratic arrogance. In another time I could imagine him flying a fighter biplane beside the Red Baron. He certainly had an enormous engine and appetite for fast-paced combat. I landed the first big shot of the fight, a thumping lead right, before switching to the body in Round 2. Mueller kept biting down hard on his mouthguard and marching forward, but I started breaking down the wall of his defence brick by brick. He was as tough as anyone I'd fought. I thought he was lucky to survive a brutal sixth round. He was cut and forlorn but he kept going until Round 9, when I hit him hard as he was leaning forward. I thought the referee was moving in to stop it. He wasn't. So I delivered the last shot that sent him through the ropes. Detroit referee, Sam Williams, stopped the fight at two minutes nineteen seconds of the round.

I had some swelling beside my right eye after beating Rico but, emerging on the horizon, I could see a bright future involving a fight with Manny Pacquiao.

Despite the ferocity of our battle, Rico and I have remained Facebook friends. It is never personal when I box and I've never really gone into a bout with a grudge because I think hate is counter-productive in boxing. That emotion can make you throw a careful strategy out the window. I hope that with all the guys I fight, I gain their respect as a tough competitor and good sportsman.

Ever since I took up boxing seriously in 2008 I have been winning friends. Now, after beating Rico, I wanted to both win friends and influence people. Especially the one person who could make a fight with Manny Pacquiao a reality.

An 85 year old who had once been good friends with John F. Kennedy and Muhammad Ali was now the most important boxing promoter in the world.

I knew Bob Arum could make my dreams come true. I wanted to meet him.

11

A few years ago Jeff was getting beaten up by school bullies and now he has the chance to shock the boxing world against one of the greatest fighters of all time. It's one of the most amazing stories I've ever heard in sport.

– Bob Arum, the most successful boxing promoter of all time

BOB ARUM SAID THAT Muhammad Ali was his great teacher, a charismatic, controversial, enthralling magician who made the world watch his every move and made fights such as the 'Thrilla in Manila' and the 'Rumble in the Jungle' epic sporting contests that will never be forgotten.

After he promoted Ali's epic win over Joe Frazier in Manila in 1975, Bob went on a two-day orgy there to celebrate. That was a long time ago and, at eighty-five, Bob said he didn't have a lot of orgy left in him. When it comes to putting together big fights though, he has the vigour of youth. For more than half a century he has promoted some of the great fights of all time involving the likes of Ali, Frazier, Sugar Ray Leonard, Roberto Durán, Marvin Hagler and Thomas Hearns. It has been estimated that he made US$50 million just from the Pacquiao–Mayweather fight.

Bob is a Harvard-trained lawyer and his first involvement with boxing came in the early 1960s. While working for President John F. Kennedy's brother Robert at the US Justice Department, he investigated the shady tax dealings involved in a world-title fight. Bob then moved to a New York law firm and met Muhammad Ali through a mutual friend, the American football great Jim Brown. At the time, the American government was planning to revoke Ali's boxing licence for refusing to be drafted into the US Army to fight in the Vietnam War and Bob's legal connections worked out a deal for Ali to continue his boxing career if he also gave boxing exhibitions at US military bases. But Ali refused, saying he didn't want to induce others to join the war.

While Ali was battling the government, Bob started promoting his boxing matches, the first being Ali against the iron-chinned Canadian George Chuvalo in Toronto in 1966. Eventually, the US government prevailed and Ali spent three years out of the sport under suspension over his army stance.

Bob says Ali was the most courageous person he ever met.

'He gave up his livelihood for his beliefs,' Bob said. 'He became the most popular sports star of all time but in the 1960s Ali was not a popular guy. A lot of people did not like his political stance – but when people eventually saw he was a man of conviction and principles, that he was willing to sacrifice everything, he gained tremendous respect around the world and he became a beloved hero. He was my great friend until the day he died.'

Fifty years after Bob promoted Ali's Toronto fight, he was ringside in a crowd of 16,132, at the Thomas & Mack Center in Las Vegas, to see another of his fighters, Manny Pacquiao, regain the WBO welterweight title from the young American Jessie Vargas, who had represented Mexico at the 2008 Olympics. The fight took place on 5 November 2016, two weeks after my win over Rico Mueller. Pacquiao won another world title eighteen years after he won his first. Showing he was still a blood-and-guts brawler, he dropped Vargas in the second round with a sizzling southpaw straight left and dominated the fight. Afterwards Vargas could only shake his head at Pacquiao's 'tremendous speed, tremendous experience'. Two judges gave Pacquiao ten of the twelve rounds and a third judge somehow had Pacquiao winning by just a point. I thought Pacquiao easily outboxed Vargas, who was a very basic fighter. He was tough but he didn't do anything special. He just stood right in front of Pacquiao with a long jab and right hand. At the time I remarked that if I was fighting Pacquiao, I would move a lot more than Vargas did and give Pacquiao different angles, the same way Pacquiao did to Vargas. I hoped that one day I would get the chance. Those hopes were starting to take root.

I was matched to fight world No. 8, Ali Funeka of South Africa, on 10 December in Auckland and, in the biggest boost to my career, Bob Arum and his fight matchmaker, Bruce Trampler, were coming to watch.

My fight would be on the undercard of Joseph Parker's WBO heavyweight-title fight with American Andy Ruiz, who was in the Arum stable. Two months earlier, when Dean Lonergan had flown to Los Angeles to do the deal for the Parker fight with Bob, he said that he also had a great young welterweight named Jeff Horn, who would be a perfect sell for a fight with Pacquaio. According to Bob, I wasn't ready for that kind of fight but he was willing to take a look at me when he came to Auckland to see what I could offer.

Ali Funeka promised to do everything he could to spoil the good first impression I planned to make on Bob. At 185 centimetres, Funeka was the tallest fighter I'd ever squared up against. He was a proven performer with long, powerful punches and plenty of experience at the top. I was now the No. 2 contender for Pacquiao's crown but Funeka said I had a suspect chin and would not last the distance against him. He'd seen the Randall Bailey fight and thought he could finish the job.

He had a dream to fight Pacquiao as well.

'Jeff Horn is standing in my way,' Funeka told reporters in South Africa, 'but I will push him aside and march on to mega-bouts. [My team has] always wanted to fight Pacquiao but [until now] it was a pipedream. We used to fantasise about what I would do to him. But now the fight is closer to realisation if I keep my end of the bargain. Without revealing much, I have observed that Horn relies too much on his right hand. He has decent punch variation but nothing to scare me.'

*

I finally met Bob Arum at Auckland's Langham Hotel where we held a press conference to announce that I would now be fighting under a co-promotion with Duco and Bob's company,

Top Rank. Bob told the press that, although I might not be ready for Pacquiao just yet, I could be in another two fights.

'Manny has told me that he wants two fights next year and we are looking at Jeff for the second bout,' Bob told reporters. 'If Jeff can win well against Funeka, I would then like him to face one of my former world champs, either Timothy Bradley or Jessie Vargas, to build up the bout. I have heard great things about Jeff and we want to see if he is ready for the best in the division or if he still needs a little seasoning.'

I knew I had to win big against Funeka. He had grown up in desperate poverty in the Eastern Cape and started boxing aged seven, using milk cartons for gloves. He was a hungry fighter in every sense. There would be 10,000 people at Auckland's Spark Arena and 100 million watching the telecast worldwide, but I was fighting to impress just one man, the promoter who could match me with the fighting senator from the Philippines.

Funeka had the same idea. With a glint in his cold, merciless eyes, the South African warhorse told journalists in Auckland that he would break my heart, if not my jaw. He had been a pro boxer for twenty-one years and, standing almost a head taller than me, he told me that he had promised his three daughters and his fans in South Africa that I would not last six rounds.

'I can hurt him and I will hurt him,' Funeka said, making a throat-cutting gesture. 'Horn is a clever boxer but I will make sure I knock him out. He has some sneaky moves but I want the opportunity for that world-title fight against Pacquiao. I will use my height and my reach to win in Round 5. He cannot pass Round 6.'

I also did not want to pass Round 6.

For weeks I had been practising a brutal body assault, and I planned to slip inside the giant's telescopic reach first chance I got to pummel his lean, spare ribs. We knew that Funeka leaned in behind his jab to further elongate his reach advantage and occasionally he overbalanced, something Glenn said would make him an enormous bullseye. My speed and timing were crucial to overcoming the size factor and making Funeka vulnerable to my counter-punches.

Two nights before the fight, Dean Lonergan hosted a sumptuous eighty-fifth birthday party for Bob Arum and about a hundred guests at a harbourside restaurant in Auckland. I rested up with Jo and my family back at our hotel, but I heard that Bob and his wife, Lovee, got a big kick out of the 'Hornet' T-shirts and caps I sent over as a gift for their grandkids. Bob regaled everyone with stories of a career that saw him outlast his great rival, the electric-haired Don King, as the biggest fight promoter of all. He talked about how he promoted more than two thousand fight shows over half a century and how at one of them, Donald Trump, then a casino owner sponsoring one of Bob's shows in Atlantic City, apparently renegotiated a fight deal down by $2.5 million after the Gulf War started, arguing that it would deter travellers from flying in to watch.

Bob was asked how Manny Pacquiao compared with Leonard, Hearns and Durán, the great welterweights he promoted in the 1980s.

'Manny is one of the great fighters of history,' Bob replied. 'Sometimes nostalgia plays tricks and you always want to think that the older guys were better. But clearly the new generation like Pacquiao and Jeff Horn have the benefit of advanced training that was unknown to Ray and Durán.'

What did the future hold for me?

'Boxing is crying out for someone like Jeff Horn,' Bob said. 'The sport is dominated by Hispanic and African-American fighters. There are a lot of good white boxers but most of them are Eastern Europeans who don't speak English. To have a white kid who has an all-action style and speaks perfect English is something that fight fans around the world will embrace. Jeff is so marketable. A schoolteacher who can fight – every delinquent kid in the world will take notice.'

At another press conference before the fight I said that although Funeka claimed I threw too many right hands, he would be hoping that I stopped throwing them by the end of the fight. I tried to sound menacing when I said it, but menace just isn't part of my make-up – I don't have the voice for it – and as usual it was down to my fists to do all the talking.

At the weigh-in the day before the fight, Funeka tried to erode my confidence by again making the throat-cutting gesture as his handlers shouted, 'Horn will fall'. As we shaped up for the cameras Funeka towered over me, but I was confident I would be looking down on him by the end of the fight.

I tried to chill in the hours leading up to the showdown, just going through the quiet, calm routine I always do. I went to a coffee shop with Jo and played poker with my corner team and Glenn's wife, Lillian. Jo and I went to see the Ben Affleck movie, *The Accountant*, which I hoped would be an omen pointing to big world-title fight paydays. I wanted to relax and avoid all possible distractions. This was a crucial fight, but I just had to remember the basics and stick to the plan Glenn had devised.

The fight night in Auckland was superb, with Joseph Parker winning the WBO world heavyweight title and my friend Shannon O'Connell, the partner of my old rival Ozan Craddock, winning a women's super-bantamweight fight.

Glenn reckoned I could get Funeka within six rounds, even though he had beaten a lot of guys who were very capable, had held the International Boxing Organization welterweight title and had gone within a whisker of winning other world titles against top-class champs such as Nate Campbell and Joan Guzmán.

The referee for the fight was a Canadian named Marlon Wright, who had been a top welterweight in the 1980s before becoming a leading international official. I didn't know it at the time but Marlon had been diagnosed with melanoma in 2014 and had been managing the cancer ever since.

Funeka came into the ring in camouflage trunks and looked ready for a long-range shoot-out. He showed his class in the opening round, clipping me with his jab a couple of times, but I was landing the heavier punches by the round's end. At the break Glenn told me I had to alter my distance. I took charge in Round 2. But then I saw stars in Round 3 – and I saw my fight with Pacquiao become very blurry.

Just as the commentator, Bob Sheridan, was saying that I looked like a choirboy but was one tough fighter, Funeka landed a right rip to my body at the same time as our heads accidentally slammed together. Lights out. I was thinking *what the hell just hit me?* I thought I was out of range of his punches. I went down – from the head clash, not the punch – and sprang up almost immediately. I did my best to show no emotion, but to my absolute horror the referee put a standing eight-count on me. A lot of the time in the ring

I don't even feel the punches coming my way because my concentration is so intense and the speed of the fight so great. But whenever there is a clash of heads, something that's increasingly common in my fights because of my aggressive style, it really hurts. It's just *BANG* and you see stars and your whole balance is knocked off kilter.

In my mind I'd won the first three rounds, but because Marlon Wright had incorrectly ruled a knockdown after the head clash Funeka was awarded that round 10–8. The judges had scored the first two rounds 10–9 for me, but now suddenly we were 28–28. I was hoping Bob Arum thought I was doing better than that.

Glenn told me in the break between Rounds 3 and 4: 'Jeff, you must win this fourth round. If they stop the fight after this round due to a cut, it goes to the judges' cards, so it's critical we remain in front.'

In the fourth round Funeka emerged from an exchange with a deep 2-centimetre wide cut over his left eye. That's when the scoring became crucial. If the fight was stopped and his cut ruled to be from an accidental head clash, the bout could end up going to him. If Funeka managed to shade a round, then he could be in front. I had to get back on top quickly. I landed a couple of hard rights at the end of the fourth but in the corner Glenn told me I had to get more of a move on.

Funeka was a dangerous guy and fought hard. I had to be smart to crack his defence. Late in the fifth I pawed a couple of times with my left hand to distract Funeka and then bowled over a right hand worthy of a Dennis Lillee bouncer which rocked him. The follow-up barrage put Funeka down. His cut eye was now starting to leak like a tap, but unfortunately I was bleeding badly too. I'd come out of an exchange just on the bell with a big wound over my right eye – a wound that was long, deep and wide. Now both of us had been down and both of us had been cut. In the break after Round 5 Glenn had one simple instruction: 'Go out and finish him.' Funeka came out firing for the start of the sixth round but I was quicker on the draw. A big right over the top and a follow-up left and right dropped him again. All the malevolence in his eyes left him. He climbed to his feet but tottered as he tried to regain his balance. Marlon Wright waved it off. It was the biggest win of my career and, as Marlon raised my hand in victory, I felt on top of the world. Sadly, that victory was one of the last fights Marlon would control. Back in his hometown of Montreal, he succumbed to the melanoma a few months later.

Immediately after the fight I told reporters that the cut eye spurred me on like an electric prod.

'You have to go for it when you see blood,' I said. 'You have to go for it like a shark in the water. I got a knockdown scored against me. It wasn't a real knockdown though. Our heads clashed and my glove touched the ground.'

The joy of victory compensated for the pain as I had seven stitches inserted over my right eye in the dressing room. At least the scar would be a match for the one over my left eye I'd received from Plotnikov. My getting cut and stitched all the time made my mum less squeamish. A decade earlier she had tried to talk me out of boxing and early in my career she would bawl her eyes out if I got hit. Now she was used to it. She didn't even flinch as my face was being sewn back together. I did a little bit, I have to be honest, but I suspected that this victory could sew up a bright future for me and Jo.

Beating Funeka was my sixteenth victory and the eleventh by knockout. I would soon be the top contender for Pacquiao's world title. I had won over Bob Arum too, at least with some qualifications.

'I thought Jeff Horn was tremendous,' he told the press. 'I love the kid. He's a real throwback fighter and he'll have a tremendous appeal to boxing fans in the States. He fought a really tough, awkward guy in Funeka and I think he has a big, big future. We want to build the best stage for him, but the truth is that back in the States where a big Pacquiao fight would probably have to happen Jeff is still not very well known, so we first have to put him in with one of the top welterweights to build his name.'

Bob repeated his plan for me to fight Jessie Vargas or Timothy Bradley before getting a Pacquiao fight.

There were no wild celebrations for us after the win – just a quiet get-together with my team and our family and friends. None of us is what you would call a party animal. Jo and I together with my mum and my grandparents, Jack and Marie Dykstra, had booked a holiday in the magnificent South Island and we had a sensational time down there doing all the tourist things at Queenstown and Wanaka.

Back in America Bob was still cautiously optimistic about my future. 'The kid is not only a terrific fighter but he looks like a movie star,' Arum said. (Thanks Bob.) 'My matchmaker Bruce Trampler was with me in New Zealand and was very impressed with him. But you can't just fight Manny Pacquiao. You have to earn it.'

I was stoked to make the cover of the *Australian Boxing Legends* magazine, under the headline 'Horn v Pacquiao' as momentum built for me to eventually face a guy I regarded as one of my idols. But 'tell him he's dreaming about Pacquiao' was the message from Manny's Australian conditioning coach, Justin Fortune, who once fought heavyweight great Lennox Lewis and now runs a gym on Sunset Boulevard in Los Angeles.

When asked about my prospects, Fortune did concede that I would beat Vargas. But Bradley and Pacquiao? Forget about it. 'Tim Bradley would be a tougher fight than Vargas,' Fortune cautioned. 'Bradley is very slick and calculating. Vargas is a good boxer but he doesn't do anything special and he's not what you'd call a great puncher either.'

Fortune said I shouldn't become overconfident about the prospect of a Pacquiao fight.

'Ali Funeka's a good fighter but he's no Pacquiao,' Fortune said. 'Pacquiao is still a live dog. He's still extremely quick – ridiculously quick – and he's still an extremely heavy puncher.'

Fortune would have a lot more to say over the next few months.

*

Bob now had me pencilled in to fight Pacquiao at the end of 2017 in what he expected to be the great champ's farewell to boxing. That was provided I was a hit against Vargas or Bradley in a fight being planned for April. But then I experienced one of those extraordinary twists of fate, something I never expected, a perfect storm of opportunities that would allow my dream to come true – in my backyard with 50,000 or so of my friends gathered around the ring.

Pacquiao's Canadian adviser, Michael Koncz, came to Bob asking for US$25 million for a bout pitting the fighting Filipino senator against another undefeated American, Terence 'Bud' Crawford. Bob didn't get rich by giving money away and he almost choked at the bill. Suddenly he could see the value in a much less expensive match-up between 'The Fighting Schoolteacher' and 'The Fighting Senator'. He called Dean Lonergan to see how much he could offer Pacquiao to fight the 'kid from Brisbane'.

At the end of December, Dean approached Peter Gleeson, the editor of Queensland's biggest selling newspaper, *The Sunday Mail*. Dean knows a lot about event tourism and marketing, having previously gained government support in New Zealand to help Joseph Parker's career and in staging the Auckland Nines. He knew if he could get the Queensland and Brisbane authorities to support a world-title fight, he could possibly put together a multimillion-dollar package that might – maybe – entice Bob and Pacquiao to agree to a fight in my hometown.

It was an enormous longshot but, in a café in New Farm, Gleeson told Dean that he could go to the Queensland government and Brisbane City Council and assure them that his paper was in my corner for the big fight. It was in keeping with News Corporation's policy of backing major events tourism as a boost for local economies. Dean then approached the city council and state government seeking sponsorship for the fight, promising 20,000 visitors to the city's hotels and a campaign promoting Brisbane to more than 150 countries taking the fight telecast.

The Queensland government and Brisbane City Council formed an alliance with Suncorp Stadium in a sponsorship arrangement and, in a world exclusive, *The Courier-Mail* revealed on 4 January that a plan was in place for me to face Pacquiao at the stadium in the biggest fight ever held in Australia. Because of Pacquiao's commitments to the Philippines senate in May and June, there was only a small window of opportunity for Dean to organise a fight – and that was in April.

I was shocked when I read the news. I had only heard a vague outline of what was happening.

But two days later there I was in the middle of Suncorp Stadium casting my eye around the vast cauldron and answering questions from a small army of journalists.

Dean was about to fly to America to sign the contract with Bob to bring the Filipino boxing icon to Brisbane. What had once seemed like a pipedream, a ridiculous fantasy, was now a reality. The biggest crowd I'd ever fought in front of in Brisbane was 2000 for the Randall Bailey fight, and now I was at a major press conference explaining how I could see myself overwhelming Pacquiao in front of 50,000.

'This is a dream come true,' I said in one interview, 'and it's a fight I can definitely win. Manny is a lot shorter than me and I fight well against guys who are shorter than me and who are coming forward. I've got youth on my side. He's thirty-eight, I'm twenty-eight. He's got the experience, but I think he's slipped a bit. He's still got very good movement and skills, but he has dropped form just slightly and that means a lot at the top level. Bob Arum seems to want the fight with me and Pacquiao now before Pacquiao retires. I think he sees it as a changing of the guard. Pacquiao's a fighter I've always looked up to. He was one of the reasons I got into boxing. I always loved the way he moved and the way he fought. He absolutely destroyed De La Hoya when I saw him the first time. I thought *wow*. I didn't really follow boxing then but I was amazed by him. It's incredible that I could soon be fighting him here in this huge stadium.'

I told the reporters I regarded Pacquiao as one of the top fighters of all time.

'Pacquiao is a machine with what he's done – coming up from 48 kilograms [light-flyweight] to be a world champ at 70 kilograms and all the divisions in between. He's a credit to his country and I'd say people who come to the fight would be coming to see him more than me. He's a huge drawcard and he's been a super champion for a long time.'

Glenn said the fight was a win–win situation for Bob.

'If Jeff wins Bob Arum has a world champ with a lot of miles left in him,' Glenn said. 'He has a great fighter for the next seven years who just beat a living legend. If Manny wins it's business as usual. But I believe Jeff will win. He's like a younger, stronger Pacquiao. He has the same deception in his moves, the angles, a very high work rate. They're both hunters. It's going to be a blistering fight. Two busy guys who can both bang and move really well. This won't be cat and mouse, like Mayweather and Pacquiao. This will be cat and cat going after each other.'

Inevitably, I was deluged with Facebook messages saying that the fight would never happen, that no one in boxing knew who I was and that, even if the fight did happen, it would be the easiest win of Manny's career. I was going to get slaughtered. Instead of the puncher, I became the punchline.

But this was no joke and I was backing myself.

A week after that first press conference at Suncorp, on 15 January, *The Sunday Mail* revealed that Queensland's top tourist destinations would be showcased to a TV audience of half a billion people as part of the deal to bring the fight to Brisbane.

The state government was about to meet with Dean. Suncorp was ready to be locked in as the venue.

According to the business plan for the fight, it would be beamed into 159 countries, including 92 million homes in China and 33 million in America. Dean had a guarantee that the telecast would include eight minutes of editorial content promoting Queensland tourism, which was worth $100 million in exposure. He was selling the fight as one of the world's great sporting events for 2017 and said the $6 million or so the Queensland alliance was being asked to pledge was a 'bargain' considering the US network CBS had charged A$7 million for each thirty-second advertisement during the 2016 Super Bowl, which had an audience of fewer than 200 million people.

The Queensland premier, Annastacia Palaszczuk, said her government would lace up the gloves if the finances were right.

'If it stacks up for the taxpayer, Queensland will be in the fight for the fight,' she said.

The Premier had just returned from the Magic Millions races on the Gold Coast when, on a stifling summer's day, the hot topic at her table had been the big fight. She had asked another guest there, Peter Gleeson, if *The Sunday Mail* was totally committed to support the government's decision to provide funding for the bout. Gleeson said I had his total backing and that he saw real substance in what Dean was offering to Queensland and the benefits it would bring to the economy.

I also received some unexpected support from Ali Funeka, who told South African journalist Mesuli Zifo that I had the 'most unconventional boxing style' he had ever seen. He said watching me on video was misleading and that Pacquiao could get the shock of his life if he wasn't properly prepared.

'I had watched his video footage and I was confident that he would not be a problem,' Funeka said. 'But wait until you get into the ring with him and you will be surprised how awkward he is. He complements his unconventional style with power as he tends to swivel all his body when throwing a right hand to generate all the power to it. Pacquiao should leave nothing to chance when preparing for Horn. That guy is not pretty to watch but he does what he does successfully. I know some people are dismissing him because he does not follow the boxing script when fighting, but I am telling you he may upset Pacquiao especially as the Filipino is not the same dynamo he used to be.'

Australia's most successful fight trainer, Johnny Lewis, weighed in, saying that I was capable of beating anyone in the world with my work rate and my courage, that I had climbed from the deck more than once in my career to overwhelm opponents, in the same manner as Johnny's most famous protégé, Jeff Fenech.

'Jeff Horn is on the way up and Manny has seen better days. I think Jeff is good enough to do the job,' Johnny said.

While I was battling my old schoolmates Nathan Millington and Kiang Lai for table tennis honours, Dean visited Bob Arum in Las Vegas and then had detailed negotiations with John Aitken from Brisbane Marketing and John Montgomery from Tourism and Events Queensland. On 29 January, *The Sunday Mail* reported in another world exclusive that the Queensland alliance had agreed to pour millions of dollars into the bout, now set for 23 April.

Pacquiao's purse would be about $10 million.

I was to get a guarantee of $500,000, plus a bonus depending on ticket sales that could push me into the millionaire category. Jo and I were flummoxed by all that.

My previous biggest purse was $20,000.

Then Manny Pacquiao landed the first big blow of our fight.

He floored me with a sucker punch I never saw coming.

12

This will be a unique sporting event in Australian history. This is the chance for a Brisbane boy to shock the world in what could be one of the biggest wins ever by an Australian sportsman.

– Dean Lonergan, promoter and former test rugby league player

'IT BLOWS MY MIND to be honest.' That's what I told *Main Event* host Eddie McGuire when he interviewed me about the prospect of fighting one of the greatest boxers in the history of the game. I was about to answer Eddie's favourite quiz question – 'Who wants to be a millionaire?' – by fighting Manny Pacquiao and he was now interviewing me as part of the telecast for the Danny Green–Anthony Mundine rematch from Adelaide Oval on 3 February. 'To think I was just teaching a year or two ago in a classroom,' I told Eddie. 'Now I'm about to fight before 50 or 60,000 people at

Suncorp Stadium in my hometown. It's just crazy. A dream come true. I can see myself winning the fight. That's what you've got to picture. You've got to picture your hand being raised – if I didn't think that now, I'd definitely lose the fight. I'm thinking positive.'

I was in a television studio in Brisbane and Eddie was doing a live cross in front of 28,000 people at a vast sports stadium in Adelaide. To think I could soon be fighting before almost double that crowd was something I still couldn't quite grasp.

As part of the interview, the great Australian world champ of the 1980s Barry Michael gave me some sage advice about beating Manny. Barry was one of Australia's toughest ever fighters, never knocked down in more than sixty fights, and he told me he thought I had a really big chance to win. I was so pleased to hear that from a great champ. Barry told me to watch how Kostya Tszyu knocked out the American southpaw Zab Judah back in 2001. The key to beating a left-hander, Barry said, was to step to the left and throw my right hand straight down the middle. It was good advice and Glenn was already working on a ten-point plan which covered that and which he said would lead to victory, provided I followed it closely.

I turned twenty-nine on 4 February and the immediate big victory I was looking for was at the ten-pin bowling alley against Kiang and Nathan and the guys from school in a tournament we had for my birthday. I was planning a lot more strikes against Pacquiao. Glenn always told me that the only way to become a legend was to beat one and, as I rolled my bowling ball into the gutter once too often, I had to pinch myself that I was really about to tackle the man described in a *Sunday Mail* editorial as a 'once in a generation sportsperson', who was up there with the likes of Usain Bolt, Tiger Woods, Rod Laver, Michael Phelps and Johnathan Thurston.

The newspaper revealed that:

> The State Government, Brisbane City Council and Suncorp Stadium had reached a financial agreement package to lure the biggest fight in Australian history to Brisbane. As part of the deal, Queensland will be showcased to hundreds of millions of viewers. It is expected as many as 6000 Filipinos will make the trip to Australia for the bout. For Horn, the mild-mannered undefeated schoolteacher, it is a dream come true.
> It's now up to the promoters of the fight to accept the financial undertaking by government agencies. This appears a formality because the promoters have made it clear right the way through that they want the bout in Brisbane. Strap your seat belts on, Queensland.

It was certainly going to be a wild ride. For days I waited for word from Pacquiao that he had signed the contract and was ready to go for 23 April.

I waited. And waited. And waited.

Dean told us it would be any day soon. I attended another of Dean's events, the Global Rugby Tens in Brisbane, where I was thrilled to have my photo taken with everyone from the Queensland governor, Paul de Jersey, to footy great Israel Folau and State of Origin coach Mal Meninga.

In the meantime, though, Manny's representative, Michael Koncz, had travelled to the Middle East to meet with the boss of a travel agency there and to talk up a Pacquiao fight in the desert. And not against me.

Then on 11 February, Manny used Twitter to send a message to his fans: 'see you in UAE for my next fight'. My heart sank. Two days later Manny kicked me where it really hurts by starting a Twitter poll asking his 165,000 followers who he should fight next – me, Amir Khan, Terence Crawford or Kell Brook. Amir Khan was the overwhelming winner of the poll for the fight to take place in the United Arab Emirates. Guess who came last with just 7 per cent of the vote? Me. I felt like tweeting an angry face back to Manny and his followers.

But Glenn told me to hold the dream, that I must not lose focus.

It was hard not to, especially when Koncz, speaking to *Gulf News* in Abu Dhabi, was adamant that I was out of the picture and that Amir Khan and Manny would generate a monster payday. 'It took us a while to get this deal together,' Koncz said. 'There was a lot of confusion whether this is going to happen here in the UAE. I'm here with full authority and power. I have been the marriage counsellor for Manny and we have developed a relationship. I'm involved in all aspects of what he does. We have executed the agreement in the morning and 100 per cent the fight will be here in the UAE.'

The Courier-Mail reported:

> In the bizarre world of boxing, a man who calls himself Manny Pacquiao's marriage counsellor and who has been known to carry the world champion's food and tuck him into bed at night, threatens to derail months of planning for the April 23 Suncorp

Super Fight against Brisbane schoolteacher Jeff Horn. Canadian Michael Koncz, Pacquiao's self-styled 'chief of staff' who follows him about as a constant minder, announced on the weekend that the world champ would be making the next defence of his WBO welterweight title, not in Brisbane, but in the United Arab Emirates. This was a bolt from the blue to Horn's promoters, Duco Events, who have successfully courted the Queensland Government and Brisbane City Council to secure funding and sponsorship.

Koncz says the fight will now '100 per cent be in the UAE' but with just 10 weeks until the proposed April 23 contest, the Pacquiao team has not revealed who will promote the bout or even the venue, saying a decision was still pending over whether it would be held in Abu Dhabi or Dubai. In Pacquiao's captivating life story, the man who became a boxing great and Filipino senator, famously ran away from his shanty home as a boy after his father cooked and ate the youngster's pet dog. Boxing, though, is even more brutal, a dog-eat-dog environment where everyone is fair game. Horn's team felt so sure that Pacquiao was about to sign their contract that they arranged a media tour of the United States in two weeks to introduce the undefeated Brisbane boxer to American fight fans. Horn's promoters say they are confident Pacquiao is playing mind games and the fight will still go ahead at Suncorp. But as he continues to push himself in training every day Horn isn't sure if he's coming or going.

Maybe that's exactly what Manny Pacquiao wanted all along.

Despite all the noise about the UAE fight and many so-called experts around the world laughing and saying, 'I told you so', that there was no way Manny would fight me – a virtual unknown down in Brisbane – Dean was unwavering in his belief that he could still deliver the fight to Suncorp Stadium.

Dean's a big, imposing bloke and there was a lot of clout to his words when he declared, 'Bob Arum is Pacquiao's promoter not Michael Koncz. The only person authorised to promote Manny Pacquiao is Bob Arum. Until Bob Arum tells me differently we are continuing with that aim of having the fight at Suncorp Stadium on April 23.'

That made me feel a bit better and, to gain support from north Queensland fans ahead of the planned fight in Brisbane, I went on a tour with a group of journalists led by well-known rugby league player manager, Jim Banaghan. The three-day bus tour started in Cairns and took in Cardwell, Tully, Ingham and Townsville. In the latter city I trained with the Cowboys rugby league team. In Cairns I opened a gym called the Hit Pit, spoke at two schools, St Joseph's Primary and St Augustine's College, and then gave boxing tips while training at a police and citizens youth club.

But all the time my head was spinning. The impasse with Manny was confusing and frustrating. We didn't know if it was him tweeting or if he had given control of his account to someone else. I told the press that all Manny's tweets were just mind games, a ploy for him and his team to show me that they had all the power and that they were calling the shots over the fight. I just wanted to get in the ring and show Manny my power and I hoped that I would.

Then Manny hit me again.

He announced that he would start training immediately for his next fight and was standing firm on the bout being held in the UAE, not Suncorp Stadium. He was still weighing up the Amir Khan proposal, he said. Publicly I said I wouldn't be sucked in by any of his mind games, but I felt I was being dragged into a giant vacuum. Manny told the major Filipino news site GMA that negotiations were still in progress and that even if I did jag a fight with him it would not be in Brisbane.

He said I was the last thing on his mind. Manny was busy in the Philippines Senate, calling for the reinstatement of death by hanging, particularly for drug traffickers. He was also arguing against an anti-discrimination proposal designed to protect the transgender community. He claimed that cross-dressing could be used to 'commit fraud'. A year earlier the born-again Christian lost a lucrative long-term deal with sportswear company Nike after he made derogatory remarks about homosexuals. He later apologised, but still confirmed that he remained opposed to same-sex marriage.

He was also opposed to fighting me.

A few days later a Manny Pacquiao–Amir Khan bout became headline news in the British press. The fight, Manny said, was set for 23 April.

The news travelled quickly around the world and hit me like a bullet. Again the naysayers came out and said I had never been in the hunt, that the fight was never going to happen in Brisbane, and that even if I did one day get into the ring with Manny I'd get slaughtered.

News of the Khan fight didn't just hit me on the chin. It also stunned Bob Arum, the man who is actually Manny's promoter.

He was fired up for a fight of his own when *The Courier-Mail* called him in Las Vegas for the real story. On 21 February Bob told the paper that the reports coming from England over the Pacquiao–Khan deal were 'total and complete bulls—'.

He said the plans for me to fight Manny at Suncorp Stadium were still 'up in the air', and that Manny was chasing an 'insane amount of money' in the UAE 'whether [the offer] is real or not real'. The insane amount of money turned out to be A$49 million. No wonder Manny had me on the backburner, as Bob said the world champ was determined to pursue that river of gold to the source, whether it was a mirage or not.

I was shattered a few days later when I read that Bob had told the TV network ESPN, 'The Australian deal is not going to happen now, because Manny is trying to get a fight done in the United Arab Emirates, and the people there favour him fighting Amir Khan. Whether it will happen or not, I just don't know, because they have to come up with a large amount of money. Manny seems to believe they will come up with the money. I have some reservations whether it will happen or not. If the money comes up, I will aid and abet the fight happening. But right now, I'm holding my powder. I don't really know. The Australian deal was a lot of money, but it paled in comparison to the ... money they're supposedly offering.'

I took my mind off the looming disappointment by going to Cirque du Soleil in Brisbane with Jo. I was invited backstage and put one of the stars, Alexander Kazeko, through the punching pads. He was pretty good, a lot better than I was when the acrobats gave me a chance on the tightrope. I'm glad the practice rope was less than a metre off the ground.

There was nothing I could do to make the Manny fight happen, but Dean refused to lose all hope. He and his team came up with the idea of a little marketing video to goad Manny into fighting me. The video featured me telling him the big offer from Dubai was an Arabian fantasy, while the multimillion-dollar offer from Brisbane was 'real money' backed by the state government. The premier, Annastacia Palaszczuk, endorsed my effort, telling Manny to man up and fight me. Politician to politician, she told the honourable Filipino senator: 'Every Queenslander knows the New South Wales league team fears a Suncorp Stadium crowd at Origin each year, but they still turn up. All Manny needs to do is book his tickets. Jeff Horn and the rest of Queensland are waiting.'

Boxing fans around the world were bagging the thought of a Pacquiao–Khan fight, as Khan was coming off a brutal knockout loss against Mexican Saúl 'Canelo' Álvarez and Manny's trainer, Freddie Roach, admitted that Manny had knocked out Khan in sparring when they trained together in Los Angeles.

Our marketing video used some footage of Donald Trump for effect, as I made the point that the Dubai money was 'fake news'. Video grabs of Trump were cut together to say, 'What the hell do you have to lose ... Manny, get the deal done.'

Manny didn't see the joke though. You could say he trumped me a few hours later when I saw this message on my twitter feed from @mannypacquiao. It said: 'Negotiations between team Pacquiao and team Khan have come to terms for the April 23 bout as this is what the fans wanted. #PacquiaoKhan'. Then there was one from @amirkingkhan which said: 'My team and

I have agreed terms with Manny Pacquiao and his team for a super fight #pacquiaokhan #April23rd'.

It looked like I'd been knocked out of the fight before a punch had even been thrown. Back at home in Acacia Ridge I told Jo that we might have to keep going on $20,000 a fight and hope that I got a shot down the track.

I refused to be completely downhearted though and put on a brave face. I always try to look at the positives and the upside, and I believed that if I continued to work hard one day my opportunity would come.

Bob Arum assured Dean that there was still no formal deal between Manny and Khan despite what they said. He reiterated that he, not Michael Koncz, was Manny's promoter. The glimmer of hope for me was that, despite what Manny and Khan were saying and despite many news outlets running with the story that I was gone, there was still no venue confirmed for any fight in the UAE and no details about television coverage.

The Courier-Mail called the Dubai kerfuffle 'a desert storm in a teacup' and the longer Manny dragged out the negotiations the more it looked like he was chasing fool's gold. Michael Koncz though was proving to be my toughest opponent.

*

On 1 March Koncz announced that Manny would now fight Amir Khan on 19 May in either Abu Dhabi or Dubai. He said the decision had been made after a two-hour meeting with Bob and that, although Bob had originally announced a Pacquiao–Horn fight in Brisbane, Manny wanted a bigger purse and a bigger name opponent to sell the fight on pay-per-view television.

'We decided to move it to 19 May here and 20 May in the United [Arab] Emirates so we'd have time to promote it properly and make it a huge success,' Koncz told *Yahoo! Sports*. 'I have to talk to both fighters to get them to approve going in May instead of in April. I don't think that will be any problem.'

Koncz said there had been considerable media criticism over me as the opponent because I was a 'no name', and that Khan's resounding victory in Manny's Twitter poll as the choice of his next opponent had sealed the deal. 'Obviously,' Koncz said, 'Amir's a big name in the US, too, as well as in England where he lives and people saw it for what it is: A toss-up fight against two fast-handed guys.'

The report stated that this final decision ended 'a bizarre several weeks in which Arum was saying one thing and Koncz and Pacquiao, who were in the Philippines, were making comments that contradicted Arum. But after the meeting in Arum's Las Vegas office, Koncz said both sides were on the same page. 'We just want to do the best and the biggest fight we can, and this makes a lot of sense for so many reasons.'

Bob had a different version of their conversation.

'It's all bulls–,' Bob said. 'All it is right now is a discussion.' He said that although he and Koncz talked about the new date, it was not even close to being set in stone and that while some investment group in the UAE was supposed to be dangling A$49 million at Manny no one had actually seen any of the coin.

'After I met with Koncz I realised everything was up in the air as far as the money [was concerned],' Bob explained with a laugh. 'They punted to me and said, "Go find the money." So far it hasn't surfaced. This could all go away like the breeze.'

I lived in hope that the desert storm would blow over. While I waited the Tourism and Major Events Minister, Kate Jones, hosted me at the big Suncorp battle when the Cowboys beat the Broncos in golden point, that man Thurston slotting over a field goal in the eighty-eighth minute to bring the 47,703-strong crowd to its feet. I could only dream of putting on a thriller in front of that many people.

As the days ticked by and still no word from Bob or Manny, I needed all the resilience that Glenn had taught me from the days I first entered his gym. But the more the clock kept ticking, the more likely it was that Manny would be lured by the bait of the best offer on the table. And that was the one being put together in Queensland.

At last. Bob finally announced that there would be no fight in the Middle East. He gave me a hint of encouragement when he told reporters late in March that Manny planned to fight in July and November and that the July fight would be outside the US. But then on 28 March, plans for our Suncorp fight hit another hurdle when, 1000 kilometres from Brisbane, Cyclone Debbie made landfall near Airlie Beach, just north-east of Proserpine, and began to wreak havoc. The premier had $4.5 million of state government money to pour into the fight, along with about $1.7 million from the Brisbane City Council. Suddenly, despite the economic benefits outlined for Queensland tourism, she was under enormous pressure to steer that government money not into my world-title shot but into an advertising campaign for the Whitsunday Islands.

She had to make a quick decision.

Ms Palaszczuk informed Peter Gleeson at *The Sunday Mail* that he had better tell Manny Pacquiao to get a move on or the fight would not happen. Dean immediately called Bob and said Koncz had to stop stalling or the deal would soon be off the table altogether, and would probably never come back. It was a firm offer, guaranteed cash for Manny, to fight a schoolteacher who the bookies said had absolutely no chance.

As Donald Trump had said on the video, what did Manny have to lose?

*

On 31 March Koncz announced that Manny had agreed to fight Jeff Horn – whoever the hell he was – in some place called Brisbane and that the deal would be finished by the end of the week. On 4 April Manny signed the deal, reluctantly, according to Koncz.

'We signed it so, yeah, we're excited about it. But again, my preference was to fight Amir Khan,' Koncz said. 'That didn't work out. We had this on the table so we decided to take it. Manny will train and do the best he can and hopefully we get the fight over with very quickly, we get out of there – we say hi to the Australian fans and media – and come home. Frankly and honestly, and nothing against Jeff Horn – I've never met the kid, I don't know him personally – but the name recognition is I guess why the fans picked Amir Khan.'

We were now twelve weeks out from the fight. Glenn and I began training in earnest even though the bout had not yet been formally announced. I went to get some new suits from the Clay Rondo store in the city because I figured I'd be doing a few interviews shortly. On 5 April Glenn told the media that if I fought at my best I would be the next welterweight champion of the world.

There were last-minute details to be finalised, over advertising and promotion and appearances and marketing and agreements, with Manny and his team. Manny was demanding a rematch in case he lost and the lion's share of the money from a return fight as well. The government still needed a filing cabinet of agreements before committing taxpayers' money. But then, on the afternoon of Saturday, 8 April, I spent the afternoon at Suncorp Stadium with Graham Quirk, Kate Jones, a heap of my nephews and nieces and photographer Annette Dew for the next day's *Sunday Mail* spread on the big fight. The report declared that I was king of the kids and could soon be king of boxing:

> It's been a rocky road to the biggest fight in Australian boxing history but Queensland Premier Annastacia Palaszczuk yesterday confirmed the Jeff Horn–Manny Pacquiao fight would finally take place at Brisbane's Suncorp Stadium on July 2. And even though 'Fighting Schoolteacher' Horn will start the Battle of Brisbane a massive underdog against one of the greatest boxers in history, he has a good chance of scoring one of the biggest wins ever in Australian sport.
>
> After months of mind games, Pacquiao has finally agreed to fight Horn in a bout which will bring the eyes of the sporting world to the River City. The Queensland Government and Brisbane City Council yesterday signed contracts to underwrite it, believing

> it will create a huge economic boost and showcase the Sunshine State to the world. Congratulating Horn yesterday, Ms Palaszczuk said that after months of speculation, 'we're finally all in the ring for this fight to go ahead'.
>
> 'Up to 55,000 boxing fans from across Australia and the world are expected to fill Suncorp Stadium to see the local teacher taking on one of the biggest names in boxing history, on his home turf,' she said. 'The match is a highlight on the state's major events calendar and is set to deliver an expected $15.8 million economic boost to the city.' Minister for Tourism and Major Events, Kate Jones said securing the fight was a major coup for Brisbane and the local tourism industry. 'We've always said we'd be keen to host a boxing match of this calibre, as long as it stacked up for Queensland taxpayers,' Ms Jones said. 'Brisbane will be pumping as the nation gets behind our local champion. This blockbuster event will raise Queensland's profile in many of our key international tourism markets including the United States, United Kingdom, New Zealand, China and South-East Asia.'

After weeks of shadow sparring between the two camps, I had finally won the opening round. Manny Pacquiao would be coming to me and I would be ready with fire.

*

A press conference was organised for the next day in New Farm Park, which was handy since, by coincidence, it was also the site for our annual Horn family gathering on that day. Graham Quirk was coming already, and Kate Jones and some of her staff and dozens of journalists also joined us under the huge Moreton Bay fig trees to talk about the biggest fight ever in Australia.

My message to Manny was, 'Be ready – because I will be.'

'I hope Manny takes me lightly,' I said. 'I hope he underestimates me because when he gets in that ring and there are 55,000 people cheering he is in for a big shock. I've underestimated opponents early in my amateur career and I ended up losing because of it. He's had a lot more experience than me and fought all the greats, but I'm hungry and I'm training to cause a big upset. I promise the people of Australia that I will train harder than ever before for this fight. Manny is one of the greatest fighters of all time, but I believe I'm getting him at the right time in his career. He's thirty-eight now and I'm twenty-nine and I'm ready to take his world title.'

I opened as a $4.30 underdog in betting markets but was happy to be the outsider in a two-horse race that was starting to grip the nation. Liam Bartlett flew to Brisbane to interview me, Glenn and my family for *60 Minutes* and I started appearing on other shows such as *The Project* and *The Footy Show*.

'I hope Manny comes out swinging with everything,' I told Sean Lawson from Fox Sports. 'He's one of my favourite fighters and his action style and my aggressive style is going to make for a very exciting fight. I'm going after him from the opening bell and the more punches he throws at me, the more openings I'll have to hit him with my counter-punches. Every time Manny throws a punch at me, his guard comes down. He's one of the best boxers of all time, but he has been knocked out and he's sometimes wide open. I'm hoping he looks at the odds and gets a little careless because I'm ready to take his world title.'

Glenn said it was a fight between two guys without a reverse gear and that I was a 'very aggressive guy with a great chin and power in both hands'. I had youth and the crowd on my side too. Glenn believed that Manny had such a busy, all-action style that it would present me with many opportunities to hit him hard. This, he said, was a variation of the Rocky story – a kid no one knows getting a chance at a legendary world champion. He was tipping I would put on a Rocky-like performance.

'It could be one of the most exciting fights for years,' Glenn said, 'and hopefully the fans will see plenty of fierce action. That's our dream anyway and so far all of our dreams about this fight have come true.'

Although I suspected that Manny and his team thought I was an easy beat, offering them easy money, Manny's trainer, Freddie Roach, said his fighter hadn't scored a knockout for eight years, 'and it's time that changed'.

He said Manny was 'working his ass off' for this fight and 'we would be keeping the world title'.

'Manny doesn't underestimate anyone,' Freddie said. 'He knows upsets can happen in boxing and that Horn is a good puncher but we are prepared for anything. No fighter in the world has Manny's work ethic. He runs for an hour in the morning and does 65 rounds of training in the gym every day. And he loves nothing more than entertaining big crowds. The bigger the crowd the more he likes it. There might be 55,000 people in the Stadium cheering for Horn but that will only encourage Manny to put on the best show he can. He will be the very best he can be for this fight because we know Jeff Horn will be at his best too.'

Freddie, who had previously trained fighters such as Oscar De La Hoya and Mike Tyson, said he would spend six weeks with Manny in Manila before the fight and then a week in Brisbane.

'There are some big fights coming up for Manny in the near future,' he said, 'and Jeff Horn is just the kind of opponent Manny needs to prepare for those. I like this fight. There's a chance Manny could be fighting Mikey Garcia or Amir Khan or Terence Crawford next. Manny needs a fight like Jeff Horn to get ready for a bigger fight. Horn is a strong guy, a counter-puncher but we're coming up with a game plan to make sure that Manny Pacquiao flies home still with that world title belt in his possession. We're going for the knockout.'

Hmmm. Me too.

I was eager to meet Manny face to face before we met fist to fist.

Finally on 24 April, after weeks of waiting for him, Manny arrived in Brisbane aboard a Singapore Airlines flight, ready for a week-long promotional tour that would take in Brisbane, Sydney and Melbourne. He arrived with his wife, Jinkee, her sister and brother-in-law and a team of managers and trainers. Manny was dressed simply in jeans and a $68 Dolce & Gabbana T-shirt with a cartoon motif. He was unfailingly polite to waiting media and, despite his ferocity in the ring, so softly spoken and unassuming that reporters strained to hear what he was saying.

He had a simple message for me.

‘Work hard,’ he said. ‘Make sure you are in 100 per cent condition on July 2 so we can give a good fight and entertain the people.

‘I am motivated and here to do my best.’

Manny claimed he hadn’t studied me closely but planned to watch my last three fights as soon as possible.

He said the prospect of me fighting before a capacity crowd at Suncorp would help me and boost my chances of scoring an upset victory.

‘That’s good for him. They’ll be cheering for Jeff Horn and that’s what I want,’ Manny said. ‘I love it. That’s what motivates me.’

Game on.

13

Life is short, but there is always time enough for courtesy.

– Ralph Waldo Emerson, American essayist, lecturer and poet

MANNY PACQUIAO WAS RIGHT where I hoped he would be. On his back, gasping for breath, crying out in pain, tears rolling down his face. He had seemingly lost all physical control and was begging for mercy. How I had longed for this moment, how I imagined him just like this during all the weeks he and Michael Koncz had played cat and mouse with me, toying with all my dreams and aspirations.

Now Manny was out on his feet.

At this exact moment, I wished that we were both at Suncorp Stadium and I was having my hand raised in victory. But instead we were in the back of a mini-bus cruising together through the northwestern suburbs of Melbourne and I was listening to Manny fall about in hysterics. There he was, one of the greatest boxers of all time, clutching his sides as he cried with laughter.

We had just left the Invictus Gym, a mixed martial arts facility in an industrial hub at Tullamarine, where Eddie McGuire had hosted a press conference promoting our fight, which was now billed as the Battle of Brisbane. AFL stars Scott Pendlebury and Jonathan Brown were there, as well as comedian Sam Pang and boxing champs such as Barry Michael and Blake Caparello, who had been top of the bill when I made my professional debut at Altona North four years earlier. It was now just a few days after the Suncorp fight was officially announced and already almost 30,000 seats had been sold.

Manny and I were both dressed in dark suits and ties but he was the star of the show, besieged by fans queuing outside the gym to meet him. They all wanted to touch this godlike figure tipped to one day become the president of the Philippines.

Inside the mini-bus, Manny did not present like a sporting deity who had earned more than $600 million from boxing. He was rocking side to side with laughter at the Australian accent of Jim Banaghan, the rugby league identity organising publicity. Manny had asked his assistant, Benjamin 'Choi' Garcia, to phone ahead and have the airport ParkRoyal, where we were both staying, prepare five lots of the only dish he seemed to eat in Australia – steak, asparagus, rice and sauteed mushrooms.

'Salted mushrooms?' Banaghan asked.

'Not salted, sauteed,' Manny replied. The way he pronounced them, the two words sounded very similar.

Then began a long comedy routine about Australian accents that lasted for more than two months until fight time. Banaghan started talking about the 'van' we were riding in and Pacquiao pointed to the artery in his wrist.

'This is a van,' the esteemed senator said.

'No that's a vein,' Banaghan replied.

'It's a van,' Pacquiao said, again mimicking the Australian accent.

'Vein!'

'This is a van!'

'It's a vein, you idiot,' Banaghan bellowed in mock fury at one of boxing's legends.

And so it went. Manny could not stop laughing. The difference between the words 'sword' and 'sawed' had him in stitches and not the sort I have had sewn into my face all too often.

It was a strange situation as the world champ and his undefeated challenger rode together in good cheer weeks away from cracking heads before more than 50,000 people. Manny was sitting in the back row of seats with Choi Garcia and I was two rows in front of them. Other passengers were Bob Arum, Bob's key lieutenant at Top Rank, Brad Jacobs, Top Rank's publicity guru, Fred Sternburg, Dean Lonergan, Michael Koncz and Banaghan. There were also a couple of Manny's bodyguards, ex-special forces guys tasked with protecting him from the big crowds everywhere we went. For days we had been travelling together on a sort of magical mystery tour, selling the fact that we would soon be tearing each other apart in front of a worldwide audience of more than 500 million people.

Yet there was never any animosity between Manny and me. Glenn had always said that this fight was the best possible showcase for boxing – it was two gentlemen at the top of their sport putting their skills, strength and tenacity on the line. I was so happy when I read that Bob Arum had said it was a battle between 'two exemplary human beings'. Every time we were asked to pose in a stare-down for the cameras, Manny and I looked each other in the eye and, without saying anything, both dared the other to laugh first. I would see his eyes shine a little bit and we would both have to bite our lips. I didn't have to feign violence or pretend fury. I knew the importance of the fight. Manny was fighting to preserve his legacy and I was fighting to make a future for my family and create boxing history. I knew that if I beat him I had the chance to make millions, and that when the first bell rang and the fight was on for real it would be non-stop action as we both threw everything we had at each other. But Manny was such a nice guy all through the press tour that I thought that it was a shame we had to punch each other.

Sitting on the bus listening to Manny laughing his head off, I suggested that maybe I could just tell him a joke before the fight and that he might not be able to recover.

*

Manny had arrived in Brisbane a few days earlier on the eve of Anzac Day and immediately went to work fulfilling his contractual commitments to publicise the bout. He won over fans wherever he went, starting at Brisbane's Sofitel Hotel early on Anzac morning when he ventured outside to take in the Dawn Service at nearby Anzac Square. He caught up with soldier-turned-fighter, Adam Lovelock, and Adam's mate, a former boxer named Steve Wijangco who was now a promoter.

Then Manny donned his running gear and met up with a film crew, which captured him at various locations around Brisbane as it put together commercial vignettes highlighting the beauty of the Sunshine State. The ads were to run during the fight telecast as part of the sponsorship from Tourism and Events Queensland and Brisbane Marketing. I would get my turn extolling some idyllic locations, including the Tangalooma Island Resort where I went surfing down the sandhills, visited shipwrecks and fed the wild dolphins as the cameras rolled.

Michael Koncz was by Manny's side throughout his day of filming and always referred to the world champ as 'boss'. Koncz tried to show everyone else that he was the 'boss' though, telling the film crew and accompanying journalists that Manny would not spend much time in the Queensland sun, that he needed water by his side at all times, that only he or Manny could open the bottles, that Manny was only going up the Kangaroo Point stairs near the Story Bridge once and that Manny would not – repeat, would not – be doing any push-ups on uneven ground. He said Manny was saving all his energy for me.

At South Bank, where Manny was filmed shadow boxing in a ring erected beside the Brisbane River, the champ was met by 3000 cheering, chanting fans waving Filipino flags and holding placards. There were emotional scenes, indicating just what an icon Manny is to the Filipino people. Some elderly women burst into tears as they threw their arms around him. Others tried to climb through the huge crowd as though they just wanted to touch the hem of his garment. Wild cheers broke out as he climbed into the boxing ring and, although Manny was clearly stunned by the size and volume of the adoring crowd in his opponent's home city, he told the large contingent of police and security personnel surrounding him that he wanted to meet all his fans. He shook all the hands that were thrown at him and hugged as many people as he could.

Later in the day at the Lone Pine Koala Sanctuary, he cuddled a koala, then finished an extraordinary day by patting a kangaroo, waving at a Tasmanian devil and risked having a finger taken off by a cockatoo. He was trying to make the bird talk and waved at it through the bars of its cage until his wife, Jinkee, reminded him he would need two good hands to beat me.

*

I had studied Manny for a long time so that, on the morning of 26 April when I finally came face to face with him at the rear of a photographic studio in the Brisbane suburb of Bowen Hills, I felt that I already knew him well. Still, he disarmed me without throwing a punch. When I arrived, Manny was there filming an interview for the fight telecasters, Main Event, with one of their hosts, Ben Damon. Peter Wallis from *The Courier-Mail* had just taken a photograph of him looking fearsome for the paper's *QWeekend* magazine, but Manny was all smiles as he stuck out his hand at seeing me and then warmly embraced me. I told him that I was really grateful for him giving me the opportunity to fight for his title and he smiled that mega-watt grin that lights up a room wherever he goes. Deep down he was probably thinking he'd knock me out in a couple of rounds, but he was gracious and very dignified.

A few hours later, flanked by Bob Arum, Dean Lonergan, Kate Jones and Graham Quirk, Manny and I attended the official launch of the fight at Suncorp Stadium. There were more people there to watch the press conference than had been at most of my fights. Manny said it was a great chance for me to make a name for myself and recalled how once he had been a young underdog too, unknown on the world stage and given no chance at the big time.

'I know what it is like to be young and hungry,' Manny said. 'Often I would lie awake and dream of my chance. I like this fight with Jeff Horn because he stands and fights, he does not run away in the ring. It will be a very exciting fight for the fans.'

He said he respected all opponents and that he wouldn't trash-talk me because he was a Christian man and did not want to set a bad example for young people.

Glenn told reporters that the big danger against Manny was that he threw punches so fast and from such a distance that it was like he was punching an opponent from the back of a truck charging towards you. This, he said, would be a bout that pitted two aggressive heavy hitters going at it.

'Hopefully this will be the fight of the year and people will come and watch and just go, "Wow, that was really something",' Glenn said.

I promised that I would do my best.

*

That afternoon Manny and I flew to Sydney on separate flights for another round with the media there. I was told that after he alighted his Virgin flight Manny wanted to use the gent's. One bodyguard stood at the entrance while another guarded the stalls. That's what you call star power.

In Sydney that night Queensland State-of-Origin great Mark Coyne and current player Aidan Guerra came to the Pullman Hotel for a chat. Mark told me all about the miracle try he scored in State of Origin in 1994 and how happy he would be if I could score a miracle win over Manny. The next day New South Wales Origin coach, Laurie Daley, added to the excitement when he gave the fighting senator a Blues jersey at a press gathering at the hotel. Radio king Alan Jones hosted the event and I told him I hoped I set an example to people everywhere that if you believed in yourself and had a definite goal you could achieve anything.

'I know Manny will come charging at me, throwing a lot of punches,' I said. 'I know I really have to watch his big left hand but if I can get him to walk on to my right cross, who knows – I might knock him out in the first round like I did to Samuel Colomban when I won the Australian title.'

Bob Arum was asked if, in all seriousness, I had any chance against his world titleholder.

'I can't root against Manny,' Bob said candidly. 'If this fight was in Vegas or Madison Square Garden in New York I wouldn't give Horn much of a chance because I think nerves would take over. But Horn is going to be fighting in front of so many of his countrymen and I think he will give a great account of himself. In 1978 I promoted a fight between Leon Spinks and Muhammad Ali and nobody gave Spinks a chance. But Spinks won. In boxing anything can happen and I have seen a lot of big upsets in fifty-one years in this business. The Fighting Schoolteacher is going to be in the news for a long time. Even if he loses against Manny, there will be many opportunities for Jeff Horn to become a world champion.'

Losing, though, was not an option for me or for Glenn.

This was the one chance that most fighters never ever get and I was going to do everything I could to make the most of it.

Another visitor to my hotel room was Cameron Williams, the Channel Nine presenter, who is another of my cousins. He has been a leading reporter for many years and told me that it was the second time he had sat on a boxer's bed for an interview. The first time was with Mike Tyson. Cameron was invited into the heavyweight champ's suite before his win over James 'Bonecrusher' Smith in Las Vegas way back in 1987, before I was born.

At lunchtime that day Manny and I flew on the same flight to Melbourne. Manny and his wife were in the wide seats up front and I was in economy. I didn't mind. I knew that I was now in the boxing big-time and was really enjoying the ride. Bob was even talking about getting Vasyl Lomachenko, the genius I had seen at the London Olympics, to spar with me in the lead-up to the fight.

All the time Bob spoke of Manny as being right up there with Muhammad Ali as one of the greatest fighters he had worked with, and one of the great humanitarians he had met.

After our press conference in Melbourne, I had dinner with Bob and Dean Lonergan in Chinatown there, and Bob reinforced the enormity of the task I was attempting and the quality of my opponent.

'Manny has won eleven world titles across eight weight divisions, from flyweight to junior-middleweight,' he said. 'No one in boxing history has come close to what he has done. But the truly great things he does are not in the boxing ring but for the poor people of the Philippines. There is a lot of poverty there and people often ask me if they have a welfare system in that country. I say, "Yes, they do, and the welfare system is called Manny Pacquiao." He has given millions and millions to his people.'

Manny and his entourage left Melbourne for Manila and Bob went home with a huge book under his arm about another famous Jew like himself, the heroic John Monash. Bob, who is an avid reader, was intrigued by the story of Monash, Australia's great World War I general and engineer. I hoped that one day he would read a book about me and I got down to the serious business of winning a world-title fight.

It had been a fascinating week on the press tour for the fight. But all along I believed that Manny, laughing all the time he was in Australia and doing very little in the way of training, was treating my challenge like a joke.

I intended to have the last laugh, but I was under no illusions about him being the star of our show.

Back home I attended a promotion with Joe Goodall in front of the Brisbane City Hall advertising the 2018 Commonwealth Games. Joe was getting ready to compete in the prestigious Feliks Stamm Boxing Tournament in Poland which he eventually won, joining a long list of great champions on the honours board there, including Lennox Lewis. Joe and I went through a light sparring session before a couple of dozen onlookers. If Manny had joined us the organisers would have needed a busload of extra security to hold back the cheering throng.

*

When he returned home to the Philippines, Manny was still not taking me seriously. A week after his Australian visit he had not started serious training. My chances of springing a massive upset were growing stronger every day he remained idle.

The website digitaljournal.com reported:

> Pacquiao has chosen to prioritize his work in the Senate over his training for the scheduled title fight. Pacquiao was set to start his formal training for the Horn fight on Tuesday but opted to attend the opening session of the Senate instead of starting his training at the Elorde Gym near the senate offices. Long-time trainer Freddie Roach has set Pacquiao's training schedule at eight weeks before the actual fight on July 2. Obviously the schedule will have to be changed in the wake of Pacquiao's preoccupation with his Senate duties. Roach, who is set to stay six weeks in Manila to personally supervise Pacquiao's training camp, has yet to announce his arrival date.

That was all good news for me. I received tips from all over on ways to beat Manny. I watched footage of another Aussie, Nedal Hussein, decking him with a straight left way back in 2000 before being stopped late in the fight, and I repeatedly watched Juan Manuel Márquez and that booming right hand that knocked Manny cold.

All the time Glenn was refining his ten-point plan that he said would lead to my victory.

On 9 May I started sparring for the fight, in my first session doing six rounds with a rising star from Mackay named Liam Paro, a slick southpaw who gave me a lot of problems for a while. I had a head cold but I still got to work on my right-hand lead which would be crucial against Manny, and I put together the sort of body shots that I hoped would slow down the world champ. Liam, coached by lawyer Alfie Di Carlo, did his best to mimic Manny's all-action style, changing levels constantly and giving an approximation of Manny's blistering attack. It was just the hit-out I needed to open my sparring campaign.

Manny began hard training that same day, beginning with a 45-minute run from his A$18 million house inside Manila's Forbes Park compound, where he lived during Senate sessions. It's in a gated community guarded at both ends by machine-gun toting watchmen. His main home is on a sprawling estate 1500 kilometres to the south in General Santos City. Manny has two other mansions in the Philippines. His wealth is mind-boggling. Three years ago he left a $780,000 watch in a hotel room, finally getting it back after posting a reward of $170,000. In 2015 he paid rapper Sean Combs $17 million for his home in Beverly Hills, where he keeps a fleet of luxury cars, including a Ferrari 488 Italia. He also has a 25,000-hectare cattle ranch in Idaho.

After his run Manny spent three hours in the upscale Elorde Gym inside the Mall of Asia shopping complex in Manila, taking a break from work in the Philippines Senate to go through a fifteen-round training session. According to the Sports Interactive Network of the Philippines, he did five rounds on the punching mitts, followed by two rounds on the heavy bag and two more on the double-end ball, before turning the speed ball into a blur for another two rounds. He finished off with two rounds of shadow boxing and two of skipping then ten minutes of stomach exercises.

His workout also contained five minutes of prayers.

The world champ was put through his paces by his assistant trainers Buboy Fernandez and Nonoy Neri. Freddie Roach had still not arrived to supervise the fight preparations.

A large gathering of reporters were at his training headquarters to welcome Manny's return to serious boxing work. 'Well, I'm glad to be back,' he told them. 'Being back in the ring gives me a wonderful feeling. There is extra adrenaline in my body. As I have been telling you, I am not taking my opponent for granted. We have been very busy in the Senate with committee hearings in the morning and the afternoon session until evening. But now it's a relatively light schedule so I can train seriously for the fight.'

After having taunted me for weeks over the Amir Khan fight, this time Manny tweeted, 'Great to be back in the gym'.

By now ticket sales for the bout were pushing the 40,000 mark. Bob Arum was amazed. He thought the fight would do well but this was record sales territory. 'Tremendous, absolutely tremendous – never seen anything like it really,' Bob told the American media. 'The whole of Australia is engaged in it. The ticket sales have been absolutely enormous. It's trending towards a sell-out. Horn has resonated with the public in Australia. I think Pacquiao is an icon. The reception that they gave Pacquiao was unbelievable and Pacquiao appeals to the Australians because of his humble nature and they fell in love with him.'

Manny continued to play mind games with me, training hard some days and taking it easy on others. A group of a dozen Australian journalists spent five days with him in mid-May. On the first day of their tour they arrived at Manny's mansion in Forbes Park because he was supposed to run in the morning. The reporters waited outside his house for two hours. Assistant trainer Buboy Fernandez came out to see them, as did Manny's younger brother, Bobby Pacquiao, a former champion, who said I would provide a difficult test for Manny but that speed and experience would prevail. A police escort turned up to follow Manny on his run, then soon after a security officer arrived on a motorbike. Some of the ten bodyguards who live at the house wandered about the yard where the champ lives with his wife and five children, eight maids and four cooks.

The reporters were told that Manny had been out late the night before after a big training session, that he normally does two or three loops of a 3-kilometre road circuit which passes his house and that he can fly round one loop in just eleven minutes.

He was so fast, in fact, that for most of the day, he vanished.

A year earlier Manny had been targeted by an Islamic terror gang and he was still terrified of his family being kidnapped. But on this morning he apparently seemed more afraid of getting sore legs than falling into the clutches of evil extremists.

After the journalists' two-hour wait, Manny eventually sent out a staff member to say he would not be running. Finally, in the early afternoon, with the air conditioner turned up high at the Elorde Gym, he arrived with a police escort in an armoured car for a two-hour training session in front of the media, displaying all that vaunted speed and declaring that he was certainly not underestimating me.

According to the observers, he was astonishingly quick in his training session. He may not have trained with the intensity that Glenn and I were working at, but the rat-a-tat-tat of his blistering punches could have been the soundtrack for a war movie as he slammed them into Buboy's punching mitts.

The fight was shaping up as two machine guns blazing away at close range, even though Manny reckoned he was still only 60 per cent fit. He said the hard work would really begin when Freddie Roach and his Australian conditioning coach, Justin Fortune, arrived in Manila six weeks before the fight.

In his workouts for the media, Manny would finish every session bathed in sweat. He said he drank six litres of water a day and had to visit the bathroom every thirty minutes. So frequent, in fact, were his toilet breaks that he had taken to keeping a bucket beside his bed in his mansion in Manila.

Buboy Fernandez, who once slept under Manny's bed in a gym when they were both dirt poor, took the brunt of the champ's fury. Several times Buboy cried out in pain as Manny's power shots detonated on the trainer's punching pads. Manny signalled his fight plan for me at the start of every round of training, charging from the corner at the bell and throwing lightning bursts of punches.

Away from the gym Manny let reporters peer into an extraordinary life. He admitted that he was not the saintly figure in which he is sometimes depicted. Speaking so softly that he was almost inaudible, he chatted to them about strippers and casinos and wild sex.

He credited his long-suffering spouse, Jinkee, for turning his whole life and soul around. Manny drinks nothing stronger than water these days but he used to be an entirely different beast, and his story of redemption is as compelling as the tale of the homeless street kid who scrapped his way through life's briars to become a sporting icon.

'I used to be drinking every night,' he told the journalists, admitting that he was once an uncontrollable wild man – reckless, feckless and dangerous to know. He was a multimillionaire by his late twenties, owned a casino and ran a strip club employing a hundred girls. He was unfaithful to Jinkee many times, he said. Although now he is a member of the Philippines government advocating the death penalty for drug dealers, he once used cocaine, methamphetamines and marijuana. He would often neglect his family to go out smoking, gambling and womanising, but now he attends Bible readings every day with Jinkee, who has encouraged the enormous transformation in his life.

Jinkee was contemplating divorce in 2011 until Pacquiao had what he calls 'a spiritual reawakening' and became a non-denominational Christian. He said he experienced dreams and visions and heard the voice of God – it was so powerful that he felt he was trembling and melting and that he had died and was born again.

Manny has a staff of about a hundred in the Philippines. One of the men closest to him is David Sisson, a 25-year-old son of American missionaries who have preached the gospel in Manny's hometown of General Santos City for more than two decades. 'Manny was a wild guy, really crazy,' the young Baptist told the Australian journalists. 'I've known him since I was eight years old. He grew up a Catholic and he and his wife Jinkee had a lot of problems in their marriage. It's amazing to see how Manny went from that lifestyle to what he has now as a devoted family man and a well-respected senator. The days of partying and drinking are over.'

It is not uncommon for Manny to spend $30,000 on a

dinner for his staff or to press wads of cash – or a newly constructed house – into the hands of the needy.

Sisson claims Manny's decision to build 1000 houses for the poor, paid for from his own pocket, shows the purity of heart in a man who spent much of his life off the rails.

*

I continued to work hard with Glenn and, for two days a week, with Dundee Kim, whose weight-training program and punch-pad work were crucial to our fight plan. Glenn is the guy who taught me how to make a fist, how to throw a punch and how to make someone attacking me miss with their punches. And Dundee is the guy who put muscle and strength on my frame, which I knew could let me overcome anything Manny threw at me. Glenn did bodybuilding for ten years himself. He knows the benefits of weight training for boxers. Much of the physical training with Dundee involved strengthening my back, shoulders, chest and arms. Much of the training I did with Glenn involved strengthening my mind and skills.

Glenn always told me that toughness isn't about how many tattoos you've got or how you act or how big you talk. It comes from belief in yourself. He said I had developed that belief through a positive focus and years of hard physical and mental training.

I knew that Manny Pacquiao would soon be coming for me.

And nice guy that he is, I knew he would test my toughness to the limit.

14

Our children are our greatest treasure. They are our future.

– Nelson Mandela, South African president

MY WIFE, JO, HAD tears in her eyes when she came rushing into our back shed with news that would change our lives forever. I was rushing myself, striding out on my electric treadmill, clocking up the kilometres on my charge towards Manny Pacquiao's world title.

Jo was more emotional than I'd seen her for a long time. She had dramatic news and wasn't sure just how to deliver it. I thought for a moment there had been some terrible accident. It was just the opposite. Some wonderful news that we'd both planned for.

'Jeffrey,' she said, her voice cracking with emotion, 'I think I'm pregnant.'

She was holding a small white plastic stick showing two clear lines. The pregnancy test had confirmed our great expectations.

I jumped off the treadmill immediately, as it continued to hum along on its own. Manny Pacquiao could wait.

'Hey, isn't that a good thing?' I said kissing the love of my life. 'This is the best news ever. What are you crying for?'

Getting a fight with Manny was a dream come true, but this made a world title pale into insignificance.

'I'm crying,' Jo said, 'because I'm so happy.'

Jo was so emotional because we'd been married for two and a half years and at that point in our lives we were afraid that we might not be able to have kids. The little white message stick told us a different story.

It was early May 2017 and I was ramping up the intensity of my campaign to take Manny's world title, busy filling in all the workout demands on the extensive spreadsheet that Glenn prepares for all my fights.

The excitement of our impending parenthood added to the thrill surrounding this golden opportunity I'd been given to set up my family for life.

My agitation went to new levels. At the best of times, I'm always looking for my keys and my wallet. Jo says one of the reasons I'm so fit is because I'm always running around the house looking for things. As I prepared to face the greatest challenge of my life at Suncorp Stadium, and as I tried to fit in seemingly endless media commitments and appearances, it was not uncommon for me to be running late for the gym and bolt out of the house only to bolt back in because I'd forgotten my towel and bottle of water. And my keys and wallet.

As Manny Pacquiao headed towards the biggest crowd to ever see him fight, he was a little more elaborate in his travel arrangements.

He left General Santos City bound for Brisbane on 24 June aboard a specially chartered AirAsia Airbus A330, along with 160 of his family, friends and members of his boxing entourage, including his wife, Jinkee, adviser Michael Koncz and his corner team of Freddie Roach, Justin Fortune and Buboy Fernandez. The aircraft's customised body featured a giant image of the Filipino icon in a fierce fighting pose, and he was given a military guard of honour as he boarded the flight, walking the red carpet to the jet while saluting a cordon of soldiers who presented arms.

The fighting pride of the Philippines was on the line. Manny declared that, 'In all my years of boxing, I have never been as motivated and fired up as for this fight. My team is very happy with my preparation. I am looking forward to this and I will be coming home as world champion. This is Jeff Horn's big chance and I know how Jeff Horn is feeling this week.'

Nervous, that's how.

I put on the best game face I could and told everyone I was supremely confident, but I knew that in Manny I was facing a mountain of Everest proportions.

He had spent the final three weeks of his preparation in his hometown of General Santos City, despite martial law operating in the area because of terrorist threats. His A-team of Roach and Fortune had arrived in Manila five weeks earlier. Back then, they had said they were disappointed with Manny's form and castigated their boss for spending too much time at his day job in the Philippines parliament rather than in maintaining his focus on me. But, by the time they boarded the flight to Brisbane, they had spent three weeks in General Santos City and were telling a different story. They said Manny had lifted his game to the point where they could laugh off my chances.

Roach said he was expecting Manny to score a spectacular knockout and that they were chasing a mega-millions rematch with Floyd Mayweather and needed an impressive win to push their case. After flattening me, Roach said, they could go on to 'bigger and better things'. 'I've been looking for a big knockout from Manny for a long time now,' he told the media, 'and I think you're going to see it in this fight.'

Manny had used four sparring partners in the closing stages of his preparation – Philippines-based Leonardo Doronio and Sonny Katiandagho, as well as the world-rated Australian lightweight George Kambosos Jnr, and the Mexican Adrian Young, who had been knocked to the canvas twice as Manny sharpened his timing and distance. Kambosos had just beaten my old rival Qamil Balla and reckoned I had no hope against the world welterweight champ.

'Manny is the best in the world, an eleven-time world champion, so fast and there's a big level of difference with Horn,' Kambosos told *The Manila Times*. 'I think Manny will knock Horn out within six rounds. Horn won't last. He can't get away from Manny's shots.' Thanks, mate.

Justin Fortune said the only way Manny could possibly lose would be if he tripped on the way to the ring. 'Manny is one of the greats and Jeff Horn is in a different league,' he said. 'If Manny puts his mind to it, he destroys anybody in the world. He's busted up some of the greats. Jeff Horn is the guy to knock out and we're in the hurt business.'

Fortune was especially critical of my decision to use Czar Amonsot as my main sparring partner for the later stages of my preparation. Czar is a Filipino southpaw based in Melbourne and he had boxed on the same card the night I knocked out Samuel Colomban. According to Fortune, I should have gone to America for sparring instead and that, since I hadn't done my homework, 'The Fighting Schoolteacher' would be totally outclassed. 'Horn won't know what hit him because Manny is that quick,' Fortune said.

But Glenn and I were very happy with Czar, who was now the No. 3 ranked junior-welterweight (63 kg) in the world and undefeated for a decade. He is a strong, tough guy and, in our torrid sessions twice a week for three weeks, he tried to push me to breaking point. It was impossible for anyone to copy Manny's style, but Glenn and I got the closest thing out there that we could.

Some critics believed I should have used multiple sparring partners, doing alternate rounds, so that they would always be fresh and fit and going at me hammer and tongs each round. But Glenn thought that it was better to use the one opponent in sparring – that would best simulate a fight situation so that I didn't have to adjust all the time to the different styles and the different timings each fighter would bring into the ring. He wanted someone who was battle-fit, someone who could do twelve rounds straight and give me the hardest sparring of my life. All the time, Glenn told Czar to 'attack, attack, attack' with everything he had. The idea was to do the most gruelling stuff possible in the gym so that I was certain I could handle anything Manny threw at me. One of my big weapons would be my unconventional style and the element of surprise it presented, but I also wanted to ensure my body and mind were tempered like the steel of a samurai sword, ready for anything. Our sparring sessions included low blows, head clashes and punches after the bell. Czar's trainer, the veteran Ray Giles, who has been involved in boxing since the days he helped the great Lionel Rose, said my timing was 'impeccable' and that I would 'definitely' catch Manny with my lightning right hand.

During my sparring sessions, which began at 1.30 p.m. – the time we were expected in the ring on 2 July – a recording of crowd noises was pumped through the gym's speakers to simulate the sound of the 50,000 fans expected. I tried to set up the mental imagery of what it would be like on the day of the fight and having my hand raised in victory.

I finished sparring ten days before the fight. My last session with Czar was the best of my campaign. Usually I don't spar that well in the last session, but I was on fire in this hit-out and felt very confident I would get the job done in the real thing.

The next day I was visited by triple world champ Jeff Fenech, who flew up from Sydney with his boxer, Brock Jarvis, who was fighting on the undercard. Standing outside Suncorp for a photoshoot beside the statue of Wally Lewis holding the Origin shield aloft, Jeff had some simple advice for my fight strategy.

'Just bash the bloke in close,' Jeff said. 'It's no more Mr Nice Guy now. I'm not saying break the rules, but you have to rough Manny up. Do everything to hurt him in close. Twist him, twist his knees, use your weight advantage, bully him – bang your shoulder into him. Manny can punch at a distance, so close the distance. Stay on his chest and make him feel all of his thirty-eight years.'

It was awesome to receive Jeff's backing – he was one boxing expert who had believed in me right from the start of my career. But Glenn was crafting and distilling his own ten-point plan for victory, which revolved around me 'controlling the gap' and avoiding Manny's big left hand. We knew it would be professional suicide for me to simply try to overpower Manny the way that fighters such as Ricky Hatton had done. They were ferocious sluggers but they ended up splattered on the canvas.

I kept a busy routine in training, fulfilling many interview requests, which I was glad to do because I saw myself as promoting a good image for boxing to the world. I helped Dundee Kim and the 'Boxing for Confidence' course that he was taking to Springwood State High School, getting the kids to do boxing training without anyone getting punched. All the work was done on the heavy bag and punching pads, which is great for fitness.

Jo and I went to see the first Origin game at Suncorp, in which the Blues ran away for a 28–4 win, gaining early bragging rights in a series the Maroons eventually won. We had tried to keep the news of Jo's pregnancy out of the media in the lead-up because of the distraction and extra pressures news of it would create. But my inner circle knew all about it. While I was punching on over twelve rounds with Czar, Lillian Rushton was in the background cuddling Jo and congratulating her.

All the time Glenn and I were going over exactly what I needed for victory. I had to have a very strong belief in my own physical capabilities. Glenn is a great proponent of self-belief but just believing in yourself isn't enough, he says. You have to be sensible and realistic and you've got to put in the hard work and craft a good plan backed with science.

Some of the things Glenn said to motivate me in the few weeks before the fight were profound.

'Manny is just a man,' he would say. 'He can't hit you with a right legend or a left experience. Let's focus on the positives. Manny is thirty-eight years of age – and, yes, he's a legend of the sport – but let's think of him as a little old man who is ready to be beaten by someone bigger, younger, stronger and fresher. Someone who is hungrier.'

Glenn said if I followed his plan I would win the fight. Such is the relationship he and I have built up over the years, if he looks me in the eye and tells me I can win I accept the fact. I had that trust, a logical plan and I knew I had done the preparation. So I didn't care what the rest of the world thought. I was happy that so many experts were writing me off because it only fuelled my desire to prove them wrong. I believed I could win and so did the people around me and that's all that mattered. Manny could not derail me so long as I stayed on the tracks that Glenn had laid down. By the time Manny arrived in Brisbane with all the pomp of a presidential visit aboard his chartered flight, I was ready for him.

When Manny read Jeff Fenech's advice to me in *The Courier-Mail*, a huge grin broke across his face at the thought of a vicious brawl.

He said he was ready too.

*

The day after Manny arrived in Brisbane, he and Jinkee and a busload of his team, as well as a convoy of media, went to the WorshipCentre Christian Church in Carina in Brisbane's south for a two-hour Sunday morning service. Manny said he had not gone to church to ask for divine help for his fight on the following Sunday but rather to thank God for all his blessings. He said his five children had stayed at home in the Philippines and were expecting to watch their dad beat me on TV.

Not everyone was so sure though. Bob Arum was warning Manny and Freddie Roach not to underestimate my strength and determination. Ring announcer Michael Buffer, a Richard Gere lookalike and the silky voice of a savage sport, had seen enough upsets in his thirty-five years in boxing to know that I could stun Manny and the odds-makers. The former male model, who has made millions from his trademark 'Let's get ready to rumble', was in Brisbane for the big fight, and said that, at thirty-eight, Manny could be getting ready to crumble. He told the press that the Battle of Brisbane could develop into a real-life Cinderella story.

The excitement over the fight had grown to unprecedented proportions. Brisbane was festooned with Pac–Horn banners and posters, and there were reports on the back and front pages of *The Courier-Mail* every day and lead items on all the radio and television news services.

I went through a public workout near the Treasury Casino three days before the fight, but such were the concerns over the crowds the police advised Manny not to appear. He did turn up at a 'legends' lunch' though, at the Brisbane Convention and Exhibition Centre two days before the fight, along with other boxing greats such as Fenech, Joseph Parker and Roberto Durán. The latter, when asked if I had any hope against Manny, replied, 'Yes. Why not? Why can't he win?

He is bigger than Pacquiao and strong. I hope it is a great fight for the public and for the world.' Durán had once held the world welterweight title I was contesting, having won it from Sugar Ray Leonard in 1980. The crowd for that epic fight at the Olympic Stadium in Montreal was more than 46,000. Manny and I had now sold more tickets than that.

At the same lunch, Tim Bradley, now a commentator for ESPN and a winner in one of three fights with Manny, also said I had a shot at winning and doing 'something great' but that I would have to knock Manny cold to do it. 'Even at thirty-eight, Manny is still lightning fast,' Bradley said. 'It's going to be so tough for Jeff to win by a decision against a guy who is so busy and has such speed and experience.'

At least that was a better chance than Bradley's co-commentator and former trainer, Teddy Atlas, was willing to give me.

Atlas told the T2T Boxing channel that the fight wouldn't even be competitive, that there was such a difference, not only in experience but talent, it was 'not a close contest'.

'With Manny you don't have a common guy,' he told ESPN. 'You have a star, a big shot, an athlete with great talent who has been successful on the world stage in some of the biggest fights of this generation. Then when you add in the charitable and philanthropic work he does, you've got something special. Not everyone has a whole country that follows them – that doesn't happen all of the time. But he's a legend and legends have huge fan bases that travel everywhere to see them.'

The penny dropped. Teddy had me getting squashed even before the opening bell. His commentary would reflect his prediction.

★

I was planning to take in a weight advantage against Manny of about 5 kilograms, an advantage I saw as a hefty head-start, but Teddy said even that would do me no good because I would simply be outclassed.

The weight limit for the fight was 66.68 kilograms – or 147 pounds in the old imperial measure – and both of us had to be on or under that for the official weigh-in at Suncorp on the morning before the fight.

According to Roach, Manny was naturally a much smaller man and had been as light as 62 kilograms in recent weeks. The weight advantage would definitely help me in the later rounds, because we would be pushing against each other all the time and Manny was going to be pushing a lot more weight than me. But Roach didn't think I would still be there for the later rounds.

I am normally about 71 kilograms in the few days before a fight, but I had been sitting at 70.2, 70.3, for the last few days as though my body instinctively knew the weight had to come down. Controlling my weight around fight time is something I've got used to over the last decade. I aim to retain physical strength while dropping weight fast.

My focus was razor sharp.

On Friday, two days before the fight and with the weigh-in approaching, I ate eggs and avocado on toast for breakfast, a small wrap at lunchtime and a small Caesar salad to ward off the hunger at 5 p.m. Then I had my very last training session. I did four rounds of pads, two rounds of shadow boxing and two rounds of skipping. It was just a light session to get me sweating and commence the dehydration process.

I wore a sweat suit made from a fabric that doesn't breathe and which really makes me perspire. I was hoping to start the session at 70.2 kilograms, but to my dismay I'd miscalculated and was 70.9.

I was down to 69.2 kilograms after the workout. Glenn said I went really well, like a racehorse chomping at the bit and ready to charge.

I hoped to drop 500 grams while I slept.

I had no dinner or water and woke up on Saturday morning, jumped on my scales and was at 68.55 kilograms. At 7.30 a.m., I drove over to Stephen Edwards' house at Holland Park. Stephen is a great cut man, fixing up my torn eyebrows during bouts, and he helps me cut weight as well.

My plan was to jump into his bath full of steaming hot water to sweat off 2 kilos as I had done for previous fights in Brisbane. Stephen said 68.55 kilograms was fine and appeared very calm. But inside his head he was screaming, *Holy crap, we have one hour to lose just under 2 kilos and then get to Suncorp Stadium by 9.05 a.m.* We are very precise in our calculations and measurements. Before getting in the bath, I jumped on Stephen's scales with my undies on. My dry weight at 7.46 a.m. showed 68.15 kilos. Stephen's scales were 400 grams different from mine. We were now confused over just how much weight was really on the line. Still wearing my undies, I jumped into the hot bath while Stephen went next door to wake up his neighbour and borrow her scales to see what they read.

At 8.05 a.m. I climbed out of the bath, a bit dehydrated, starving and light-headed from the heat. Stephen insisted I'm the only man he has ever helped out of a hot bath, but he steadied me to make sure I didn't fall and split my head open on the steps, which would have stuffed up the biggest fight in Australia's history. Both Stephen's scales and those of the neighbour's registered 67.20 kilos. I was breathing a little easier, but I still had a way to go. Stephen boiled the kettle and poured it into his bath to spike it back up and I went back to poaching myself. Stephen took a photo of me in the tub, promising to think up a good meme to embarrass me. Again, he assured me I was the only man he had ever photographed in a bath. At this stage I thought he was protesting a bit too much.

At 8.15 a.m. I climbed out of the bath again and weighed 66.80 kilos. I knew that I would continue to sweat on the way to the stadium but we were still not sure if the scales were correct. If my scales at home were right, then I was still 67.20kg. We had to weigh in at or under 66.68. My wet undies weighed around 150 grams. It was all very close and we were nervous about which scales were correct. So it was back in the bath and another kettle of hot water for good measure.

By 8.25 a.m. I weighed 66.40 kilos on both scales. We were now good to go even if they were out because I could always ditch the undies on the official scales if I had to. Stephen said he would take a large orange towel embroidered with 'Jeff the Hornet Horn' to screen me from the cameras and preserve my modesty if that happened. I got dressed in dry undies and shorts, donned a Hornet T-shirt and jacket and headed off to Suncorp. My plan was to get there around 9 a.m. and jump on the official scales for a test run. If I was well under, I would have a small measured amount of water – 100 millilitres, equalling around 100 grams. If I was a bit over, I was ready to go nude.

There was a media frenzy awaiting us at Suncorp. The weigh-in was being beamed live around the world and we were told we had to be on the scales in five minutes. Holy crap, no test run. If we weighed in over the limit, it would be witnessed by millions live. Stephen was absolutely churning inside as I jumped on the scales, surrounded by Glenn and the rest of my team. Hundreds of cameras and microphones were recording everything. I weighed in at 66.35 kilos, well inside the limit, and did a muscle flex. Stephen gave me a bottle of Powerade and I started chugging it down as media from all around the world grabbed me for live feeds. Manny weighed in at 66.1 kilos but said he'd had no problems with the weight and had just eaten a big breakfast. I had lost 4.6 kilos in just fifteen hours. Some of the media commented that I looked gaunt and drained, but I knew that after rehydrating and fuelling up on carbohydrates the only thing I would be starving for would be victory.

Asked to pose for a face-off, Manny and I stared at each other close up as the sound of camera motor drives resembled an aircraft taking off in the background. This time neither of us was laughing. Manny's eyes were no longer shining, but instead glinted with the prospect of imminent battle and what would be a fight for survival. 'Tomorrow is going to be fun,' Manny told the press, but despite the fact that he would start the fight a five-to-one favourite, deep down in his soul he must have known that this could be a life-changing moment for both of us.

Glenn told the media this was going to be a 'Sunday, bloody Sunday' and that we were ready for war.

I said, 'The game face is on now, school's out. I can't wait to get out there and get the job done.'

*

After the weigh-in my team went through my normal pre-fight routine. We had lunch together and then I played poker with Glenn, Dad, Ben, Stephen Edwards and a few others. I had played poker before previous fights and won and I liked that routine. I was hoping they might let me win this time, given the fact that I had a fairly important assignment the next day, but they are all very competitive like me and would concede nothing. I think it was the first game I ever lost to them. Jo was fretting that my luck might have run out and was saying, 'Oh my gosh, I hope this isn't a bad sign.' But Mum put me in a much better mood when she came over to make me a pasta meal for dinner. Then Jo and I sat together on the couch like we do most nights and chilled watching some light-hearted movie interspersed with a fair bit of channel surfing. I wanted a clear head so that in the morning my mind was centred on just one thing – winning the world welterweight title.

At the same time as Jo and I were relaxing together in our little house, Manny Pacquiao was holed up at the Sofitel Hotel, one of Brisbane's grandest establishments, with many of his 'closest friends' and family and was leading a prayer gathering. The glaring disparity in our lifestyles was obvious.

I never wavered in my belief that I would win. Three days before the fight, my auntie Kathy Chambers cut my hair and I'd asked her to be extra careful with the style because half a billion people would be watching. Kathy had broken her ankle and was cutting my hair while perched on a little scooter to aid her mobility. I don't know if it was nerves or not, but she fell off her scooter as she was doing my hair and had to grab me by the collar to stop from hitting the floor.

Dad and I had talked a lot about using a win over Manny to catapult me into more big fights, to strike while the iron was hot. As Jo and I sat on the couch after dinner, we talked over a couple of announcements I planned to make the next day to a worldwide TV audience, rehearsing exactly what I should say. I had some visual props prepared – a walking stick and an extra set of boxing gloves to take with me. I normally drive myself to fights with Jo, but in the morning a limo was coming to pick me up so that I could relax and not worry about people cutting in on me on what were expected to be crowded roads heading to the stadium. The limo turned out to be a party van, but that was still okay.

I went to bed at about 10 o'clock and I was asleep by 10.30. Jo reckons I was snoring by 10.33. Loudly. But she let me have as much shut-eye as possible.

Jo's pregnancy was a life-changing event for both of us. At Suncorp Stadium I would try to give her and our new baby a performance to remember.

I wanted it to be a victory that all of Australia could celebrate.

15

Rhythm is everything in boxing. Every move you make starts with your heart, and that's in rhythm or you're in trouble. Your rhythm should set the pace of the fight. If it does, then you penetrate your opponent's rhythm. You make him fight your fight, and that's what boxing is all about.

– Sugar Ray Robinson, world welterweight and middleweight champ

IT WAS THE WALL of humanity that hit me long before Manny Pacquiao. People everywhere – the biggest crowd ever for a boxing match in Australia and about 50,000 more than had ever seen me fight in my home city.

As I came out of the dressing room on that brilliant, breeze-less Sunday afternoon at Suncorp Stadium and headed towards the boxing ring, it was as though I was marching through an enormous tunnel constructed out of people. The noise of their cheering literally hurt my ears. I had my game face on though and, as Glenn nodded and waved at the large sections of the crowd, thanking them all for coming out to support the nerdy kid made good, I stared straight ahead at my future. It was right there in front of me, inside the ropes of a boxing ring erected in the middle of the huge footy ground where I had only ever been as a spectator. Now the eyes of the sporting world were upon me.

I marched forward resolutely, the cheers washing over me like waves and only once did my composure crack – when I saw my pop, Ray Horn, all eighty-nine years of him and still punching. He was sitting beside the blue corner which would be my base camp as I launched this most audacious ascent towards the top of boxing's elite. I stopped briefly and patted Ray on the forearm with the gloves that I would soon hurl at Pacquiao. Then I climbed the four blue wooden stairs and I was standing on the canvas where I hoped to paint my masterpiece.

All around me there were people yelling and cheering and chanting 'Horn-et, Horn-et'. As much as I tried to simply focus on the job at hand, the atmosphere was so electric I felt as though I'd been zapped.

*

Even before I made my entrance into the wall of sound out in the middle of the stadium, this had been a monumental day in the history of Australian boxing. Jeff Fenech had overcome the death of his mother, Mary, a day earlier to lead Brock Jarvis to another victory on the undercard, my old amateur peer David Toussaint had beaten American Shane Mosley Jnr, and my London Olympic teammate Damien Hooper had scored the biggest win of his career with an upset points decision over the big, bearded Russian Umar Salamov.

Our team had also been involved in a couple of bitter fights in the dressing rooms. Stephen Edwards' day had started with him working in Damien Hooper's corner. Damien was cut in the second round and Stephen went to work, staunching the bleeding with a combination of the coagulant adrenaline, a jumbo swab and Vaseline, and using a small cold, flat iron called an end-swell to slow the swelling. It was good practice for what was to come in my fight.

After that bout, Stephen moved into my room and started getting ready for the Pacquiao fight. About ninety minutes before I was due to fight, there was a big altercation over the tape used to cover the gauze on my hands. Glenn was wrapping my fists in the time-honoured practice that fighters go through before a bout to stop their hands breaking. We were using a tan-coloured tape that would not have raised eyebrows anywhere else in the world. But Freddie Roach who was watching on in our dressing room – more to unsettle our team than to ensure everything was above board – insisted that only white tape be used and that was the rule in world title fights. This was a new one on us but the local boxing commission supervisor accepted this claim, despite the rules of the WBO not saying anywhere that the tape had to be white. Ben laughed at the idea that we had to change tape because of the colour and Freddie, who is notorious for playing mind games with opponents, exploded with anger, using a series of expletives that would have earned him a lengthy suspension if he'd been in my classroom. Freddie's performance was farcical and unprofessional. He became unhinged when Ben niggled him further and he threatened to punch on there and then with my brother. I know Freddie was a pretty good lightweight in his day, but if they'd come to blows my money was on Ben. I sat through Freddie's tirade impassively and, because Glenn didn't want to cause any further upset for me, he agreed to change the tape.

Manny's team had been trying to win the mental battle against me ever since the fight was signed. At the official press conference for the fight a few days earlier, during speeches by Kate Jones and Graham Quirk, Manny had spent most of the time transfixed by his mobile phone in what I took as a signal that the fight was not that important to him. On fight day though, I couldn't help but sense a degree of panic among those tasked with steering him to victory.

The level to which they stooped in trying to rattle me was quite extraordinary.

While the tape kerfuffle was going on, Stephen Edwards was preparing adrenaline to use on cuts that I might suffer in the title fight. Based on a twelve-round bout, and knowing that there was a massive chance of head clashes, he prepped around thirty vials of adrenaline. This involves breaking tiny 1-millilitre vials of liquid into sealed containers for use at ringside. Stephen, who had used about sixteen vials in the Hooper fight, did this in front of the WBO dressing-room supervisor.

Around ten minutes before we were to go out to the ring, Stephen was summoned by a local commission official, Philip Holiday, who is a former world lightweight champion. The WBO corner supervisor was nearby with a Pacquiao representative. Freddie had sent his representative to lodge a formal complaint about Stephen preparing the adrenaline in the dressing room rather than at ringside. A big argument broke out, with the Pacquiao camp saying that they couldn't tell if Stephen was really using adrenaline. Stephen said that this was bull, that if they had an allegation to make they should make it to the World Anti-Doping Agency, and they could take a sample and get it tested.

After five minutes of finger-pointing and chest-thumping from the Pacquiao team, Phil Holiday ruled that Stephen had to tip all the carefully prepared adrenaline down the sink. Stephen asked Phil if there was a specific rule that said the adrenaline vials could only be broken ringside as he had never heard of this rule. Phil said there was, but his voice and facial expression showed uncertainty.

Phil was obviously bluffed by Freddie and the Pacquiao team. Stephen has since confirmed with John Hogg, president of the Australian National Boxing Federation, that Phil didn't have the authority to make this ruling, that there was no such rule and that if he had been consulted, John would not have ruled in favour of ditching the adrenaline. There was even an argument about the type of containers Stephen was using, but Phil finally allowed them after watching Stephen wash them out.

Stephen believes that at this stage Freddie Roach thought we would have no adrenaline left and would be unable to repair any damage to me once the fight began because there was no hope of sourcing any adrenaline so close to fight time. Fortunately Stephen is slightly obsessive-compulsive and he had stuffed twenty extra vials into the bottom corner of his bag just in case. Stephen scrambled to grab those vials just as we were given word by the television producers that it was time to walk out to centre ring.

*

We posed for one final photo of the team in the dressing room – me, Glenn, Ben, Dundee Kim, Joe Goodall, Adam Copland, Sam Banney, Steve Scanlan and Stephen Edwards. Then we headed out the door and into the labyrinth of tunnels under Suncorp Stadium.

Glenn's words were ringing in my ears as we got ready to go. All along he had said Manny was underestimating me.

'They don't know how good Jeff is,' Glenn had said on the eve of the fight, 'but they will find out tomorrow how tough he is, and how competitive and technically proficient he is. It will be a gruelling fight and we plan to grind Pacquiao down.'

I had read and re-read Glenn's detailed ten-point plan in the lead-up to this moment many, many times. Now it flashed before my eyes like a neon sign.

Gap control. Maintain the correct distance from him, Glenn said.

Recovery, he said. When you throw punches make sure your hands are up on the way out.

Constant head movement, he said. Keep Manny guessing and off balance.

Keep moving to the left, he said. Avoid Manny's big straight left at all times.

Rhythm, he said. Break Manny's rhythm. Keep him frustrated.

Glenn said that the gap control – taking charge of the distance from Manny – was the secret to nullifying his electrifying speed. Once I had adapted to his speed and power, I could then start to break him down. It was all based around the gap. Glenn had always told me that if the opponent was faster, I needed more reaction time and that meant staying at the right distance. I had to be a constantly moving target.

I had to get in front on the scorecards and stay in front, he said. I couldn't let Manny get two or three rounds in the bank early on.

So, I was ready for a fast start.

*

Even though I had visualised this moment so many times in the weeks leading up to the fight, nothing quite prepared me for the massive sea of fans cheering as I came out onto the ground. I walked to the ring surrounded by a large team of security staff and my team, who were all dressed in their black-and-orange Hornet uniforms. I felt relaxed and I was soaking up the atmosphere as Glenn guided my steps, making sure I didn't trip or stumble.

On the loud speakers Jack White was blasting out 'Seven Nation Army', my entrance song. The people lining my pathway were right on top of us and all around. It was just as well I could see light at the end of this human tunnel or I might not have found the ring. It felt like I was going through a maze of people. Glenn was annoyed that the sun was streaming all over the ring – we thought the canopy above the canvas would be much bigger. He had to put on his sunglasses to stop squinting. I stopped briefly at ringside to say hello to my pop.

Then I was in the ring, under the white hot incubator lights and the glare of a worldwide audience.

Manny came out moments later to AC/DC's 'Thunderstruck' and the crowd was rocking as he walked through the wall of people, smiling and waving without a care in the world. I caught sight of him coming to the ring on the big screen and vowed to wipe that smile off his face.

As Manny made his way to the Battle of Brisbane, commentator Bob Sheridan was telling his audience, 'Here he comes, one of the best fighters who ever lived,' and he started rattling off the names of all the men Manny had mugged. It was an impressive list. Manny had twice as many knockout wins on his record as I had fights. Fifty-nine wins, six losses, two draws, thirty-eight knockouts.

It was the six losses that interested me. Three of them were in his last eight fights. I was ready to make it four from nine.

As I waited with my team in the corner, bouncing on the soles of my orange-and-black Everlast boots, I tried to stay centred and not get emotional or caught up in the excitement.

The sun bathed the ring in a golden glow as Manny dropped to his knees in a corner and prayed that he and I would get through the fight safely.

By now 'Eye of the Tiger' was erupting from the stadium speakers. Glenn told me just to stay cool as we waited for Michael Buffer, the iconic announcer, immaculate in his dinner jacket, to take centre stage.

'Ladeeez and gentlemen,' he began, 'from Suncorp Stadium in Brisbane, Queensland, Australia – this is the moment we've all been waiting for ...'

I had mentally prepared myself for all of this – standing there with my team in the corner, seeing Manny across the ring. I had imagined what they would say to me – the fight felt very déjà vu because it was going exactly as Glenn and I had planned.

'It is brought to you,' Buffer continued, 'by Hall of Fame promoter Mr Bob Arum with his Top Rank Incorporated and Duco Events in association with the Queensland government and Brisbane City Council.'

All the time Manny was across the ring from me smiling and chatting to his corner team as if this was a walk in the park. In his sunglasses Glenn looked like a cool hipster, though Manny probably thought Glenn was trying to send a Mafioso look to the opposition.

'This is it, twelve rounds of boxing,' Buffer declared, 'for the WBO welterweight championship of the world ...'

Dundee Kim gave me a quick swig from a bottle of Mount Franklin water. If I was worried about getting a big head from all of this attention, it was too late because I looked out at the big screens around the ground and my face looked about six storeys high.

'And now the officials are ready,' Buffer said. 'The fighters are in the ring and they are ready.'

The cheering boomed around the stadium. Nine years earlier, in one of the first fights I ever saw, Buffer had introduced Manny Pacquiao and Oscar De La Hoya before their super fight. Now it was my turn before a much bigger crowd.

'Boxing fans, are you ready? For the thousands in attendance and the millions watching around the world – ladies and gentlemen ...'

Buffer paused briefly for effect and then ... *'LET'S GET READY TO RUMBLE!!!!'*

As focused as I was, the hairs stood up on the back of my neck. Sitting beside the ring Mum and Jo were holding hands, ready to cheer their lungs out or to comfort each other in their distress.

Then Buffer looked towards me.

'Introducing first, fighting out of the blue corner, with his head trainer, Glenn Rushton. Wearing orange with black. Official weight 66.35 kilograms or 147 pounds. This Australian Olympian now has an undefeated professional record consisting of seventeen fights. From Brisbane, Queensland, he's the fighting pride of Australia, the undefeated WBO No. 2 ranked welterweight challenger in the world ... Jeff "The Hornet" Hooooooorrrrnnnnn.'

It was a battle not to jump for joy. I don't usually get overawed but this was astonishing.

'And across the ring, his opponent, fighting out of the red corner, his head trainer, Freddie Roach. Wearing red and blue and weighing in officially at 66.1 kilograms, the fighting pride of the Philippines, the reigning defending WBO welterweight champion of the world ... Manny "Pacman" Pacquuioooooowwww.'

The roar was just as mighty.

The referee for the fight, Mark Nelson, a diminutive print operator and picture framer from Maplewood, Minnesota, summoned us to centre ring. Manny was still smiling like a school kid hiding a naughty secret from the teacher. The referee told us to touch gloves and, as we did so, Nelson gave us a final, 'Good luck to both of you'.

We went back to our corners and waited for the opening bell that would define the rest of our lives.

Manny was bouncing in his corner, still smiling as he high-fived his team. To me he wasn't focused. He was just too relaxed for the brutality that was about to go down.

I shuffled my feet in the corner and gave a steely gaze across the ring. I was all business. In my head over and over again was Glenn's mantra.

Gap control, recovery, head movement, stay away from the left hand.

Gap control, recovery, head movement, stay away from the left hand.

Gap control, recovery ...

BING

Round 1

Here we go.

I attacked immediately. I came out to show Manny that I was the boss, not him. Feigning with my jab, moving to the left, I threw a big looping hook that he took on the gloves. I wasn't intimidated by him at all. I knew I had to take the initiative, that if I gave him too much respect he'd get the upper hand. When you're in there with a fast guy he already has an advantage, so you can't wait and let him dictate. You're much better to go on the attack.

I maintained the gap and was already frustrating Manny with my movement. A lot of people think boxing is just about punching but the legs are vital. Fifty-five seconds into the round I trapped Manny against the ropes and put some fast punches together, ending the volley with a looping right that snaked around the gloves and clipped him on the side of the head. He danced away with that big grin as if to say, you got me, you bugger.

Already I felt I was breaking his rhythm. Manny seemed confused. He is famed for his aggression and fighting on the back foot must have felt weird to him. He couldn't get set because he didn't really know when I was coming in to attack. Halfway through the round I had him against the ropes again and I unloaded with a burst of punches to the body and head that finished with a hard left uppercut through the gloves he was holding tight against his face.

Bob Sheridan was yelling at ringside, 'Horn is all over him.'

With seventy-five seconds left in the round I nailed him with a solid right hand, which I felt was my best punch against him. Somehow my mouthguard dropped out. It gave Manny a brief break as the referee took me to my corner to have it replaced. But I was soon attacking again and forty seconds before the end of the round I had Manny against the ropes once more. In close I was pushing his head down in the hope of stopping head clashes. I was manhandling him. All the weight training with Dundee Kim was paying off big time. My constant movement to the left was also rattling Manny's timing so that he was like a misfiring engine. The smile left his face.

Glenn had predicted this would be a war and the most gruelling fight of Manny's career. Commentators were astounded that someone was hitting him with five- and six-punch combinations and that he was unable to fire back. By the end of the round Manny had a big frown on his face.

Now Manny knew it was going to be a tough day in the office for him. In the corner, as Stephen Edwards pressed a cold pack against my neck, Glenn waved his forefinger in my face sternly.

'Discipline,' he said. 'Remember the gap. Moving. Good recovery. You did a great job. You won that round clearly. Just be smart. Move away. Don't get carried away. Don't get careless. Stay in the moment. That was a great first round. Let's keep doing this.'

Round 2

I was starting to really impose my size and strength on Manny now. His big gun was the straight left and I knew I had to shut that down. Because of my movement away from him, he was unable to land the lead right hooks which had been a dominant punch for him for many years. Manny had a look of grim resignation on his face as he tried to up the tempo. The casual attitude was gone. I sensed he was waiting for me to make errors and burn up all my energy before launching a counter-attack. But I had plenty in the tank and midway through the round I pummelled him against the ropes again.

With a minute left in the round our heads banged together. There would be a lot more unfortunate meetings like that before the bloody battle was over. Manny caught me with a fast straight left, the first significant punch he'd landed and followed it up with another couple as he tried to accelerate. But I dug in a really hard, long straight right to the body and by the end of the round he was again in retreat.

I was walking through his punches and I have to say that at that stage I didn't really feel anything that he threw. But

I did feel the clashing of our heads and at the end of the round I was cut over the right eye by another head clash. In the corner Glenn pressed a swab soaked with adrenaline into the cut and Ben went to work on swelling around the eye. Stephen worked on the left-hand side of my face while Adam Copland was tracking the time. He called out time intervals between rounds and with fifteen seconds to go, Ben would fill the cut with Vaseline. This process continued for the remainder of the fight and Glenn and Ben did a magnificent job in controlling what was an ever increasing cut.

In the opposite corner Freddie Roach was giving Manny many sips of Fiji brand spring water – his favourite – and Buboy Fernandez was imploring him to fight in and out, in and out.

That's what Manny was trying to do, but my unpredictable rhythm was breaking his.

Round 3

I could hear the crowd roaring as I went after Manny right from the opening bell. His pre-fight plan was probably to box along with me, then throw a rapid flurry and catch me coming in as he had done against so many champions in the past. But my movement wouldn't let him get set to throw his combinations. For the first time anyone could recall, Manny was being consistently backed against the ropes. He kept trying to land the left hand but I was making him miss by a few inches nearly every time.

I could see the frustration growing on his face, like he was sitting for an exam and didn't know the answers. He was landing very few punches and when they did land they were having little effect. Manny landed another couple of lefts late in the round, but I had dominated for most of the three minutes. When I went back to the corner though, the guys had to work overtime. I was bleeding badly from the cut eye.

Round 4

Manny started to complain to the referee that I was roughing him up, which I thought was a bit rich coming from one of the most vicious fighters of all time. As it was, I was the one faring worse from the head clashes with the big cut over my eye.

I opened the fourth round with a hard straight right and he could only smile when I helped him to the canvas with a solid push after we came together in another close tussle. He just wasn't used to being treated like this and Glenn was stoked that, while Manny continued to have a perplexed look on his face, my expression didn't waver.

Blood continued to trickle down my face from the cut above my eye but I could see the finish line to this fight clearly. Although I felt I was in charge, I was still mightily impressed by Manny because no matter how many big shots I was landing he remained calm, even though his frustration was obvious. One of the commentators calling the fight for British television even went so far as to say it looked like Manny was feeling embarrassed. I was standing at a range where his speed didn't bother me because I had the reach on him. I think Ahmed El Mousaoui was just as quick as Manny, so I had seen that sort of speed before. My main concern was that the damage to my right eye was worsening. In the break between rounds, as the corner went to work plugging up the cut, Glenn said I was in front, three rounds to one, but that I had to remain disciplined.

'Keep zoning to the left,' he said. 'We've got this fight, Jeff.'

Round 5

Again we went at it and Manny tried to fight fire with fire, but I was still landing the bigger punches. After one exchange early in the round, he banged his fists together as if to say, come on, keep coming. He was rattled. I knew that he was hoping I would throw caution to the wind and charge at him recklessly. Instead I was just staying out of his range by a few centimetres and striking when it suited me.

In the times when we would throw punches and then finish in a clinch, he would say to me, 'Break, break'. Like an idiot I did what Manny told me. It happened again soon after and like an idiot I did it again. I'm just so used to hearing the 'break' call from a referee or sparring partner. Finally, I wised up and the next time he told me to 'Break, break', I said to myself, *Stuff this, you don't tell me what to do – that's the ref's job.*

At times Manny was missing wildly and with thirty seconds left in the round, he staggered and lost his balance after I clipped him with a right hand.

Round 6

Glenn and I had practised to straighten Manny up with body shots, particularly the left rip. Invariably that punch got him out of a crouch and raised him into the gun sights for my right hand.

At this stage of the fight, I felt that I was boxing my way to victory. I started the sixth as violently as any round, battering Manny against the ropes and landing a big right uppercut that snapped his head back. I roughed him up pretty badly against the ropes and, with forty-five seconds gone in the round, Mark Nelson temporarily stopped the action as blood started cascading from the right side of Manny's head after yet another accidental clash of heads.

He had sustained a wound about 3 centimetres long and looked totally bewildered. I've heard that Manny gets squeamish at the sight of his own blood and after the ringside doctor, Ben Manion, allowed the fight to continue, I put Manny under enormous pressure immediately. This was certainly the bloody Sunday that Glenn had predicted.

At the halfway mark of the fight, the British commentary team had me up five rounds to one and one of them, Barry Jones, the former world super-featherweight champion from Wales, said I was 'boxing out of my skin'. Danny Green, calling the fight for Main Event in Australia, said I was 'all over Manny Pacquiao'.

Round 7

There was a note of panic in Manny's corner now and a degree of chaos. His Argentinian cut man, Miguel Diaz, was talking to him in Spanish as he worked on stemming the blood flow from Manny's head wound. Buboy Fernandez was speaking to Manny in the Filipino language, while Freddie Roach and Justin Fortune were trying to inspire him in English.

My right-hand lead was causing Manny all sorts of problems. He now had a big wad of Vaseline inserted into the wound on the side of his head as a sort of greasy plug. It looked like a patch of grey hair. The pace of the fight and the pounding of my punches were ageing the world champ quickly. With forty-five seconds remaining, Manny emerged from another head clash with another gaping wound, this time on the left side of his scalp. If he was squeamish about the sight of his own blood he should have been used to it by now. Manny was a mess and I was making him look worse.

At the end of the round Buboy Fernandez was screaming at the referee while smacking himself repeatedly over the head protesting about the head clashes. But there was now precious little wisdom coming from Freddie Roach and Justin Fortune. They had plenty to say about me before the fight but now they were mute. Severe cases of shock can apparently do that to people. All their pre-fight bagging of me was backfiring.

After the seventh round my dad came up to Pop at ringside and said, 'Dad, in a few minutes your grandson will be the welterweight champion of the world.'

Round 8

Manny stepped up the pace now and looked more dangerous. He got onto the front foot more and had more success connecting. But I was still coming forward strongly.

Halfway through the round Manny landed a solid left hand and then pushed me to the canvas. I was on my back for the only time in the fight, but the referee correctly ruled no knockdown. The Filipino fans though, saw the fight pattern starting to change and became even more vocal in support for their hero. I had set a cracking pace but I could feel myself slowing ever so slightly. The British commentary team had me way in front, Bob Sheridan and Danny Green had me slightly ahead, and Teddy Atlas somehow had Manny Pacquiao winning a landslide. Go figure that out.

In my mind I was a mile in front, but I knew all along that great fighters find a way to win when their backs are against the wall. Manny was badly cut and weary. But faced with a humiliating defeat and a loss of face in his nation, he started to lift a gear for one final surge.

Beware the wounded beast.

Boy, did I get savaged.

Manny had one surprise after another for me as he now pushed me to the brink of defeat.

Mum and Jo were very nervous and quiet amid the roar of the crowd.

They held each other's hands more tightly than ever.

16

Rounds 10, 11 and 12 were the three greatest rounds ever seen in an Australian boxing ring.

– My dad, Jeff Horn Snr

MY FACE WAS A gory mess at the end of the eighth round and Manny could smell blood. It was not from the two deep wounds on either side of his head, but rather the sniff of victory which I now presented to him. My sisters, Mum, Dad and Jo were all on their feet applauding me, but Manny now had a glimmer of hope that he could snatch victory. His flashing burst of punches were what had made him one of the greats and he was revving the engine.

In my corner, Glenn worked on the cut over my right eye as Stephen wiped my face of the blood that was coming from my nose and around my left ear. This had been an especially brutal fight as Manny and I pushed each other to the outer limits of mental and physical endurance. We both looked the worse for wear. But Manny had made a career out of winning world title fights – this was my first. A few days before the bout, as he trained at Brisbane's Lang Park PCYC, he had said that although I might be a teacher in the classroom, he was a teacher in the ring. I knew I had to get back on top, but Manny sensed I was starting to wilt.

My dad sensed it too.

Round 9

There was still time for Manny to take control of the fight so I had to nip his renewed vigour in the bud. Immediately I went on the attack, driving him to the ropes and ripping in a big left downstairs to the body. I was still moving well and making him miss. Manny tried to throw a lead right hook, thought better of it and directed a left-hand missile at my head, but I ducked under it. With a minute gone in the round I thought I was gaining the ascendancy again, but then he timed one of my attacks beautifully and got me with a long, straight left counter-punch.

BOOM.

My head started to buzz. This was just the way I'd felt when Randall Bailey clocked me with his big right haymaker. Manny had been waiting all night for this chance. I managed to bounce away from him, using my legs to stay out of danger, but he was dogged and he started to attack constantly, firing away with that big left and just waiting for me to walk onto it. He was starting to measure me accurately and I was beginning to weaken under the fusillade of bombs. One after another. Boom. Boom. Boom. I was disorientated and for a moment felt shots hitting me everywhere. I knew I had to get on my bike and move away to recover.

Don't go down, I told myself. *Don't go down.*

With every punch that Manny landed, my head was spinning and my equilibrium was out the window. My eyesight was blurry from the cut and my legs felt like jelly.

I knew there were half a billion people watching this and I knew I could not go down.

But it was so hard to stay upright. I wasn't moving to the left like I had been earlier in the fight. Glenn was roaring at me to stick to the plan, but I was starting to go straight back and I was paying a heavy price.

With eighty seconds left in the round, my legs wobbled again from another of Manny's two-handed bursts. He was now the guy in charge and I was being bullied again for the first time since high school. With a minute to go, Manny must have heard the words of one commentator, who said I was 'spent, knackered'.

A couple of weeks before the fight, a shudder had gone through my dad and brother, Ben, as they watched the sickening television footage of a boxer losing his life after a brutal fight in Sydney. I can honestly say I have never gone into the ring trying to damage an opponent, but boxing is obviously a gruelling sport where accidents happen and people can get badly hurt, or worse. One of Manny's great friends had died in the boxing ring.

Dad said he felt sick watching a *60 Minutes* segment about Davey Browne's death. He made Ben watch it because he wanted him to realise that no matter what, everyone in my corner had to make sure that I did not get badly hurt against Manny, world title or no world title. Dad knew everyone in my corner loved me, but he didn't want any of them to have their judgment affected by excitement in the heat of battle.

In Round 9 I was hurt and my dad knew it.

As Manny unloaded on me, I was thinking about Jo sitting ringside. I could hear her and Mum shouting encouragement. They were holding hands, their grip on each other growing tighter with every punch Manny landed. They have a secret code that they say to each other if they're really stressed during my fights, but it wasn't working.

I was still thinking clearly despite being rocked. I was thinking, *If this keeps going like this I'm about to get stopped. I'VE GOT TO KEEP MOVING. I've got to hit him back.*

I knew I could set up my family for life and there was no way I was going to lose. At least that was the plan.

Commentator Teddy Atlas couldn't hide his joy at the thought I was about to be knocked out.

Whether he actually said it or not, Winston Churchill is credited with declaring, 'If you're going through hell, keep going' – and that's what I felt. In the end my mobility helped me when I got into trouble, thanks to the thousands of hours I had spent in Glenn's gym learning to move when I got tagged, learning to survive no matter how bad the storm.

'Come on Jeffrey,' Mum, Jo and Lillian Rushton yelled. 'You can do it. We believe in you.'

I was in trouble but despite the cut eye I could see my way out of it.

CLANG.

The bell mercifully tolled to end Round 9 and I breathed a sigh of relief. Manny was trying to destroy me, but I still had the utmost respect for him as a man and as a competitor.

We were both bloodied and bruised. But after those tumultuous three minutes, I couldn't help but pat him on the stomach to acknowledge his Herculean effort. Buboy Fernandez raised his fist in triumph as Manny returned to his corner with a spring in his step that I hadn't seen before in the fight.

I went back to my corner worn out and looking like I'd been hit by a car. Dad came to the corner and said, 'Ben, now you look after him. You look after him, son.' I took a deep breath though, and the oxygen was like some potent elixir. Within a few seconds I had regained my composure. It was just like when I got tagged by Randall Bailey – I was buzzing for a little while and then I came good.

As my corner went to work on my war wounds, Ben was telling me, 'Come on, Jeff, suck it up, breathe. This is what you've worked so hard for, brother.'

Manny had really shocked me. But his big left cross was nowhere near as stunning as what referee Mark Nelson did next.

Glenn was telling me, 'Come on, Jeff, just three rounds to go now,' when all of a sudden Nelson pushed through the pack of corner men around me. 'Jeff,' he said, 'listen, I'm here to protect you, okay. I think you've had enough.'

'I'm fine,' I shot back, as Glenn, Stephen, Adam and Ben all protested that I was fighting back and that I was good to go.

But Nelson was adamant. He knew about boxers who had been badly hurt too, and he didn't want to risk a calamity on his watch. He must have forgotten my performance in the first seven rounds because he said, 'Show me something in this round or I'm going to stop the fight.' I thought I'd been showing him what I could do all afternoon. Okay, I had a little rough patch for a minute or so in one round, but I was fine and ready to fight on with everything I had.

I thought the subject was closed. But just in case I'd suddenly had a bout of deafness, Nelson reappeared like a gate-crasher at a party to remind me. 'Show me something or I'm stopping the fight.'

Glenn assured Nelson that there was still hunger in my heart and fire in my belly. But he told me I had to get back on track, back on the plan, or our dream was dead right there and then.

In the time since that round, a lot of experts have said it should have been a 10–8 round for Manny because he was dominant, rather than 10–9 the way the judges had it. I've watched it many times and I disagree. Sure, he rocked me in the middle stages of the round, but if you watch it closely I was the guy who was dominant in the first minute. Then in the last minute, Manny missed more punches than he landed.

Still, he had made a huge impression on the referee and, I feared, on the three ringside judges too. Nelson was scared I was about to be knocked out, but instead he woke me up.

You want me to show you something – well, get a load of this.

Round 10

I came out and not only showed Nelson something, but I demonstrated to Manny that he had fired his best shots and I was not only still standing but throwing them back just as hard.

I think that's when Manny's heart broke. He was a 38-year-old who had thrown a lot of heavy blows without achieving the desired result and his fuel gauge was starting to flash empty.

Before long I felt that I was back on top and that I had slammed shut Manny's window of opportunity. I might have looked spent at the end of the ninth round, but three minutes can be an eternity in boxing.

Glenn had programmed the survival skills into my brain and I hit the run mode. The fact that all the physical and mental conditioning had made me extremely tough, even by the huge demands of boxing, was a surprise to Manny.

Later Bob Arum would say, 'That's what happens when you go in over-confident, and you have the morons in Manny's corner saying that the only way Horn could win the fight is if Manny trips on his way to the ring. What kind of bull is that? I saw the kid fight in New Zealand. I knew he was a competent fighter. I knew it would be a tough fight, that it wasn't a walk in the park, and that's what happened.'

In Manny's corner Freddie Roach and Justin Fortune seemed perplexed over how to handle me.

Round 11

In the corner, as the boys worked on me feverishly after Round 10, Glenn kept me positive but was firm that there could now be no mistakes. 'Two rounds, okay?' he said, reminding me that just six minutes and one dangerous titleholder stood between me and boxing history. 'That was a great round, Jeff,' he said. 'You won that round, you came back to win it. Let's lift the work rate a bit but don't become predictable. You've still got to watch your recovery, zone left, go left, move your head, go to the body that little more. Use that left rip to the body to set up the right hand.'

Glenn said that the fight was either even, or that I was up by one point. He later told me he was being generous to Manny, giving him any of the close rounds. Glenn said we needed a big finish, just as we had trained for. In all of our sparring sessions he had asked me to lift the work rate for the last two rounds, and now he wanted me to do that again, but without getting careless or predictable. I had to remain disciplined until the final second of the fight. He certainly didn't want me to think I could coast to the finish line, only to lose by a point.

Mark Nelson was taking some convincing, coming back yet again to check on me. In hindsight, I appreciate that the welfare of the fighters should be a referee's top priority, but before Nelson could open his mouth I shouted to him, 'I'm fine.' Glenn told Nelson he didn't have to be concerned. 'He won the round,' Glenn said, 'he won the bloody round', as all my corner joined in the chorus, 'He won the round.' Ben had the final word as Nelson was leaving, telling him to 'Get outta town.'

I put the pressure on Manny at the start of the eleventh. He boxed well in retreat but I still felt that I was the aggressor and the guy forcing the action.

But I was saving the best for last.

Round 12

Glenn hoped that the judges had me in front, but really we had no idea how they would score the fight. Each judge is different. Glenn knew I had to impress them with a big finish just to make sure. The official judges were Waleska Roldan, a woman from New York, and two male judges, Chris Flores from Arizona and Ramon Cerdan of Argentina. To fire me up for one final surge, Glenn told me that the points were very close and I had to lift the pressure in the last round. Manny had been an immensely popular world champ for nearly twenty years and we didn't know what effect that would have on what the judges were seeing. It certainly had some effect on Teddy Atlas, who seemed to only notice the punches that Manny landed.

I knew I had to put an exclamation mark on my performance.

'Ladies and gentlemen,' Michael Buffer's voice reverberated around the stadium. 'This is the twelfth and final round.' The crowd rose to its feet and Manny and I marched to centre ring to touch gloves. Despite this being a gruelling, torrid, brutal fight, we had both conducted ourselves like fine sportsmen. We would still try to knock each other cold though. Halfway through the round, I bombed Manny with a right and he was firing nothing back. I hit him with another big right. He came back with a flurry that missed.

With a minute to go in the last round, Manny had blood seeping into both his eyes and he was fighting like an alley cat to preserve his reputation. Despite the desperation I saw on his face, he couldn't match it with me physically in the dying embers of what had been a boxing firestorm. He landed a good straight left as the clock ticked down, but I thought it was fitting that at the final bell, as more than 51,000 voices boomed in a cacophony around me, Manny was again backed against the ropes and I was unloading with both hands. That had been the scenario for much of the fight.

*

At the final bell, Manny and I, two proud fighters who had given their all, embraced in centre ring and our corners both lifted us into their arms. Manny went over to a neutral corner, then dropped to his knees to give thanks to God for our safe passage through the fight. He rested his head against the white-and-purple Oxmar Properties sign, which Phil Murphy still has as a souvenir, blood smear and all.

Both teams paced nervously in centre ring as we waited for the judges' verdict. Forget what you might have heard about other sports – in boxing winning is everything.

Dad and Glenn embraced me and told me I'd done a great job. Glenn said he thought I'd won by a couple of points.

'Ladies and gentlemen,' Michael Buffer announced, 'before we go to the scorecards, a round of applause for a great display of courage in this ring here today.' The crowd erupted.

'Here are the score totals.'

Manny and I stood on either side of Mark Nelson in centre ring as he prepared to raise one of our hands in victory. Buffer continued.

'Waleska Roldan scored 117–111. Chris Flores scored it 115–113.'

A pause.

'... same score from Ramon Cerdan, 115–113 to ...'

Long pause. It seemed forever. If Buffer said 'new', I was the world champion. If he said 'still', I'd lost.

'... the winner by unanimous decision ... and *NEW* ...'

A wave of joy like a tsunami crashed over me as Nelson lifted my arm. Manny's gaze lowered to the floor. I didn't hear anything else for some time after that, but apparently Buffer continued after the word '*NEW*' with '... WBO welterweight champion of the world, the fighting pride of Brisbane, Queensland, Australia – Jeff "The Hornet" Hoooorrrrnnnnn.'

Glenn lifted me into his arms as though I was weightless and all around me my friends in orange and black danced and hollered and whooped for joy. It had been a long, hard and at times gut-wrenching journey.

Manny and I embraced. He looked much older than he had at the start of the fight, although I was no oil painting either. He accepted the decision with good grace.

Stephen shook Mark Nelson's hand and thanked him, very much, for not stopping the fight. Nelson told Stephen that he had approached the corner after Round 9 with every intention of stopping it, but because I and my corner were so adamant that I was okay, he gave me one last chance. Like I say to people all the time, never give up on your ambitions no matter how grim things might seem. Those few words we said to Nelson in the corner after Round 9 changed my life forever.

Ben Damon, the Main Event host, put a microphone in front of me and asked how on earth I was able to win after such a dramatic ninth round.

Normally, I get a bit embarrassed because, as I approach the age of thirty, my voice still sounds like a school kid's. But with all the excitement of victory, I went up another half an octave. It sounded like I'd just gulped down a mouthful of helium when I answered.

'I dunno,' I said, looking around at the great sea of people applauding. 'I guess it was all the crowd behind me, all the support. Thank you, everybody.'

Then I threw a punch I'd been rehearsing for a long time.

The day before I had sent Stephen an email with a speech I wanted to read out regardless of the result. He'd printed it out and had it in his back pocket throughout the fight. Now he passed it to me to read.

'One quick thing,' I started, as my team handed me a walking stick and a pair of spare boxing gloves. 'First, I'm just having a bit of a dig overseas to Floyd Mayweather, but this is no joke – which one does he want, the walking stick or the gloves? Come and have a real fight.' At the time Mayweather was in the process of hyping his fight with Conor McGregor, and I was letting him know that I would present a far more formidable challenge than the boxing novice from Mixed Martial Arts (MMA). If Floyd wants it, I'm here.

'I just believed from when I was very young that I could do this,' I told Ben Damon.

When I was asked whether I'd fight Manny again, I said, 'Bring it on. I'd love to fight in front of you guys again.' I thanked my team for all their hard work and support and I thanked all my family and Glenn and Lillian Rushton, who had been like a second set of parents to me ever since I wandered into that boxing gym as a shy, nervous teenager.

'But this is not the best moment of my life,' I said. 'That is yet to come with my beautiful wife, Joanna. She's pregnant with our first child, so thank you for all your love and support.'

While I was caught up in interviews, Stephen went to the stand to celebrate with his wife, Daochula. When he saw her crying, he started too, crying for probably the first time in more than thirty years. What we had all achieved together and the pride we felt as a band of brothers hit Stephen all at once. It was overwhelming for him. Sometimes people mistake Stephen or Glenn for my dad. I'm very lucky I have all three of them who love me like a son.

★

Back in the ring, Ben Damon asked Manny, his expression weary and both sides of his head caked with blood, if I was tougher than he'd thought.

'Very tough,' he said. 'I didn't expect that, but it is part of the game. That's the decision of the judges. I respect that.'

Did he want a rematch? 'Absolutely – yeah, yeah, definitely.'

Beside the ring, Teddy Atlas's head was about to explode. At the judges' decision, he had gone into some sort of meltdown. 'You don't get points for trying,' he screamed. Even though former world champ Tim Bradley, sitting beside him, was saying that it was a close fight and I had proved myself as a dangerman for any welterweight in the world, Teddy had been deriding me since the fight was announced and had written me off from the opening bell. Now his worst fears had come to pass. Not only was I not an easy beat, like he said, but I was now the world champion. He had to cover his tracks.

Manny and I were asked to step outside the ring for an interview with the ESPN commentary team of Atlas, Bradley and Joe Tessitore.

'Listen, congratulations,' Teddy said, 'great effort. I thought you lost but great effort.'

Manny started laughing and Jeff Fenech, standing nearby, said later if Teddy had spoken like that to him after the greatest moment of his career, he would have punched Teddy so hard the loudmouth would have swallowed the microphone.

But Teddy wasn't finished.

'I thought this guy,' he said, pointing to Manny, 'was landing the punches. You were throwing a lot that were missing but you showed great heart, the heart of a champion, no doubt about that. Did you really think you were winning that fight?'

'Yes,' I said, taken aback by this in front of a huge audience around the world. 'I thought I was outpointing him and I thought I was coming forward more and landing the cleaner blows.'

I was too kind to Teddy.

'That's just my opinion,' I said. 'I respect your opinion too, of course, Teddy.'

I don't anymore. Looking back, I think Teddy's comments weren't just rude and disrespectful to someone who had just fought their heart out and realised a life's ambition, but they were plain wrong. Watching and re-watching the fight, I thought I won clearly.

Teddy has been described as 'a natural trouble magnet' and I can see why. He spent time in gaol for an armed robbery and claims he once pulled a gun on Mike Tyson. In his book, *Atlas: From the Streets to the Ring*, he said that he wanted to kill his former charge, the Canadian boxer Donny Lalonde, after Lalonde dumped him as coach. Teddy claimed that he took a gun and waited outside the fighter's apartment in New York, but Lalonde wasn't home at the time. 'If he had opened the door, he was dead. I would have pulled the trigger, turned around, and walked away.' According to the website *Fightnews*, Lalonde called Teddy a 'certifiable nutcase' who 'may not be the most stable person walking around'. Lalonde said that the address Teddy listed in his book was wrong, so if he really did try to shoot him he was waiting outside the wrong apartment in the wrong part of town. So it may not be just fight results that Teddy gets wrong.

My promoter, Dean Lonergan, has demanded that ESPN not use Teddy for any of my future fights.

Back at ringside, Manny told Tim Bradley that he felt my power during the fight and it was strong. Manny said he didn't want to make excuses, but reckoned he caught a cold when he arrived in Brisbane. That was the first any of us had heard about it.

As Manny and I parted ways, I shook his hand again and said, 'Manny, you're an absolute legend, mate, thank you.'

I shook the hands of the ESPN team, too, unaware that Teddy and someone named Stephen A. Smith back in ESPN's US studio were continuing their hatchet job on me. Smith, who knows next to nothing about boxing and was calling me 'Joe Horn' in the lead-up to the fight, asked Teddy in a live cross what the 'angle' was for such a blatant robbery of Manny. 'It's a corrupt sport,' Teddy said. 'I've been in the sport for forty-five years, I'm sorry.' Boxing has been Teddy's livelihood for decades, but there he was crapping on the sport. His ranting certainly created enough controversy to fuel a possible rematch with Manny.

*

Back in my dressing room, my face was very sore. I was pretty busted up. My right eye was swollen shut and there were now seven stitches of blue thread in my torn right eyebrow. I had a big lump the size of an apricot between my eyes, bruises all over the top of my scalp, a small cut under my left eye and a bruise on the side of my left eye. My left cheekbone was badly discoloured and, although my nose wasn't broken, it was purple and swollen. At least my hands were fine. All the hand strengthening had worked.

I was lying face up on a massage table, motionless, as Ben pressed an ice pack against my skull. One concerned onlooker called for an ambulance. But I was fine. I was just lying there quietly with ice cooling my head, enjoying the calm after the win and the silence after all the noise. There was so much excitement around beating Manny, and all the adrenaline was pumping so fast that I just wanted to lie still and rest.

Because I'd been denying myself treats for so long, in the knowledge I might just need that extra skerrick of fitness in an emergency, I'd been fantasising for a long time about eating a whole jar of Nutella. I planned to get into some as soon as I could.

'It's all worth it, all the pain and sacrifice,' I told reporters as I surveyed them through my one good eye. 'I wanted to make my family and my friends proud. Manny was trying so hard in there and I really appreciate him giving me the chance to fight for this world title.

'He hit me hard a few times in that ninth round and our heads banged together causing the cuts. Those head clashes buzzed me a few times, but there was nothing Manny could do that would stop me from my dream. You saw today the power that comes from believing in yourself, from having good people around you and working towards a dream.

'I mightn't look too good, but I feel so happy. I went through a rough patch but I'm a Queenslander and I found a way to push through.'

In Manny's dressing room, Dr Jeffrey Roth stitched up the head lacerations on the now former world champ. The right-side cut was 5 centimetres long and it took nine stitches to close it. The cut on the left side was 3.5 centimetres long and took eight stitches.

Freddie Roach told the media that, 'I have to go along with Manny and say I respect the decision of the judges. Well, two of the judges. I did think Manny won but Jeff Horn showed a lot of heart. He is a big, strong fighter and I congratulate him.'

Mum had been an emotional mess just like Lillian and my aunties sitting ringside. 'I'm just overcome,' she said. 'I'm so proud. I know how hard he has worked for this. It's hard to believe this is the same boy who was picked on at school.'

Dad was walking on air. He told reporters that, when he told Ben to look after me following that terrible ninth round, his heart was in his mouth. He added, 'This has been a remarkable journey and it just shows what anyone can achieve with determination and a plan. The way he fought back after Round 9 was breathtaking. Rounds 10, 11 and 12 were the three greatest rounds ever seen in an Australian boxing ring.'

Dean Lonergan said there was a provision for a return fight 'if Manny wants to go again'.

'It was just an unbelievable performance from Jeff,' Dean said. 'To fight that well against Manny, a true legend of the sport, was amazing. But we always knew he was capable of doing that. The fight was an incredible spectacle and a great piece of sporting history for Brisbane and Australia. To have that Brisbane crowd, that noise, behind him ... that just made a difference for Jeff. You cannot underestimate what this has done for Jeff's profile and appeal worldwide.'

I posed for a photo with Dad and my pop, three generations of Horns, with the WBO world welterweight title belt – the spoils of war. 'Seeing Jeff become world champ is the thing that's kept me going these last few years,' Pop said. 'He's always been such a lovely young bloke and I've always wished the very best for him. Nothing will top what he did today. It's been one of the best days of my long life.'

*

In a quiet anteroom underneath Suncorp Stadium, away from all the other cameras, notebooks and microphones, Glenn and I gave an interview to *The Courier-Mail.* I was asked what was the secret formula to my dramatic turn-around from Round 9 to 10.

'Belief,' I said. 'That's heart. Getting through that ninth round. Being able to get hit, to get caught with a shot and continue on. I knew in my heart that I could beat Manny and nothing was going to stop me.'

Glenn agreed and, though he was worried by my slump in the ninth round, he said he had looked into my eyes and could see I was still hungry. I still had that fire in my belly, I still wanted the win. Glenn knew that I wasn't spent.

'If Jeff was spent, I'd have said, "Jeff, you're done", but I know him like a son. I know how tough he is and I know what he can do,' Glenn told the newspaper. 'He was being smart. He knew he'd been clipped with a few from Pacquiao but he wasn't that bad. But he knew he didn't want to keep getting hit. I wanted him to breathe and relax and recover and get back on my ten-point plan for victory. That's what he did.

'For me, this has been as big as Australia winning the America's Cup – one of the great moments in Australian sport. You just think there's a young lad who has represented us, who has punched above his weight, who has come back from a torrid Round 9 and found that drive from within him.

'Jeff Horn makes you proud to be an Australian right now. And it couldn't happen to a nicer bloke.'

In between my interviews, Peter Wallis from *The Courier-Mail* took a beautiful photograph. To me it summed up the fight even more than the pictures that went around the world of me with my arms in the air in triumph and my corner celebrating wildly. The photo was just of me and Jo, husband and wife, sitting quietly together on a wooden bench, enjoying each other's company after every piece of emotion and exertion had been extracted from me and telecast around the world.

The lives of Mr and Mrs Horn, and the baby we were expecting, had been changed forever by what had just happened at Suncorp Stadium. But we were still the same people, just an ordinary suburban couple caught up in an extraordinary moment.

Jo and I fell in love when I was a geeky kid who knew nothing about boxing and had never even seen a proper fight. I was a long way from world champion in the days when she would console me after I'd been beaten up at school. We both have to pinch ourselves now to remind ourselves that we're not in some weird movie, that this is real life. We have loved each other through thick and thin and, while I grew to believe in myself over time through Glenn's training, as I sat with Jo in the quiet of the dressing room I knew there had been an even bigger factor in my success.

It was that my beautiful wife always believed in me.

17

I haven't been so proud of an Aussie sportsman for so long. Jeff Horn doesn't act tough, he doesn't talk tough because he doesn't have to. I've never seen a braver performance in sport than his win over Manny Pacquiao.

– Johnny Lewis, Australia's International Hall of Fame boxing trainer

A FEW HOURS AFTER the fight, we headed to the Treasury Casino to celebrate the victory at an after-party for 300 family members and friends. I received a congratulatory message from Prime Minister Malcolm Turnbull – who said he wanted me to fight Floyd Mayweather – but my battle with Manny was not over yet.

Manny had concocted a sneaky scheme to put me through another tough and bitter round of fighting. He had accepted the judges' verdict immediately after the fight with good grace, and at the time I never pictured him as a sore loser. But there you go. I believe it was the people around Manny persuading him to challenge. I guess a guy as fierce as he is would do anything for victory.

I was unaware of his face-saving plan as I rode the immediate post-fight euphoria.

I certainly didn't overdo the celebrations. I don't drink much as a rule and, because I had been hit hard in the head a few times during the fight, I didn't want to drink any alcohol. I wanted to look after my brain cells. But I celebrated with some chocolate for breakfast after staying at the casino that night. I really enjoyed destroying a block of it at long last. My friends Donna and Melvin brought some Nutella donuts to the Treasury and I ended up eating a fair bit of Nutella out of a jar. Six people gave me jars of the chocolate-hazelnut spread at the time, so I was stocked up for a while.

The aftermath of the fight was pretty much a blur as I spent nearly the whole party posing for photos with family and friends, most of whom remember me when I was a bullied schoolboy. To say some of them are still a bit confused about me being a world boxing champion would be an understatement.

While my critics continued to fan the flames of controversy, the influential website BoxRec.com now ranked me in the world's top ten fighters pound for pound, which I thought was pretty amazing for a veteran of just eighteen fights. They also rated me above my two American rivals at the top of the welterweight pile – Keith Thurman, who holds the World Boxing Council and the World Boxing Association titles, and London Olympian Errol Spence Jnr, who holds the International Boxing Federation version.

For the first time in many years, Manny had dropped out of the top ten and was now ranked No. 11 pound for pound and No. 3 at welterweight.

Johnny Lewis, the great Sydney trainer, said that I certainly deserved the decision over Manny and that in more than fifty years of involvement in high-end sport – in boxing and as a trainer for the Australian rugby league team – he had never seen anything braver. That was a great compliment from Johnny, whose fighter Jeff 'Hit Man' Harding rose from the canvas to win the world light-heavyweight title against Dennis Andries back in 1989 with a big-noting casino owner named Donald Trump ringside. The promoter back then was also Bob Arum.

'Jeff Horn clearly won the fight against Pacquiao,' Johnny said, adding, 'He won most of the early rounds 10–9 on my card. He dominated the first half, although he was badly hurt in the ninth round. He doesn't want to take that sort of punishment ever again. I thought the referee did a really great job. I was concerned that Jeff was hurt and I was scared that after doing so well and being way in front he was about to lose. But Jeff is a really special athlete. He doesn't act tough, he doesn't talk tough because he doesn't have to. All that toughness comes from deep within. I've seen in a couple of his earlier fights when he's gone down and you can see him trying to get up even before he hits the canvas. That's pure guts. Every boxer who steps in the ring has to be brave – but Jeff Horn's bravery is at the highest level. This kid just beat an all-time great in his eighteenth fight and with just four years as a pro. Anything is possible.'

Johnny said that Manny looked 'like a garden gnome' against me because I was so much bigger and stronger than him and that I was able to 'rag-doll' him throughout – throwing him around all the time.

'The whole country should be proud of what Jeff Horn has done and the way he conducted himself,' he said. 'His polite demeanour and graciousness are more than a breath of fresh air for Australian sport. He's a blast of greatness. I haven't been so proud of an Aussie sportsman for so long. I'm walking around like I'm 10-feet tall after that win – it's like I've won the world title and I reckon that's the effect he's had on a lot of people in this country.'

Johnny also said I'd have a good chance of beating Floyd Mayweather. Even though getting that fight is a longshot, Glenn was already working on a scheme to hand Mayweather his first defeat. Critics around the world laughed loudly when Glenn first revealed details in *The Courier-Mail* of his masterplan to beat Manny two weeks before the title fight, but I had the last laugh. We believe it would be the same story against Floyd.

Glenn's plan to beat Mayweather would be very different from the Pacquiao plan and I think I could rattle Mayweather in the same way I flummoxed Manny. I'd love the chance to try. We see flaws in Mayweather's style that I can definitely exploit. He's a great defensive fighter, he's incredibly quick, he has a great eye and good control of distance. But we can beat him. Marcos Maidana from Argentina put on a great performance against Mayweather, but he couldn't continue it in the later rounds. I'd fight like Maidana for twelve rounds, not six. Mayweather is beatable and, with the win over Manny, I believe I can now beat anyone my size in the world at welterweight or junior-middleweight (70 kg).

Glenn and I would also have no qualms tackling the great Mexican Saúl 'Canelo' Álvarez either. I'd especially like to unify the titles against Thurman and Spence.

I've said all along that I only want big fights. Glenn has taught me to be confident about my boxing ability without being arrogant, and I am willing to back myself against the toughest opponents in the sport.

*

Manny and his huge entourage flew out of Australia from the Gold Coast on his chartered AirAsia jet a day after the fight. He was smiling for the cameras with wife, Jinkee, as he left, but frowning and whingeing when he arrived home.

There was trouble in the camp as soon as the scorecards were announced with me as the winner – everyone on Team Pacquiao was looking for a scapegoat. Freddie Roach feared that Manny was mad at him and publicly complained that he hadn't received his cut of the boss's purse, although Manny said there was no problem and the money would be paid by Bob Arum. Then Roach bleated to *USA Today* that I had a very 'dirty' style. 'Headlocks, pushing a guy down,' he said, 'using his elbows, head butts, and the referee didn't say nothing about nothing. The only thing [referee Mark Nelson] said to me was, "Freddie, when a southpaw fights a righty, it's going to happen."' Roach said, 'Not when he leads with his head. Those are intentional head butts.'

They weren't intentional and Freddie knows I was only pushing Manny's head down to stop the butts from occurring. Glenn has always taught me to be a tough fighter, not a dirty one. As it was I got a badly cut eye from the head clashes. The butts also caused the two big gashes on Manny's hairline. They also spooked him.

'He doesn't get a lot of cuts, and when he does cut he panics a little bit,' Roach said. 'In between rounds when the referee was talking to him, Manny wanted to have the ring doctor look at them. For a fighter to say that, he knows where he's at and he wants to know how bad the cut is. The doctor okayed it, so Manny fought on pretty well. He's never done well when he's had those issues, you know, blood in the face. It affects everyone differently.'

Roach said Manny may also have over-trained, which is a pretty sad indictment on the trainer.

'His work ethic is still very, very good,' Roach said, 'and he trains very hard, but he probably trains too hard. He tries to do what he did when he was younger, and you can't do that. It's part of life, getting old ... He's got to realise he's thirty-eight years old now and not twenty-eight. Basically, he's a senator, a fighter and a father. He has a wife and kids. So the last thing I want to see is for Manny to get hurt.'

Roach also refuted Bob Arum's complaints that he and Manny's other handlers were overconfident coming into the fight and that the corner was out of control during the battle. 'It's hard when Buboy [Fernandez] is yelling, and Miguel [Diaz] is telling me he has to get in the middle to work on the cuts,' Roach said. 'And to get my message across to Manny, what he should be doing, is very difficult. Miguel is getting older and he has trouble getting in and out of the ring, and Buboy gets excited. Control in that corner has always been a little difficult.'

I don't know if they could find any more excuses, but Justin Fortune replied to Bob calling Manny's corner team a bunch of morons by trying to make a joke of it all, saying that although they weren't all that smart 'moron' was a bit harsh.

Manny wasn't laughing. He grew savagely critical of the result once he was back on home soil. Teddy Atlas's fervour – and the resulting storm on Twitter and Facebook it created – got Manny all hot and bothered too. Even though I had the WBO belt in my possession, Manny was coming up with a sneaky plan to steal it back. I thought I'd won fair and square but, prompted by the fact he is such a public figure and felt he needed to do something to save face, he was now claiming that he'd been robbed.

A day after the fight, the Philippines' sports regulatory body for boxing, the Games and Amusement Board (GAB), wrote to the WBO calling for a 'thorough review' of the decisions of the referee and judges. 'We are making this request for a review, which may call for sanctions on the referee and judges if so warranted, in furtherance of our mutual goal of protecting the integrity of the sport,' the board wrote.

Manny attached a copy of the letter to his own statement, saying, 'The WBO should take appropriate action on the letter sent by the Games and Amusement Board so as not to erode the people's interest in boxing.'

Rather than accept the decision, Manny was willing to damage the reputation of boxing – by calling into question the integrity and competence of officials – to get what he wanted. I thought it was very selfish. It was not a good advertisement for the sport at all, despite him saying he was only interested in boxing's reputation.

The following day the WBO responded to the controversy through Twitter, declaring that 'the discretion of a referee or judge cannot be reversed, except in a case of fraud or violation of laws which is not the case in Pac vs Horn. The contract for Pac vs Horn provides a rematch clause, which the WBO is in accordance if the promoters decide to move forward.'

*

Manny and his shenanigans were the least of my worries though. Four days after the fight I was going the distance again – this time for a ticker-tape parade just 500 metres up Brisbane's Queen Street Mall in the heart of the CBD.

Going the distance with Manny had been a dangerous ordeal, but this was one of the great pleasures Jo and I have enjoyed. I'd done this once before after coming home from the 2012 Olympics, but the crowd this time was much bigger and the spotlight was just on me. It was all a bit wonderful. Jo and I were in an open-top Cobra convertible followed by Glenn and Lillian in the same type of car. Thousands of people surrounded us, cheering and waving.

It was a surreal moment – a week earlier Jo and I could have shopped there anonymously. Now, as we cruised along slowly in the powerful sports cars, the engines rumbling lustily and the chrome glinting in the sun, fans were holding up babies as though to be blessed, grandmothers were taking photos to show the grandchildren, old men and small kids were cheering. People threw coloured streamers at me and showered me with goodwill. Teddy Atlas had whipped up a lot of animosity towards me overseas and I was copping hell from social media trolls who claimed, usually with a great deal of rudeness, that Manny had been ripped off. But here, in the middle of my home city, everyone was on my side.

All of them knew that a big storm was brewing over the scorecards and they had my back.

From deep within the big crowd, one young man yelled out, 'You won the fight easy, Jeff – I had it 115–113, seven rounds to five.' Thanks, mate.

Another guy, with the frantic, fervent expression of someone who has just survived combat, shouted, 'Jeff, you're an inspiration, an inspiration to us all.' Thanks again.

I was dressed in a three-piece suit and open-neck shirt. My wounds were healing and I waved to everyone, signed autographs until my right hand hurt and posed for selfies with as many of the multitude as I could.

The parade concluded at the end of the mall, at Reddacliff Place. A few days earlier I had given a boxing exhibition there as the No. 1 contender for the world welterweight title. Now I was the champ.

I was greeted by Alan Jones, who was the MC for the day, Premier Annastacia Palaszczuk and Lord Mayor Graham Quirk. Graham awarded me the ceremonial keys to the city, an honour I could never have imagined in my wildest dreams. What made it even more bizarre is that Graham has known me all my life and remembers me well from family gatherings when I was a kid who wouldn't bruise a grape. Now I was a world-famous boxer. Go figure.

Graham said he had been worried for me in Round 9, but that it was my 'calm and steely resolve … that capacity to fight back from despair that saw the history books rewritten'.

The premier had just been in talks with Dean Lonergan and she said that any rematch with Manny would be in

Brisbane and that I was now a hero to all of Australia. 'As a teacher you know how to deliver lessons and Manny learned his – don't ever underestimate a Queenslander,' she said.

I was asked to address the huge crowd. I hoped my words made the same sort of impact as my fists did at Suncorp. Knowing that victory meant so much to all my supporters had spurred me on, and I told the crowd that, 'You've all been part of this. Everyone who ever gave me a thumbs up, or a wave or sent me a message of support – it all counts. You all contributed to the win in some way, so thank you very much.'

As a schoolboy who was cast as an outsider by bullies, I faced dark times, even some times when I didn't think I had anything left to live for, but my message to everyone was that you just have to keep pushing forward. I hoped that people took a lesson from my win over Manny. I'm a Queenslander and I won't give up and if you refuse to give in, amazing things can happen. I'm proof of that.

My corner team – Glenn, Ben, Stephen and Adam as well as Dundee Kim – were all presented with awards from the Brisbane City Council for being part of a historic event that had contributed significantly to the city and state economies. The fight also showcased Brisbane to the world as a great city capable of staging a monumental sporting event.

All around, photographers and cameramen jostled each other to get the best shots and reporters wanted to know every last detail of my life. I'm grateful for the attention, but sometimes it can seem overwhelming. I'm still getting used to being in the public eye. I've even had a paparazzo on my tail, motor-drive running, to get photos of me putting out the rubbish bins.

I am doing my best not to get carried away with the victory and what it means.

Lillian Rushton, very kindly, told a reporter that world champ Jeff Horn will be little different from the Jeff Horn of a month earlier or from the 'shy, polite boy' – as she called me – who first came to her husband for boxing lessons.

'He's always been such a lovely, calm young guy who represents the best of Australia,' she said. 'Wouldn't it be great if all of our sports stars were gentlemen like Jeff Horn?'

I was really touched at the end of the parade ceremonies when Glenn took the microphone and said, 'I'd like to thank Jeff from the bottom of my heart for what he did on Sunday. The courage and strength of character he showed will never be forgotten by anyone who saw it. Not many people gave us a chance against Manny Pacquiao, but the best is yet to come. We dared to dream, and it just goes to show when you dream, you can do anything.'

Throughout my boxing career, which began so inauspiciously at the Acacia Ridge Hotel, Glenn has told me to 'hold the dream' and never forget my goals.

When I arrived at Glenn's house back in 2006 looking for someone to show me how to defend myself, I was starting a journey that has taken us and our families and friends to astonishing heights. Dream big, everyone, because big dreams can come true.

*

While I was now literally living my dream, Manny Pacquiao was going through something of a nightmare. Before the fight Michael Koncz had said that I was an inferior opponent and that Manny was coming to Australia to score a quick win before going home with the cheque. Now he laid the blame squarely with Manny's team for the loss. 'The corner didn't have a strategy,' he said. 'They were all amazed Jeff Horn was such a tough, rugged fighter and they didn't adapt to it.'

But Manny wanted to blame the judges – not his team who had treated me like a joke – declaring that the result was 'unfair'. He no longer had a world title, but he still had plenty of clout and his agitation was getting results. Given his lofty status in the sport for so many years and his position as a high-ranking politician, the WBO announced on 6 July, four days after the fight, that it would re-score the contest.

Some of my fans feared that the title could be taken from me, but I knew that no re-score could change the result. Back in 2012, when Tim Bradley had beaten him by a close decision, Manny kicked up an epic stink and a re-count by WBO judges had him winning. Bradley still kept the title until a rematch, even though Manny had scored a decisive psychological victory. The only real danger for me in this re-count was that it could possibly back up the childish ravings of Teddy Atlas and Stephen A. Smith. I didn't want Teddy and Stephen getting any more ammunition. They'd done enough damage to me and boxing's reputation as it was.

The Philippines GAB said it made the request for a re-score because it wanted to protect 'boxing's integrity', citing 'possible miscalls by the referee and judges'. The WBO president, Francisco 'Paco' Valcarcel, had been the official supervisor at Suncorp Stadium to ensure all rules and regulations were followed, so he was taking no nonsense over the attacks on his referee and judges. The WBO repeated its statement that the only way to revoke the judges' decision rested on proving fraud in match officiating – and there was no fraud to prove.

In a letter to the GAB and Manny, Valcarcel, a Puerto Rican lawyer, said, 'I would be very grateful if the GAB can provide any evidence indicating fraud or violation of law. The purpose of this review is to be able to give the fans certainty of who was the winner of the bout, even though we do not have the power to reverse the decision of the judges.'

Five anonymous judges would review the bout, assigning their own scores to rounds, Valcarcel said. 'Then, we will tabulate the results to ascertain clearly which rounds each fighter won using an average scale based on 60, 80 and 100 per cent,' he said. 'This means that three of the five officials have to agree to determine which fighter won the round.'

Valcarcel was strong in his support of the three judges at Suncorp, noting that each had scored hundreds of fights. 'The officials who participated in this fight are all professional, distinguished, honest and honourable human beings,' he said.

In a statement issued from his Senate office, Manny said, 'I love boxing and I don't want to see it dying because of [an] unfair decision and officiating. I had already accepted the decision but as a leader and, at the same time, fighter I have the moral obligation to uphold sportsmanship, truth and fairness in the eyes of the public.'

Manny changed opinions as quickly as I had changed angles in our fight. He had called for a rematch, but now he told journalists he would also 'think hard' about retiring. Then he started to explore the option of a rematch in the Philippines.

Although initially saying he respected the fight outcome, Manny now questioned the referee's decisions and made disparaging comments about me. 'He's not really good but he's really strong,' he said. 'It's as if the referee wanted to help my opponent.'

I was really disappointed in Manny for saying that because the fight had been so exciting and he knew in his heart that I had outfought him. If he had any complaint, why didn't he say something in the ring after the bout?

Three-time world champ Jeff Fenech, who was the victim of a highly controversial decision against Azumah Nelson in Las Vegas in 1991, backed me up, saying, 'There shouldn't have been any controversy at all about this fight. Jeff Horn won – end of story. He dominated the first six rounds and Manny is just trying to save face now. The American commentary was ridiculous – they said Pacquiao got ripped off. What fight were they watching? All they are trying to do is rob Jeff Horn of the glory he deserves. This was one of the greatest wins ever by an Australian boxer.'

The Courier-Mail offered the opinion that, 'by constantly complaining Manny Pacquiao is tarnishing Jeff Horn's victory. He's also staining his own reputation and that of the fight game he has served so well for so many years.'

It was an anxious wait as the five WBO judges were assigned to re-score the bout. Horn–Pacquiao was the biggest fight ever in Australia, but would it now be the biggest black eye Australian boxing had ever suffered? A re-score in Manny's favour would be an embarrassment for everyone involved in staging the fight. Who knew how the five new judges would see it?

Finally, on 11 July the WBO published this statement from its headquarters in San Juan, Puerto Rico:

The Jeff Horn vs. Manny Pacquiao bout results were controversial, causing disputes among fans. For this reason, transparency is so important. The WBO does not have power to reverse the Judges' decision based on discretion as it can only be revoked when fraud or a violation of Law has occurred, which is not relevant in this case.

Based on this, five (5) anonymous, competent Judges from different countries were asked to watch the bout without sound. Then, the independent results were tabulated to ascertain clearly the rounds each fighter won using an average scale based on 60, 80 and 100 per cent.

To determine the winner of each round, 3 out of the 5 officials have to be in agreement.

Upon the analysis, the findings stated that Pacquiao won the 3rd, the 8th and 9th by 100%; the 5th round was won by 80%; and the 11th round by 60%. Horn won the 1st, 6th and 12th rounds by 100%; rounds 2nd, 4th, and 7th by 80%; and then, the 10th round by 60%. From the results, it can be established that Pacquiao won 5 rounds while Horn won 7 rounds.

The next step of the analysis was to combine the independent Judges with the Bout Judges to find the percentage agreement by round. Upon doing this analysis, the findings of the Judges stated that Pacquiao won the 3rd and 9th by 100%; the 8th round was won by 87.5%; no rounds were won by 75%; the 5th round by 62.5%; and the 10th and 11th were even rounds. On the other hand, the Judges' findings stated that Horn won the 1st, 6th, and 12th rounds by 100%; by 87.5%,

> he won the 4th and the 7th; the 2nd was won by 75%; none were won by 62.5%; and the even rounds were the 10th and the 11th. The analytical method utilized was also used in the decision of ... Pacquiao–Bradley.
>
> Based on this analysis, Jeff Horn was the winner of the bout.

Did you get that Manny and Teddy? 'Jeff Horn was the winner of the bout.' Two sets of judges and still one winner. A thorough review had shown that I deserved the decision.

The Courier-Mail offered the opinion that Teddy Atlas's mad ramblings after the fight now looked like a John Cleese skit from *Fawlty Towers*.

And Manny didn't fare too well either, the newspaper declaring:

> Give yourself an uppercut Manny Pacquiao. You turned into a sore loser only to cop another beating after an independent review of the judges' scorecards from your loss to Jeff Horn declared the Aussie battler victorious for a second time. And put your microphone away Teddy Atlas and go stand in the corner for a while. As the most vocal critic of the decision – you insulted Horn. You've shown that you're a goose and when it comes to scoring a fight, you've got no idea.

It's significant to note that while judge Waleska Roldan received a lot of criticism for her score of 117–111 for me, she was backed up totally by the re-score. When you look at her scorecard, at least one judge, either from the original panel or from the second re-score panel, agreed with her scoring of each round. She was never alone on her scoring of any round.

★

One of my management team sent a news report on the result of the WBO review via Facebook to Teddy Atlas, Stephen A. Smith, actor Samuel L. Jackson and basketballer Kobe Bryant, who had all mocked the result on social media. None of them replied. I guess they were Manny fans and only saw what they wanted to see. No matter what the re-score found, some people just don't want to change their opinions.

I felt vindicated though, because the re-count gave me official evidence to back up my opinion on the fight. Instead of saying I think I won, now a heap of other people – professionally – thought I won the fight too.

I think that deep down Manny believed I deserved the decision as well. Not that he would ever admit it.

He was upset about the first lot of judges and just as unhappy with the second lot, declaring, 'Let the people judge for themselves. People saw what happened. We have seen worse judgments in the past where judges manipulated results. Nothing surprises me now.' Don't forget Manny is an elected politician. He has to maintain popularity in his country to keep his place in the Senate.

I believed the best way to settle the score between us was of course with the planned rematch, something Manny seemed keen on.

In a series of interviews in the Philippines, he said his whole fight plan would be different the second time – 'more disciplined' and 'throwing a lot of punches'. He reckoned he would pick up in the rematch where he left off in Round 9 at Suncorp.

I welcome him trying to do that. I am sure Manny would be better prepared for a return fight with me. He knows now what I bring to the table and he would be training differently to cope with my aggression and power.

But I would be a far more dangerous opponent for Manny the second time around. Glenn would prepare me to give Manny more surprises than in the first fight, more of the unexpected to keep him on the back foot. And although Manny says next time he wants to pick his own referee and judges, I'm sure a stoppage win by me would settle any of his lingering doubts forever.

Manny has other pressing commitments, though.

A few weeks after losing to me, he lifted the spirits of Filipino troops on a visit to a southern city where soldiers had been battling pro–Islamic State (IS) militants for more than two months. The boxer-turned-senator was made a lieutenant colonel in the military reserves in recognition of his boxing achievements and he is a real inspiration to his soldiers. Dressed in military camouflage and beret, he said that he would join the fight in the city of Marawi where militants had been on a rampage, holding hostages, burning buildings and flying the black IS flag.

'You are the real heroes, not Manny Pacquiao. I am just a boxer but you give your lives for our country,' he told soldiers in a camp in Marawi. 'Hopefully, I can come back here and greet you again when the fighting is done and if it isn't finished when I come back, then I will be the one who will go over there.' Manny was referring to a battleground outside the camp where gunshots and explosions could be heard. The fighting in the Mindanao region, where Manny was born, had already claimed nearly 650 lives, including a significant number of civilians.

As that conflict raged and Manny continued to play games over the return fight, Jo and I boarded a plane to attend the ESPYs, the ESPN sports awards in Los Angeles. While I was in America, I left the WBO title belt in the safe keeping of my dad. He knows how much work, how much real blood, sweat and cheers went into winning it and how much it means not just to me but to every other kid who ever had a dream.

I was asked by reporters at Brisbane airport if I would look up Teddy Atlas when I got to America.

'I have nothing to say to Teddy Atlas,' I said. 'I'm not a fan anymore. He kind of annoyed me a little bit after the fight. I'm on a high after winning and he's tried to drag me down straight away. It's disappointing.'

My dad said our family were all hurt by the controversy Teddy had whipped up and that Teddy 'was totally unprofessional'.

'He let himself down and he certainly let ESPN down,' Dad said, adding that he'd like an apology from the blowhard.

He's still waiting.

*

The ESPYs was a sensational night, held at the Microsoft Theatre in Los Angeles on 12 July and hosted by the great American football quarterback Peyton Manning. It was just like the Academy Awards. Jo and I were like kids with stars in our eyes, getting the red-carpet treatment. We were seated right in the very front row near swimmer Michael Phelps and the great Olympic and world boxing champion Vasyl Lomachenko, the fighter my mate Luke Jackson and I had so admired at London in 2012. It was certainly exalted company and to be with champions of that ilk was a real honour.

Usain Bolt won an award and MMA star Demetrious Johnson was voted best fighter for the year, ahead of boxers Terence Crawford, Gennady Golovkin and Andre Ward and MMA's Conor McGregor. Bob Arum was already talking up a fight between me and Crawford.

Maybe Conor McGregor might fight me in the future. I can only live in hope. I'd like to think I could stop Conor inside six rounds. He's come from the UFC, not boxing, and he's not professional with his hands. He gives an opponent a lot of openings and drops his guard. He doesn't have that tidiness of a boxer and I hit hard. I was surprised he lasted ten rounds with Floyd Mayweather, but Floyd hadn't fought in two years and took his time to get going.

I had a lot of media commitments in the few days I was in America. I appeared on the Rich Eisen talk show and gave dozens of interviews in Los Angeles where Lomachenko was preparing for a fight at the same venue as the ESPYs. Bob Arum and his team, including publicity boss Fred Sternburg, really made a fuss over Jo and me, taking us out on the town.

We then headed to Las Vegas for a few days, travelling in more style than a year earlier, even splurging on a suite at the beautiful Bellagio, which was really nice. It's about the only splurge of this magnitude on a hotel room we've ever had and we are very lucky to get the opportunity to enjoy the perks of being world champ.

At the Luxor Hotel we saw a display on the human anatomy, which included one on the development of a baby. Big fights might be one thing, but a baby on the way is the most exciting thing for Jo and me. While I was talking business with Bob in America and discussing the big battles ahead in 2018, the birth of our first child was the topic that most interested us.

The years ahead promise much more excitement to come.

*

Manny Pacquiao and I were set to fight a rematch on 12 November at the same venue, but on 1 September he pulled out, saying he was too busy with Senate commitments. I was really keen to fight Manny again and was training hard. The Queensland premier, Annastacia Palaszczuk, whose government was ready to support the rematch, said she was disappointed by his withdrawal, adding that, 'frankly, I think he's a bit too scared to come and face Jeff Horn. For Manny not to reappear really says to me that he knows Jeff is the world champion.'

The Courier-Mail lampooned Manny in an illustration, putting his head on a chicken's body with the headline 'PACQUI-OUT'.

Dean Lonergan summed things up well too. 'I don't think for one second Manny Pacquiao is running scared of Jeff Horn,' he said. 'He has been in the ring with the greatest boxers of our generation. He's not going to be inducted into the Boxing Hall of Fame for ducking fights. I just don't think the timing suited him so we will look at other options. Manny has decided that he will not be competing in a rematch with

Jeff in 2017. On behalf of the Philippines government he will be part of a delegation that will visit China in the middle of his proposed preparation period for the fight. Pacquiao is committed to fighting again in 2018, and a rematch with Jeff for the WBO world welterweight title.'

Bob Arum warned the welterweight division though that I'm in for the long haul.

Bob said that I am a 'tough, tough kid' and 'probably the strongest welterweight in the world'. 'If it was just an alley fight, I would pick Horn against any welterweight out there,' he told American journalists. 'Obviously these are not alley fights, but Manny Pacquiao has never fought a fighter as strong, physically, as Horn.'

18

I was very wild when I was younger. It was street fighting. There weren't really any rules. You would just fight until someone won – punching them, kicking them, headbutting them. Anything to beat them.

– Gary Corcoran, explaining his determination to take my world title

THE WEEKS IMMEDIATELY AFTER my upset victory over Manny Pacquiao were almost as frenzied as the fight itself. In all the controversy that the now ex-world champ and his team generated, Glenn and I were eagerly awaiting a summer rematch when I could really turn up the heat and scorch Pacquiao again.

But as the days morphed into weeks, Manny finally took himself out of all calculations for the contracted rematch in Brisbane.

The hunt was on for a new opponent, with the Queensland premier saying she'd like to see me take on Conor McGregor.

My old sparring partner Anthony Mundine and the rising American star Terence Crawford both loomed large on my horizon, too. Mundine was making plenty of noise, as he had done throughout his career, telling anyone who would listen that he could give me a boxing lesson.

Before long, he was turning up the volume and the vitriol, saying I had only been given the chance against Pacquiao because I was white and that I was 'only the flavour of the month' because of my skin colour.

I looked forward to discussing that point with Mundine in the near future but, for the time being, I was only interested in defending my world title and there was no way Mundine could boil down to fight me at the welterweight limit. He was more than 12 kg above that weight when he lost a controversial decision against Danny Green earlier in 2017 at Adelaide Oval.

A fight with Crawford seemed more likely following the American's powerful performance against Namibian Julius Indongo on 19 August in Lincoln, Nebraska, Crawford's home state.

Crawford became the first man since Aussie great Kostya Tszyu to unify all major championship belts at junior-welterweight (63.5 kg). He fought well, switching from orthodox to southpaw like I often do, though Indongo, a lanky long-armed power-puncher, didn't put up much resistance.

It was the first time I had seen Crawford fight and he landed a debilitating body shot in the third round. Crawford was now looking towards moving up to welterweight and his promoter Bob Arum was keen to match him with me.

He certainly looked a formidable opponent but, to be honest, Jo and I were too busy preparing for the birth of our first child to worry much about him.

I helped my mate Dennis Hogan get ready to climb further up the world ratings in the junior-middleweight division against a lanky Japanese star named Yuki Nonaka, and my great mate Joe Goodall, who had walked with me to the ring for the Pacquiao fight at Suncorp, came home to Stretton from Hamburg after winning Australia's first medal at the world amateur boxing titles for twenty-six years.

As her pregnancy advanced, Jo and I set some time aside to holiday on the Gold Coast, before she quit work to become a full-time mum.

In October, I travelled to Melbourne where I was thrilled to win the Don Award at the Crown Palladium. I was the first boxer to receive the award, which is presented to the individual judged as Australia's most inspirational sportsperson.

Among the other finalists was hurdler Sally Pearson, a friend from the London Olympics, who had coached herself to a dramatic second world title in London. Sally had already won the Don Award twice, so I didn't feel too bad that she missed out this time. Other finalists included the Australian women's football team, swimmer Emily Seebohm, surfing world champ Tyler Wright, AFLW star Erin Phillips and rugby league champion Johnathan Thurston.

As the year wound down, I was named *GQ Magazine*'s Athlete of the Year and Queensland's Sports Star of the Year and I was profiled in a great documentary by Kristine Taylor for the ABC TV program *Australian Story*.

But I knew I could only dine out on the Pacquiao victory

for so long. I had to get back into the ring to defend that world championship for a purse of $1 million.

While a bout with Crawford was shaping up as superfight in America for 2018, the search had been going on for weeks to find a suitable opponent to fight me in Brisbane at the end of 2017. The opportunity finally went to a gritty Englishman named Gary Corcoran, who came from the rough and tumble world of the Irish 'travellers', known colloquially as 'gypsies'. Corcoran was born in London but spoke with an Irish accent, as his family hailed from Galway.

He was tough and a fraction taller than me, with a rugged walk-up all-action style that promised fireworks. He was confident and cocky, too, as befitting his nickname of 'The Hellraiser'.

The match was set for 13 December at the Brisbane Convention and Exhibition Centre. Corcoran said the fight gave him the chance for revenge on a teacher after he had been suspended from class nineteen times during his schooldays for fighting and other misbehaviour.

He promised his two-year-old daughter, Summer, and wife Jennifer that he would bring my welterweight title belt back to the 12-metre caravan that was home to his young family at a traveller's camp near London's Wembley Arena.

'I've been fighting all my life,' Corcoran told *The Courier-Mail*. 'I've got eight brothers and they are all champion boxers, too. Jeff Horn is a good fighter, but I am just so hungry for this win. I know I can stop him inside the distance.'

The 26-year-old had watched my win over Pacquiao from inside his caravan, surrounded by friends and family from the traveller community, and he predicted a rough fight with lots of head clashes. In his previous bout, Corcoran had overwhelmed Larry Ekundayo, one of the hottest prospects in Britain, and he tipped that I would be surprised by his physical strength.

'The plan is to overpower Horn,' he said. 'This is the biggest opportunity of my career and we're going to meet in centre ring and punch it out. I'm expecting a war, that's what I want and it's going to be a good fight. The two of us are not going to take a back step. It's going to be a thriller. Toe to toe. I'm a brawler but I can box. I'm very strong and I just keep coming.'

Corcoran reckoned I had suffered such a physical and emotional toll in the gruelling war with Pacquiao that I was ready to fall apart.

For our first press conference, seven weeks before the fight, I arrived late because I had taken Jo for pregnancy scans. I told the media that my young family was the main reason why I would not let Corcoran leave Brisbane with the world title belt that I fought so hard to win.

*

Corcoran set up his training camp at the Fortitude Gym in the Brisbane suburb of Newstead, the same gym where my old rival Todd Kidd was based. Todd wasn't about to give Corcoran any tips on beating me, but Corcoran had some of his own ideas about how to cope in a tough fight. He made headlines when he said that if I hit him with a headbutt he would turn around and bite me. Glenn and I posed for photos on the eve of the fight wearing earmuffs made from boxing gloves with false teeth stuck to the padding. In response,

Corcoran gave me a cap with a boxing glove on it, suggesting that I use my head as a third fist.

Corcoran was actually quite good fun in the lead-up to the fight; we went on a press tour that included us each facing four deliveries from the great Shane Warne, for a segment with Mark Taylor and Michael Slater on the *Cricket Show* during the First Ashes Test at the Gabba. Corcoran proved better than me with a piece of willow, but I was confident I could hit harder than him with the boxing gloves.

I knuckled down to the hard work with Glenn at Stretton, sparring with Dennis Hogan and the former champ Michael Katsidis. I continued to do my strength and conditioning work at Dundee Kim's gyms in Yeronga and West End. One of Dundee's assistants, Tay Otene, was a former Year 10 pupil of mine when I taught physical education at Springwood High School. One of the fighters who trained alongside me at Dundee's was Nathaniel May, the brilliant featherweight from Western Australia whose trainer Peter Stokes had terminal cancer and only weeks to live but who bravely carried on, determined to see his young champ win one more big fight.

Three weeks before facing Corcoran, I suffered a deep cut over my left eye when I copped a hard jab against Marcus Nelson in sparring. It required eight stitches and naturally disrupted my training by curtailing future sparring sessions. Despite trying to disguise the injury with a little make-up whenever I had to make public appearances, Corcoran spotted it and said it would be a huge bullseye.

I knew that I had to use a very high, tight guard against him to protect the damage and the mass of scar tissue over my right eye from the win over Pacquiao.

*

At the weigh-in for the Corcoran fight, I met Britain's former world champ Amir Khan, who was in Australia filming the TV show *I'm a Celebrity ... Get Me Out of Here* on the Gold Coast hinterland. There has long been talk of us fighting one day and it would be a great match-up as he is lightning fast. Khan said that while he supported his fellow Englishman he believed I would be too strong and aggressive for Corcoran and that my pressure would break him down.

We would find out on the next night.

Even though she has never liked the brutality of boxing, there was no way Jo was going to miss cheering me on in the fight, and I had real fears that our baby might arrive while she was ringside.

So we arranged for Dr Brad Robinson, one of Australia's leading obstetricians, to be at the bout just in case.

Brad had delivered more than 2000 babies and, although none of them had ever arrived at a world title fight, he was keyed up in case Jo gave him the wave to signal that our baby girl had decided to come early. Jo would be in her thirty-eighth week of pregnancy at fight time, and Brad reckoned that in her state of 'advanced gestation', there was 'a real possibility that she could go into labour during the fight'. Dean Lonergan had an ambulance on standby to rush Jo to hospital if the excitement of the fight brought on her contractions.

Jo was resplendent in a vivid blue dress ringside as Corcoran and I got ready to turn on a lively 'blue' for the fans. At the opening bell, a capacity crowd of 7000 cheered me on, but no one was cheering louder than Jo, who was seated next to my mum. I also sensed that, somehow, our little unborn daughter was cheering too.

Unfortunately, because I'd missed so much sparring due to the cut over my eye, my timing was out and I quickly realised the fight would prove much tougher than I'd imagined.

In Round 1, Corcoran was down from a slip after ninety seconds and I then rocked him with a straight left and big left rip to the body to finish the round. But he was rugged.

My best shot early came in Round 2, when I nailed him flush with a big overhand right and I followed it with a savage uppercut.

Corcoran was warned by the referee, a little New Yorker named Benjy Esteves, for hitting me in the back of the head in a clinch, and Esteves had to repeat the warning to him in Round 3.

Corcoran was fighting hard, though, with plenty of legal punches too, and he landed a peach of a straight right on my chin in Round 4. He got me with a big right after the bell to end Round 7, as well, but it wasn't enough to make me deviate from Glenn's fight plan.

Even though Corcoran and I were both cut, I could sense Corcoran starting to come apart at the seams. Finally, his resistance cracked. I shook him in Round 8, I hurt him badly in Round 10 and as his cornermen threw in the towel in Round 11, the referee called a halt.

Corcoran needed six stitches in one cut and four in another and I needed eleven to seal three wounds of my own.

We had tried to tear each other apart but, when it was all over, Corcoran and I embraced backstage and gave one another our very best Christmas wishes. I congratulated him on a great effort and told him that he was an extremely tough guy with a lot of heart and determination and I wished him all the best for his life.

★

Three nights after beating Corcoran, Jo and I had a wonderful time at the 90th birthday party for my pop, Ray Horn. It was a beautiful gathering of family and friends at the Belmont Bowls Club in suburban Brisbane. Ray was honoured as the much-loved patriarch of the Horn clan and everyone was thrilled that we were about to welcome a new member. It would be the culmination of the most extraordinary year of my life. Two weeks after Pop's birthday, Jo and I counted off the last days of 2017 in a room at the Greenslopes Private Hospital as we prepared for the happiest new year of all. After eighteen hours in labour, Jo gave birth to our beautiful baby girl, Isabelle Kate, at 7.40 p.m. on Saturday, 30 December. It was frustrating and frightening seeing Jo in pain and not being able to help, but it gave me an insight into how my wife feels when I fight and she is powerless to do anything.

Isabelle weighed in at 3.58 kg and I burst into tears seeing her born. For me and Jo, it was the greatest thing ever in our lives.

We thought Isabelle was just perfect.

We couldn't stop staring at our little girl and thinking, 'Oh my gosh, we created her with love.'

19

Jeff is an incredibly talented boxer and a hardworking, humble hometown hero we are all proud of. Now Jeff, the local legend from Queensland, will fight under the lights of Las Vegas, putting the spotlight and the eyes of the world back on our home state.

– Kate Jones, Queensland's Minister for Innovation and Tourism Industry Development

IN JANUARY 2018, Dean Lonergan announced that I would defend my title against Terence Crawford at the spiritual home of world boxing, Madison Square Garden, in New York, on 14 April. Crawford had watched my bloody win over Gary Corcoran and was confident. It seemed nothing could slow down Crawford, as he compiled a run of thirty-two fights for thirty-two wins leading into our bout.

The fast and cocky American shaped up as the toughest opponent of my career and I needed my family with me for moral support. Our beautiful daughter, Isabelle, was only a few weeks old when we organised her passport so she could travel with Jo and me to America for the fight.

Crawford had a superb resume as a fighter and an intimidating personality. He and his beefy coach, Brian 'BoMac' McIntyre, were the masters of trash talk and disrespect.

The circumstances surrounding Crawford's early career put his grit into perspective. He had grown up fighting for survival and knew all about violence and guns. Crawford had turned professional in 2008, five months before I had my very first amateur fight. In September 2008, in his hometown of Omaha, Nebraska, Crawford was sitting in the driver's seat of his 1986 Pontiac Cutlass Supreme, under a streetlight, counting his winnings from an illegal dice game. He had just won his fourth professional fight and was getting ready to box on national television for the ESPN network. As Crawford counted his cash, a gunman, taking aim at another player in Crawford's group, fired a 9-mm pistol through the rear window of the car. Unfortunately for Crawford, the trajectory of the slug changed after it hit the glass of the rear window, veering slightly, and Crawford was hit. He slumped over the steering wheel.

With blood cascading down the back of his head and holding one hand against his gaping head wound, Crawford somehow came to his senses, turned on the ignition and drove himself to the nearest hospital, using his mobile phone to call his mother, Deborah, and BoMac along the way.

The bullet had exited through his neck. After having the

wound stitched, Crawford then drove himself home. What did not destroy him only made him stronger. He won his next fight a few weeks later on national television. By knockout.

Crawford later learned that the man who shot him was, in turn, killed by a gunshot wound to the head.

In 2014, Crawford won the World Boxing Organization lightweight (61 kg) title from Scotland's Ricky Burns, who boasted a victory over Queensland's former world champ Michael Katsidis.

He followed that victory with superb defences against Yuriorkis Gamboa and Ray Beltran. Then he invaded the junior-welterweight (63.5 kg) division and went on an astonishing run beating the best at that weight to unify all four major world title belts. No one stood a chance – Thomas Dulorme, Dierry Jean, Hank Lundy, Viktor Postol, John Molina, Felix Diaz, and in his last fight before facing me, big-hitting undefeated Julius Indongo of Namibia.

Crawford was pretty much good at everything in the boxing ring, plus he had an awkward style, switching between orthodox and southpaw. He could hit hard and take a punch, so it promised to be a really exciting fight. I was backing my constant pressure and physical strength even though the bookmakers had me very much as an outsider.

I was getting more than $2 million for the fight and I had the chance to beat the guy being touted as the best fighter in the world pound for pound.

I began sparring the slick southpaw Liam Paro who had helped me so much in my preparation for Manny Pacquiao, and I did a lot of work with Dennis Hogan as he prepared to beat Englishman Jimmy Kilrain Kelly, another world-rated junior-middleweight.

My training was going very well when Crawford landed a big sucker punch by gaining an indefinite postponement of the bout, citing a hand injury suffered in sparring, though we never saw a medical report about it. Glenn made the Americans explode with anger when he said I had fought with much worse injuries than a 'bruised hand' and that Crawford was 'soft' and needed to 'harden up Princess.'

BoMac threatened to knock Glenn out when he saw him, but I could guarantee that Glenn would not have had any trouble with the big-talking American, and BoMac himself later conceded that Glenn would 'kick his ass'.

But the postponement definitely derailed my preparations for a while before the fight was finally set for 10 June (Australian time) at the huge MGM Grand Casino in Las Vegas. The big fight shaped up as the ultimate test for me – an even tougher challenge than Manny Pacquiao.

In the midst of all this, I had a huge thrill at the end of March when I was given the honour of carrying the Queen's Baton on the last leg of its relay into Brisbane's South Bank ahead of the Gold Coast Commonwealth Games. It was an amazing experience and over the next two weeks I got to see so many top Aussies representing their country at the Games, including a couple of guys I had sparred with, Liam Wilson and Clay Waterman. At the end of April, Jo and I were on hand for my sister Bianca's wedding to Tim. Family has always meant the world to me and I love supporting my brother and my sisters in the same way they have backed me through my life.

*

In May, I started sparring with a slick American named Ray Robinson, a lanky southpaw who had beaten Terence Crawford in the amateur ranks. We spent two weeks slugging it out as I honed my speed and fitness for what Glenn and I knew would be a fast-paced battle. Ray gave me a little nick beside my eye and hit me with some good shots but he hit nowhere near as hard as the car that rammed me from behind on Granard Road, Rocklea, after a gruelling training session with Dundee Kim. My car was involved in a three-car pile-up and, while I suffered whiplash, I was lucky not to be seriously hurt. Fortunately, Jo and baby Isabelle were not in the car at the time. The man in the centre of the crash had his head buried in his hands and was in shock. Someone called an ambulance, and it arrived very quickly.

Thankfully, the trip to America with Jo and Isabelle at the end of May was a lot more pleasant, though I can't say everything about Vegas was a breeze. Crawford and his team were less than welcoming, with him tweeting that he planned on 'f....g me up'.

We were very different people. I was born into a loving family and grew up on acreage in Pallara in Brisbane's leafy southwest and have a bachelor's degree in education; Crawford was born and raised in a tough northern suburb of Omaha, Nebraska, a few kilometres across town from the home of Warren Buffet, once the world's richest man, but a million light years away in circumstance.

Crawford comes from a fighting family – his father, grandfather, uncles and cousins were all boxers – and he began fighting at age seven. He has had his share of fights outside the ring as well. In 2016, while already a two-division world champ, Crawford was sentenced to ninety days in jail along with two years' probation after being found guilty of disorderly conduct and damage to property for his actions at a panel beaters where his 1984 Chevrolet Monte Carlo was being repaired.

He had told the panel beater he was unhappy with the paint job on his classic car and violently took it back without paying the bill, causing $5000 damage to a hydraulic lift. Crawford was led away in handcuffs after the hearing.

Two months later, he reportedly pulled out a gun to break up a brawl between two female acquaintances, prompting the Omaha police to detain him for questioning. Crawford produced a concealed-carry permit.

He is a father of five, and while boxing has made Crawford a rich man he has never left the gritty environment in which he grew up.

I tried to keep my time in Vegas as close to my family life in Brisbane as possible. Jo's parents, Mark and Leigh Buckley, took a room adjoining ours at the MGM Grand to help look after Isabelle if her crying during the night woke me up. In hindsight, having Isabelle in the room with me so close to a world title fight wasn't the best idea and I had a bit of a sniffle by fight time.

Still, Jo and I took Isabelle on regular strolls in Vegas, and guests at the massive hotel/casino complex were often surprised to see a world boxing champ helping his wife carry a baby's pram down the steps outside our accommodation and hugging Isabelle to my chest. They would also have been surprised to see me and Jo rushing through Vegas on foot like anonymous tourists to pick up our tickets to see illusionist Mat Franco perform. Jo and I even had a romantic cruise on a replica of a Venetian canal, complete with a gondola and a tenor singing Italian arias.

One of the real highlights in Vegas was when Jo, Mum and I went on a 230-kilometres-per-hour helicopter ride from Las Vegas along the Colorado River into the Grand Canyon with Brisbane's *Sunday Mail* photographer Peter Wallis to take some front-page shots for the Australian press. The grandeur of one of nature's most awesome sights was almost as beautiful as the smile on Isabelle's face when we got back to the hotel that afternoon.

But I wasn't in town for a holiday. I was on a search and destroy mission.

Things did not go well for that from the start.

I was disappointed to see that I had been given second billing on all the advertising for the fight as though I were the challenger to Crawford, rather than the defending world champ.

To get the fight with Pacquiao back in 2017, I had had to sign a contract with Bob Arum, allowing him to promote my next two bouts. The first was against Gary Corcoran. The second and last was with Crawford. But Arum had Crawford signed to a long-term contract and made no secret of the fact he wanted me to lose since I was becoming a free agent. I told the press in America that I felt like I was just a pawn in the game.

The desert heat at the height of the American summer was intense and our first gym in Vegas was inside a dilapidated building just off Dean Martin Drive. It had no air conditioning and we had to train there in the heat of the day while Crawford trained there in the cool of the night. It wasn't long before Kevin Barry, who trains my old friend Joseph Parker the great Kiwi heavyweight, offered us the use of his terrific gym in another section of town. I had also left my normal training boots back in Brisbane and started using a new pair in the gym. They rubbed me up the wrong way, literally, and the subsequent blisters hampered my movement.

There was a lot of controversy over the choice of gloves for the fight, too, with Crawford using the old-fashioned horse-hair gloves that sometimes allow boxers to manipulate the padding so that there is very little protection over the knuckles, dramatically increasing their punching power. In the end Crawford wore the gloves he wanted but we checked them out and found that there was not much chance of the stuffing having been moved around. As it turned out the gloves weren't really an issue.

I was the biggest opponent Crawford had faced but he is a smart tactician, a brilliant boxer and he had done his homework on me, declaring: 'A lot of people don't look at the real details. They don't see his feints, his angles, his punch selection. Things like that, those are the things that I look at, the things that he does that are different, that are unorthodox and can frustrate a fighter.'

Crawford said he expected me to use my size and strength to intimidate him and, as Kevin Barry urged me to 'bring out the mongrel', he was prepared for me to try and overpower him.

'That's something that we're gonna be up for,' Crawford said. 'Horn fights to win. I love a person to fight to win, because I'm coming in there to fight to win and that's gonna make for an exciting fight.'

Making the 66.68 kg weight limit continued to be a problem for me and once again I had to drop 4 kg in a day to comply.

Anthony Mundine was watching the telecast and sent

me a 'good luck' message through *The Courier-Mail* saying: 'Crawford is a beast but Jeff has such an unusual style that he can pull off the upset. I really want him to do well. Jeff gets hit a few times, but he's tough, unconventional and awkward. He has to make it a real brawl like he did when he beat Manny Pacquiao and he has to disguise his attacks. He can't come in square on. He has to feint with his feet a lot to keep Crawford off balance and guessing.'

I was relaxed and confident in the dressing room before the fight and my eyes lit up when the great actor Mark Wahlberg paid me a visit. But I couldn't follow the script Glenn had written out for me when it came to fight time and Crawford forced me to make a lot of mistakes.

I rushed too much, I failed to maintain the gap between us and sometimes when I was attacking I ended up too stationary, meaning Crawford could rip me with some brutal body shots before I got away.

Not being able to move freely in the week before the fight due to painful blisters on my feet was not helping my footwork. I was moving my head but my legs were not moving like they were against Pacquiao, which enabled Crawford to target my body. And despite Glenn's repeated protests, the NSAC officials positioned Glenn a couple of metres away from the ring, seated down low on a short stool, so he was struggling to get clear vision of the ring and said he could see only half the fight. In every other fight, Glenn had been right beside the ring – but not this time. This frustrated Glenn, as he said he felt disconnected from me, and our usual connection enables him to keep me on plan.

The first round was fairly even. I got clipped early, but I came back strongly. I was landing punches on the way in, but I was having trouble catching Crawford with clean shots, as his defence was very good. I was thinking what someone like Jeff Fenech would be saying; it would have been 'stay on his chest, stay on his chest'. But I just couldn't stay on him, and when I did catch him, he would clinch his way out of trouble. If he got me with a clean shot on the way in he was prepared to trade with me, but if he missed me and I hit him on the way in he would clinch. I knew he would be going backwards, but I thought I could get in easier and beat him on the inside. What was particularly frustrating for both Glenn and me is that Crawford wasn't doing anything we didn't expect – I just felt off.

Right up to the end of Round 7, Glenn kept saying the rounds were close, but I felt I was probably narrowly losing them. Glenn had said before the fight that we should assume all the close rounds would go to Crawford and I knew I wasn't convincingly winning the rounds. Between rounds, Glenn was trying to get me back on plan – move more laterally, come in faster, lift my intensity when in range and get out smarter, as we had trained to do. Glenn had developed a really good plan that had worked well in sparring against southpaw Ray Robinson – but I couldn't execute the plan on this night. Glenn wanted me to be more mongrel on the inside, as I was with Pacquiao, but I felt flat and was accepting Crawford's clinches rather than going up a gear in close and shaking him off. Don't get me wrong, Crawford is a great fighter. I knew I had to bring my A game to beat him, but it just wasn't there that night.

In Round 5, Crawford started poking his tongue out at me, but it was his fists that I was more concerned about. I tried to swarm him in Round 6, but he countered very well and I now started fighting with more desperation, knowing that while I had taken the early rounds against Pacquiao, I knew I had not received the early rounds against Crawford.

The few hundred Australians who came over to support me tried to lift me with chants of 'Hornet! Hornet!' but Crawford wasn't listening.

In Round 8, he set me back on my heels but I came back, only to be rocked at the end of the round. Then, in Round 9, with fifty-five seconds left in the round, I zigged when I should have zagged, stepping to the right just as Crawford threw a left hook. It wasn't a massive punch, but it was well timed and unbalanced me. While I didn't go down, my gloves touched the canvas, which resulted in Crawford being awarded a knockdown. Inspired by this, Crawford's confidence spiked and he started pouring on the pressure. As I backed away towards the ropes, he hit me with a good shot. I then evaded a couple of punches and as I was stepping off the ropes, Las Vegas referee Robert Byrd halted the action at two minutes thirty-three seconds into Round 9. Glenn said he couldn't see the stoppage at all from where he was forced to sit, but he immediately leapt into the ring, looked into my eyes and asked if I was okay. I said I was fine and he then asked the referee why he had stopped the fight. Some of my fans also said that as the world champion defending my title I should have been given more of a chance to fight back. I definitely felt I still had more in me, but that's boxing. Jo and my parents were just glad that I was okay.

While I felt like I was having an off night, Glenn would later break this down piece by piece, as usual, and explain to me exactly why I was having an off night, not in any way to put me down – but to learn from the experience and ensure the mistakes didn't happen again. He referred to the loss as 'a series of unfortunate events'.

I had suffered my first professional loss in twenty starts, but even with twenty-six stitches in the torn skin around my eyes I was still smiling, still grateful for all the great things I had in my life.

After the bout, I left for Canada for a three-week holiday with Jo, Isabelle, my mum and Jo's parents. As we took in the magnificent vistas of Vancouver, the Rocky Mountains and Lake Louise, I relaxed after the fight proud that I had given it my best shot against a great boxer. Crawford had a lot more professional experience than me and the home advantage. He taught me a lesson, but I'm a fast learner and I hope that one day I get the chance to fight him again and hopefully even the score.

*

Before I had even boarded the plane in Vegas bound for Vancouver and our Canadian holiday, Anthony Mundine ramped up the pressure to fight me in a big outdoor battle at Suncorp Stadium. I liked the idea straight away. When I was growing up, Mundine was the biggest star in the sport. The first fight I ever saw was his win over Danny Green in 2006. It would be a thrill to face the man who had been an Australian sporting legend for a quarter of a century. As soon as I had lost to Crawford, Mundine's manager Emaid Dib contacted *The Courier-Mail* to say that he and Mundine were ready to make me an offer of a 50/50 split for what could be the biggest all-Australian fight of all time.

Dib, whose brother Billy once held the world featherweight title, told *The Courier-Mail*: 'I have spoken to Anthony and he has instructed me to run with the proposal. I have advised him that we make a very strong offer straight off the bat and show Horn and Rushton that we are being genuine and not playing games. Anthony and I are happy to sit down with Jeff's Dad and Glenn Rushton within days.'

Emaid then phoned Glenn in Las Vegas and together they started planning a huge night of boxing that was eventually set for 30 November at Suncorp Stadium.

The weight limit of 71 kg would be much more comfortable for me than having to boil down to welterweight again.

Mundine has made a lot of noise and sold a lot of tickets throughout his career by being controversial and sometimes that has masked what a great athlete he is, one of the very best dual-sport athletes Australia has produced.

He left rugby league in 2000 as one of the game's most exciting players and within a year was giving three-time Olympian and world boxing champ Sven Ottke a hell of a tough fight in Germany. He boasted wins over some terrific fighters including Danny Green, Daniel Geale, Lester Ellis, Antwun Echols, Sam Soliman and many more. And even though Mundine was now forty-three, I anticipated he would still have plenty of tricks to show me. He had rocked some big strong guys all the way up to cruiserweight (90 kg) so I had to be on my game every second of every round.

Mundine went old school in his preparation, too, determined to do everything he could to cause an upset against me.

He slashed his entourage, staying in Brisbane with just his dad and trainer, Tony, and his mum, Lyn. He made his training base at Chris McCullen's Logan Boxing Club, basically a big garden shed at the back of a house in Slacks Creek. His ice bath was a plastic garbage bin, which gave new meaning to all his trash talk.

Mundine had his first tattoo inked on his arm at age seventeen – a small Playboy symbol that he says he should get lasered off sometime – but as he flexed his muscles for pre-fight publicity pictures it was the other tattoos adorning his body that were most prominent – the names of his children – Rahim, Malik, Lilant (Anthony Jr), Ayishah and above his heart, Jada. They were his motivation to beat me, and the chance to be remembered for one last great win after twenty-five years at the top of Australian sport.

As the fight got closer I could sense Mundine's anxiety levels rising every time we came together.

Then at the prefight weigh-in his tension exploded. We were eyeballing each other up close after weighing in for the fight when Mundine suddenly grabbed me by the chin and throat and pushed me.

'I'm like a caged tiger,' Mundine snarled at reporters after we were separated, 'I'm ready to kill, man. My back is to the wall. And I'm ready to fight back.'

Mundine had a look of wild desperation as he lunged at me, bizarrely saying that I represented 'white privilege in Australia'. Later, he even said that I represented 'injustice'.

'He stands for all the things I'm against. He wants to wave the flag, he wants to play the anthem. He doesn't even understand what all that means.'

I refused to retaliate because I was saving my punches for the fight.

I knew Mundine was a former three-times world champion, an incredible athlete ranked by the WBO as the number 9 middleweight in the world, two divisions above where I had fought all of my previous fights, so I wasn't expecting an easy night. We had prepared for a 30-year-old

Mundine at his prime, as all reports were that Mundine was in great shape and had worked harder for this fight than he had for a very long time. This time, we were ready.

But not even Glenn could have foretold what would happen that night. Glenn had been telling me in the lead-up to the fight that I had to make a statement against Mundine. He said a win was not good enough. He said I had to prove to the world that the Crawford fight was not the real Jeff Horn – that it was just an aberration. He told me to get my foot on Mundine's throat early and keep it there for the whole fight.

On fight day, my team-mates Joe Goodall and Cameron Hammond both won bouts on the undercard but sadly, after starting well, my brother Ben gassed out against a Townsville fighter named Lachlan O'Shea and lost his professional debut.

Ben was still in my corner, though, when the main fight of the night began.

As soon as I went after Mundine I found him easy to hit and realised that he didn't have a lot of resistance. I was wary of his speed and while he did tag me with a left hook, every punch I landed seemed to hurt him.

A big right to the body in the opening stages made him wince and then I went for him. For weeks I had been practising softening up Mundine with body shots and then going for the chin. Midway through the round I pressed forward and banged in a big right and left rip to the body. Mundine instinctively backed off trying to protect his chin with his shoulder but I was too quick and I cannoned over a left hook that dropped him. Referee Phil Austin reached the count of seven before waving the fight off, as it was obvious Mundine wasn't getting to his feet unaided.

The bout had lasted just ninety-six seconds.

Mundine was gracious in defeat, saying the torch had passed to a new era and that if he was going to lose like that he was glad he had lost to a 'good dude' like me. Before long, though, he was calling for a rematch.

I was absolutely elated with my performance as it put me squarely back into the frame for a world title shot at light-middleweight or middleweight. It was a relief not having to boil down to welterweight again; I feel much stronger and more comfortable fighting at 70 kg or above.

*

While the win over Mundine brought me a great sense of joy, there was even better news ahead for Jo and me in the immediate aftermath.

Late in 2018, we bought a lovely new home in the Brisbane suburb of Sunnybank, with plenty of bedrooms for us to raise a large family.

On Isabelle's first birthday, 30 December 2018, we were delighted to announce that Jo was pregnant with our second child.

We couldn't have been happier for our little family.

I married Jo in 2014, when I was a struggling part-time teacher, but I have also married a dream with determination, and I found that is the basis for success in any endeavour.

I have a wonderful family, tremendous friends and loyal fans who I love dearly and who have lifted me to heights that still boggle my mind.

I have to say my life is truly blessed and I wish you all the very best with whatever dreams you wish to pursue.

20

I never set out to make Jeff a world champion. I set out to make him a legend. I know what's inside him. He's not just a brilliant boxer. He's much more than that. He is one of the finest young men you would ever know and he does every Australian proud.

– Glenn Rushton, who taught me how to defend myself and how to find the champion within

THANK YOU FOR READING my story. I hope this part is a good bit because I want everyone looking at these last few pages to understand my simple message.

I have been in the news a lot because of my wins over Pacquiao and Mundine, and great things are possible for you too, if you really want that. Having risen from a very low base to become a famous sportsman, I believe that anything is possible in life if you put your mind to it and work towards a goal. For me and for you.

Really?

Yes. As Glenn would say, 'Yeah, really.'

You might not even like boxing, you might not be interested in it. But no matter what field of endeavour you are pursuing, I think my story proves that dreams can come true – even big, ridiculous, absurd crazy dreams like those of a wimpy schoolboy with no interest in boxing becoming the No. 1 welterweight in the world one day. It's only a decade ago that I learned what a welterweight actually was.

Jo and I are not flashy people, and our daughter was born into a world very different from the one we imagined when we were married in 2014, while I was still working as a schoolteacher. I hope our children realise that hard work and discipline are the keys to success. That's what it's all about and those attributes are the foundations of what Glenn and I established in our early years together.

Still, you can also have fun on your journey.

I drive myself pretty hard in training, but I'm not hung up on body image or fanatical about diet. In the six weeks after beating Manny, I put on 10 kilograms with a regimen based around chocolate and doughnuts. But I know that when fight time comes around, I'm ravenous for success and experienced and disciplined enough to shut the door on all the treats so I can get in terrific physical and mental condition.

My family and my friends are what my life is all about.

It's gratifying to be recognised and appreciated in the street and, I'll be honest, yes, sometimes I even get a buzz out of being mobbed. But Jo and I aim to maintain a simple life despite the glare of the world sporting spotlight. These days,

Jo has to go shopping by herself because if I go with her it takes forever to get the groceries. People want selfies with me and sometimes it's hard to accommodate everyone, given that I have so many commitments now. Jo knows I hate grocery shopping, in any case. And I hate to ever appear rude.

I have received all sorts of honours outside the boxing ring, which I'm really proud about. A few weeks after I beat Manny, a Queensland police dog was named Hornet in honour of me. The little puppy was a cute fella when I cuddled him, but I reckon he'll have even more bite than I do when he's chasing lawbreakers. He looks like a real goer.

Jo and I still do the things we have always enjoyed – quiet get-togethers with friends and family, barbecues, table tennis tournaments against my old schoolmates and board games. Not long after the Pacquiao bout, a good friend of mine, Jo Christiaans, a fine actor who taught alongside me at Pallara for a while, visited our house with Drace Illusionist, a terrific magician, who showed me a whole raft of new tricks.

*

My reasons for becoming a boxer were never about making money. Thirteen years ago I began fighting for a little trophy, although the bigger trophy was the fact that I had conquered my fears to become a real boxer. I ended up competing at the Olympic Games just four years after deciding to concentrate on my sport. As a professional I made $1500 – less expenses – for my debut. It was not a lot of money, but I always had the big picture in mind. Before beating Manny Pacquiao, I was making $20,000 a fight and, although that is good money by the standards of Australian boxing, financially the world-title win has set up my family with a comfortable financial future. At the moment, my fame still outweighs my fortune by a long way, though, and Jo and I are definitely not rich. But we have been able to update the 2004 Toyota Camry that Jo used to drive to the train station on her way to work.

*

Boxing has often copped a bad reputation, but I hope that Glenn and I have changed the image of the sport for the better with our success.

Glenn likes to focus on the positive aspects of the fight game and he's changed thousands of lives through boxing and martial arts, helping people whom he has taken from depressive states and given confidence. He has assisted so many people to overcome their fears, particularly kids who might otherwise have ended up on drugs or alcohol. There are countless parents who thank him for saving their children and at least one nerdy, geeky kid who is grateful that Glenn turned him into a world boxing champion.

You learn a lot about yourself in the boxing ring. It teaches you a great deal about life and, in a lot of ways, is a metaphor for life – the struggles, the determination, the low blows, the big hits, the fightbacks. Triumph and tragedy. You develop courage and resilience, which can then help you in every aspect of life. As the great old Aussie champ of the 1940s, Vic Patrick, once said, 'Even if you're just a prelim boy it takes a lot to lace on a glove.' And even if you never actually have a fight, boxing offers enormous health benefits, from the discipline of training to the confidence that helps you to become a better person. It's a message I give to schools as I advocate boxing training just for fitness.

If all the fighting in Australia was done in the boxing ring, the streets would certainly be much safer and there would be a lot less crime.

I believe that a lot of young people lash out simply because they're afraid, they lack the confidence to handle stressful situations and they over-react or panic. Glenn taught me to handle the most difficult situations you can imagine, such as having blood dripping down your face from a cut eye, one of history's greatest boxers coming at you like a runaway train and a referee saying he's going to stop the fight.

Glenn taught me that high level of confidence by slowly building up my physical and mental strength over time. He says my self-belief comes from my heart and not my tongue because I let my performances speak for me.

*

Even if people don't like boxing, I think they could learn a lot from what Glenn and I have achieved together.

Right from the outset he told me that a person could create their own future and that feeling sorry for yourself, as I had done when I was bullied, would get you nowhere. You had to be proactive. He says whatever things hurt you in life, you have to do something to overcome them, not become a victim. Glenn likes to use me as an example of the benefits of boxing training for personal development, pointing out how far I've progressed from the days when other kids were regularly beating me up.

My rise from the bottom of despair to the top of boxing has been described in the press as not so much a fight as a fable – a fairy tale even – about a bullied boy who saw a vision of himself as something better than just a human target.

How did I achieve this and how can you also realise whatever goals and ambitions you have?

Well, firstly, let me say you have the power within you to achieve great things. We all do.

I'm just an ordinary guy from the suburbs. Nothing special. I'm certainly no superman. It still hurts when I have to get a needle, I still feel lousy when I get a cold and my heart still jumps when an aeroplane bucks a bit. At the core I'm just like everyone else. I had no boxing background and no head start in sports. I just worked hard and stayed focused on my goals. I surrounded myself with good people, and because I had a good coach I listened to him, practised what he taught me and never let go of my dream. Then I gave it 100 per cent every time I went to the gym.

I had definite objectives and a systematic approach to realising them step by step, all the time improving myself and strengthening my belief that I could climb the next rung on the ladder – and eventually every rung between me and the top. In the amateurs it was a progression through state, Australian, Oceania and world titles and the Olympics. Step by step. Gradually I improved my skills and I empowered myself. In the pro ranks Duco's matchmaker, Stuart Duncan, found opponents who would challenge me and bring out my best as he and Glenn stepped up the level of competition with each bout.

It was a course of self-improvement and on-the-job training. Glenn likens it to tempering steel.

I hope that you see my story as being not just about boxing but about the power of hope and what can be accomplished by the unwavering belief in a dream.

I've had career-threatening injuries, disappointments, defeats and other setbacks along the way. But although they wobbled me at times, I never got off course for too long.

When I was a kid, bullies would sometimes make me so sad that I would think to myself it was pointless going on. My win over Manny Pacquiao was a victory for everyone who has been bullied or beaten or depressed or downhearted. I say that, no matter where you find yourself in life, there is always a way up and a way out of your situation.

Never give up. No matter how bad things look, never give up.

At the end of Round 9 against Manny, the referee was ready to stop the bout and deny me a chance at history and the opportunity to be world champion. After I had come so close to triumph, it looked like it was curtains for my dream. I was hurt and knocked around. I could have hung my head and resigned myself to being a 'nearly' man, but Glenn and I refused to give up on my dream. Because of that, because of fighting hard when it looked like every last chip was down, my life changed dramatically over the next few minutes.

Yours can too if you refuse to quit.

Find a way to win. Don't stop. You might be hurting, you might be downhearted, you might have everything going against you. But don't quit. Hang in there. If you don't believe me, I have a big, shiny red-and-gold belt that says 'WORLD CHAMPION' on it to prove what can happen when you keep going against the odds.

I've been very lucky in life. I had good parents and a good mentor in Glenn, great people in my corner, and supporters from all walks of life who believed in my boxing ability and, more importantly, appreciated my character.

I hope I have set a good example for other sportsmen and women to follow. You don't need to be arrogant or petulant or rude or obnoxious to be successful in sport. In fact, if you are decent, polite and dependable, people might appreciate you even more.

As 2017 ended, I was content that I had married the love of my life and was about to become a father. And I have also beaten one of the best boxers who ever stepped into the ring. By doing that, I think I proved to the whole world that in life anything is possible.

Anything.

Thanks so much for sharing my journey, which I believe will continue with more big wins in 2019 and beyond.

I am so happy that I have realised many of my dreams.

And I know that you can, too.

Career Record

of

Jeffrey Christopher Horn

Born: 4 February 1988, Brisbane Qld

MY ROAD TO THE WORLD WELTERWEIGHT TITLE AND BEYOND

Amateur Fights	66 (48 wins, 18 losses)

Professional Fights	
1 March 2013	TKO 2: Jody Allen
27 April 2013	KO 1: Torin Rophia
9 May 2013	TKO 1: Rangson Poonsang
8 August 2013	Tech Draw Rd 3: Rivan Cesaire
12 September 2013	KO 1: Samuel Colomban **Wins vacant Australian welterweight title**
16 November 2013	TKO 2: Aswin Cabuy
6 December 2013	W Points 6: Naoufel Ben Rabeh
19 March 2014	TKO 9: Rivan Cesaire
5 July 2014	W Pts 12: Fernando Ferreira da Silva
6 December 2014	KO 5: Robson Assis
13 June 2015	TKO 3: Richmond Djarbeng
1 August 2015	W Tech Decision 7: Viktor Plotnikov
15 October 2015	W Pts 10: Alfredo Rodolfo Blanco
5 December 2015	W Pts 10: Ahmed El Mousaoui
27 April 2016	TKO 7: Randall Bailey
21 October 2016	TKO 9: Rico Mueller
10 December 2016	TKO 6: Ali Funeka
2 July 2017	W Pts 12: Manny Pacquiao **Wins WBO welterweight title**
13 December 2017	TKO 11: Gary Corcoran **Retains WBO welterweight title**
9 June 2018	Loss TKO 9: Terence Crawford **Loses WBO welterweight title**
30 November 2018	KO 1: Anthony Mundine

Grand Star Receptions, Altona North, Victoria
Fortitude Stadium, Newstead, Queensland
Royal International Convention Centre, Bowen Hills, Queensland
Southport RSL Club, Queensland
The Melbourne Pavilion, Kensington, Victoria
Royal International Convention Centre, Bowen Hills, Queensland
Metro City, Northbridge, Western Australia
Jupiters Hotel & Casino, Broadbeach, Queensland
Vodafone Events Centre, Manukau City, New Zealand
Claudelands Arena, Hamilton, New Zealand
Arena Manawatu, Palmerston North, New Zealand
Stadium Southland, Invercargill, New Zealand
The Trusts Arena, Auckland, New Zealand
Claudelands Arena, Hamilton, New Zealand
Convention & Exhibition Centre, Brisbane, Queensland
Sleeman Sports Complex, Chandler, Queensland
Spark Arena, Auckland, New Zealand
Suncorp Stadium, Brisbane, Queensland
Convention & Exhibition Centre, Brisbane, Queensland
MGM Grand, Las Vegas, Nevada
Suncorp Stadium, Brisbane, Queensland

JEFF HORN v MANNY PACQUIAO

2 July 2017

Suncorp Stadium, Brisbane Qld

Official Judges' Scorecards						
	RD 1	RD 2	RD 3	RD 4	RD 5	RD 6
W. ROLDAN	9–10 HOR	9–10 HOR	10–9 PAC	9–10 HOR	9–10 HOR	9–10 HOR
C. FLORES	9–10 HOR	10–9 PAC	10–9 PAC	9–10 HOR	9–10 HOR	9–10 HOR
R. CERDAN	9–10 HOR	9–10 HOR	10–9 PAC	9–10 HOR	10–9 PAC	9–10 HOR

WBO Review Judges' Scorecards						
	RD 1	RD 2	RD 3	RD 4	RD 5	RD 6
JUDGE 1	9–10 HOR	10–9 PAC	10–9 PAC	9–10 HOR	10–9 PAC	9–10 HOR
JUDGE 2	9–10 HOR	9–10 HOR	10–9 PAC	9–10 HOR	10–9 PAC	9–10 HOR
JUDGE 3	9–10 HOR	9–10 HOR	10–9 PAC	9–10 HOR	10–9 PAC	9–10 HOR
JUDGE 4	9–10 HOR	9–10 HOR	10–9 PAC	10–9 PAC	9–10 HOR	9–10 HOR
JUDGE 5	9–10 HOR	9–10 HOR	10–9 PAC	9–10 HOR	10–9 PAC	9–10 HOR

RD 7	RD 8	RD 9	RD 10	RD 11	RD 12	Total
9–10 HOR	10–9 PAC	10–9 PAC	9–10 HOR	9–10 HOR	9–10 HOR	111–117 HOR
9–10 HOR	10–9 PAC	10–9 PAC	10–9 PAC	9–10 HOR	9–10 HOR	113–115 HOR
9–10 HOR	9–10 HOR	10–9 PAC	10–9 PAC	10–9 PAC	9–10 HOR	113–115 HOR

RD 7	RD 8	RD 9	RD 10	RD 11	RD 12	Total
9–10 HOR	10–9 PAC	10–8 PAC	9–10 HOR	10–9 PAC	9–10 HOR	114–113 PAC
9–10 HOR	10–9 PAC	10–9 PAC	10–9 PAC	10–9 PAC	9–10 HOR	114–114 DRAW
10–9 PAC	10–9 PAC	10–9 PAC	9–10 HOR	9–10 HOR	9–10 HOR	113–115 HOR
9–10 HOR	10–9 PAC	10–8 PAC	10–9 PAC	9–10 HOR	9–10 HOR	113–114 HOR
9–10 HOR	10–9 PAC	10–8 PAC	9–10 HOR	10–9 PAC	9–10 HOR	113–114 HOR

Jeff Horn's story is one of the most inspiring in sporting history. A quiet schoolboy who suffered at the hands of bullies, he started taking self-defence classes one night a week. At the age of twenty-four, Jeff made the quarter-finals of the 2012 London Olympics. Five years later, on 2 July 2017, he defeated all-time great Manny Pacquiao of the Philippines to win the World Boxing Organization welterweight title. Jeff is married to his high school sweetheart, Joanna. They live in Brisbane.

An award-winning journalist, Grantlee Kieza OAM has held senior positions at *The Daily Telegraph*, *The Sunday Telegraph* and *The Courier-Mail*. He is a Walkley Award finalist and the author of fourteen acclaimed books, including the recent bestsellers *Bert Hinkler*, *Monash*, *Mrs Kelly* and *Banjo*. In 2017, Grantlee was named Queensland's Sports Journalist of the Year and in 2018 inducted into the Australian Boxing Hall of Fame. He lives in Brisbane.